'For us it wa

The Passion, Grief and Fortitude
of Patience Darton

The Cañada Blanch / Sussex Academic Studies on Contemporary Spain

General Editor: Professor Paul Preston, London School of Economics

Dacia Viejo-Rose, *Reconstructing Spain: Cultural Heritage and Memory after Civil War.*

Richard Wigg, *Churchill and Spain: The Survival of the Franco Regime, 1940–1945.*

Published by the Cañada Blanch Centre for Contemporary Spanish Studies in conjunction with Routledge / Taylor & Francis

1 Francisco J. Romero Salvadó, *Spain 1914–1918: Between War and Revolution.*

2 David Wingeate Pike, *Spaniards in the Holocaust: Mauthausen, the Horror on the Danube.*

3 Herbert Rutledge Southworth, *Conspiracy and the Spanish Civil War: The Brainwashing of Francisco Franco.*

4 Angel Smith (editor), *Red Barcelona: Social Protest and Labour Mobilization in the Twentieth Century.*

5 Angela Jackson, *British Women and the Spanish Civil War.*

6 Kathleen Richmond, *Women and Spanish Fascism: The Women's Section of the Falange, 1934–1959.*

7 Chris Ealham, *Class, Culture and Conflict in Barcelona, 1898–1937.*

8 Julián Casanova, *Anarchism, the Republic and Civil War in Spain 1931–1939.*

9 Montserrat Guibernau, *Catalan Nationalism: Francoism, Transition and Democracy.*

10 Richard Baxell, *British Volunteers in the Spanish Civil War: The British Battalion in the International Brigades, 1936–1939.*

11 Hilari Raguer, *The Catholic Church and the Spanish Civil War.*

12 Richard Wigg, *Churchill and Spain: The Survival of the Franco Regime, 1940–45.*

13 Nicholas Coni, *Medicine and the Spanish Civil War.*

14 Diego Muro, *Ethnicity and Violence: The Case of Radical Basque Nationalism.*

15 Francisco J. Romero Salvadó, *Spain's Revolutionary Crisis, 1917–1923.*

16 Peter Anderson, *The Francoist Military Trials. Terror and Complicity, 1939–1945.*

To Paul Preston

In acknowledgement and gratitude for his personal
commitment and hard work through the Cañada Blanch
Centre to enrich the historiography of twentieth-century
Spain by bringing about the publication of so many
books that, like this one, might otherwise have
languished unpublished in the digital limbo
of their authors' computers.

'For us it was Heaven'

The Passion, Grief and Fortitude
of Patience Darton

FROM THE SPANISH CIVIL WAR
TO MAO'S CHINA

ANGELA JACKSON

**International Brigade
Memorial Trust**

sussex
ACADEMIC
PRESS
Brighton • Portland • Toronto

Cañada Blanch Centre
for Contemporary
Spanish Studies

2 4 6 8 10 9 7 5 3 1

First published in 2012 in Great Britain by
SUSSEX ACADEMIC PRESS
PO Box 139, Eastbourne BN24 9BP

and in the United States of America by
SUSSEX ACADEMIC PRESS
920 NE 58th Ave, Suite 300, Portland, Oregon 97213-3786

and in Canada by
SUSSEX ACADEMIC PRESS (CANADA)
8000 Bathurst Street, Unit 1, PO Box 30010, Vaughan, Ontario L4J 0C6

Published in collaboration with the Cañada Blanch Centre for Contemporary Spanish
Studies, with support from the International Brigade Memorial Trust.

British Library Cataloguing in Publication Data
A CIP catalogue record for this book is available from the British Library.

Library of Congress Cataloging-in-Publication Data
Jackson, Angela, 1946–
"For us it was heaven" : the passion, grief and fortitude of Patience Darton; from
the Spanish Civil War to Mao's China / Angela Jackson.
p. cm.
Includes bibliographical references and index.
ISBN 978-1-84519-514-4 (h/b : alk. paper) —
ISBN 978-1-84519-515-1 (p/b : alk. paper)
   1. Darton, Patience, 1911–1996. 2. Spain—History—Civil War,
1936–1939—Medical care. 3. Spain—History—Civil War, 1936–1939—
Women. 4. Spain—History—Civil War, 1936–1939—Participation, British.
5. Nurses—Spain—Biography. 6. Nurses—Great Britain—Biography.
7. Communists—Great Britain—Biography. 8. Darton, Patience, 1911–1996—
Travel—China. 9. China—History—1949–1976. I. Title.
DP269.7.J34 2012
946.081'7—dc23
   [B]   2011040273

MIX
Paper from
responsible sources
FSC
www.fsc.org FSC® C013056

Typeset & designed by Sussex Academic Press, Brighton & Eastbourne.
Printed by TJ International, Padstow, Cornwall.

Contents

The Cañada Blanch Centre for Contemporary Spanish Studies

In the 1960s, the most important initiative in the cultural and academic relations between Spain and the United Kingdom was launched by a Valencian fruit importer in London. The creation by Vicente Cañada Blanch of the Anglo-Spanish Cultural Foundation has subsequently benefited large numbers of Spanish and British scholars at various levels. Thanks to the generosity of Vicente Cañada Blanch, thousands of Spanish schoolchildren have been educated at the secondary school in West London that bears his name. At the same time, many British and Spanish university students have benefited from the exchange scholarships which fostered cultural and scientific exchanges between the two countries. Some of the most important historical, artistic and literary work on Spanish topics to be produced in Great Britain was initially made possible by Cañada Blanch scholarships.

Vicente Cañada Blanch was, by inclination, a conservative. When his Foundation was created, the Franco regime was still in the plenitude of its power. Nevertheless, the keynote of the Foundation's activities was always a complete open-mindedness on political issues. This was reflected in the diversity of research projects supported by the Foundation, many of which, in Francoist Spain, would have been regarded as subversive. When the Dictator died, Don Vicente was in his seventy-fifth year. In the two decades following the death of the Dictator, although apparently indestructible, Don Vicente was obliged to husband his energies. Increasingly, the work of the Foundation was carried forward by Miguel Dols whose tireless and imaginative work in London was matched in Spain by that of José María Coll Comín. They were united in the Foundation's spirit of open-minded commitment to fostering research of high quality in pursuit of better Anglo-Spanish cultural relations. Throughout the 1990s, thanks to them, the role of the Foundation grew considerably.

In 1994, in collaboration with the London School of Economics, the Foundation established the Príncipe de Asturias Chair of Contemporary Spanish History and the Cañada Blanch Centre for Contemporary Spanish Studies. It is the particular task of the Cañada Blanch Centre for Contemporary Spanish Studies to promote the understanding of twentieth-century Spain through research and teaching of contemporary Spanish history, politics, economy, sociology and culture. The Centre possesses a valuable library and archival centre for specialists in contemporary Spain. This work is carried on through the publications of the doctoral and post-doctoral researchers at the Centre itself and through the many seminars and lectures held at the London School of Economics. While the seminars are the province of the researchers, the lecture cycles have been the forum in which Spanish politicians have been able to address audiences in the United Kingdom.

Since 1998, the Cañada Blanch Centre has published a substantial number of books in collaboration with several different publishers on the subject of contemporary Spanish history and politics. A fruitful partnership with Sussex Academic Press began in 2004 with the publication of Christina Palomares's fascinating work on the origins of the Partido Popular in Spain, *The Quest for Survival after Franco. Moderate Francoism and the Slow Journey to the Polls, 1964–1977*. This was followed in 2007 by Soledad Fox's deeply moving biography of one of the most intriguing women of 1930s Spain, *Constancia de la Mora in War and Exile: International Voice for the Spanish Republic* and Isabel Rohr's path-breaking study of anti-Semitism in Spain, *The Spanish Right and the Jews, 1898–1945: Antisemitism and Opportunism*. 2008 saw the publication of a revised edition of Richard Wigg's penetrating study of Anglo-Spanish relations during the Second World War, *Churchill and Spain: The Survival of the Franco Regime, 1940–1945* together with *Triumph at Midnight of the Century: A Critical Biography of Arturo Barea*, Michael Eaude's fascinating revaluation of the great Spanish author of *The Forging of a Rebel*.

Our collaboration in 2009 was inaugurated by Gareth Stockey's incisive account of another crucial element in Anglo-Spanish relations, *Gibraltar. A Dagger in the Spine of Spain*. We were especially proud that it was continued by the most distinguished American historian of the Spanish Civil War, Gabriel Jackson. His pioneering work *The Spanish Republic and the Civil War*, first published 1965 and still in print, quickly became a classic. The Sussex Academic Press/Cañada Blanch series was greatly privileged to be associated with Professor Jackson's biography of the great Republican war leader, Juan Negrín.

2011 took the series to new heights. Two remarkable and complementary works, Olivia Muñoz Rojas, *Ashes and Granite: Destruction and Reconstruction in the Spanish Civil War and its Aftermath* and Dacia Viejo-Rose, *Reconstructing Spain: Cultural Heritage and Memory after Civil War*, opened up an entirely new dimension of the study of the early Franco regime and its internal conflicts. They were followed by Richard Purkiss's analysis of the Valencian anarchist movement during the revolutionary period from 1918 to 1923, the military dictatorship of General Primo de Rivera and the Second Republic. It is a fascinating work which sheds entirely new light both on the breakdown of political coexistence during the Republic and on the origins of the violence that was to explode after the military coup of July 1936. The year ended with the publication of *France Divided: The French and the Civil War in Spain* by David Wingeate Pike. It made available in a thoroughly updated edition, and in English for the first time, one of the classics of the historiography of the Spanish Civil War.

An extremely rich programme for 2012 opened with Germà Bel's remarkable *Infrastructure and the Political Economy of Nation Building in Spain*. This startlingly original work exposed the damage done to the Spanish economy by the country's asymmetrical and dysfunctional transport and communications model. It is followed now by Angela Jackson's rich and moving account of an extraordinary life – that of the left-wing nurse Patience Darton. It is the first of a trio of books concerned with the International Brigades and the Republican medical services in the Spanish Civil War. The others are a comprehensive account of the Republican medical services by Linda Palfreeman and a life of Tom Wintringham by Hugh Purcell and Phyl Smith.

PAUL PRESTON
Series Editor
London School of Economics

Series Editor's Preface

Unusually, I find myself writing a preface to a biography of a woman whom I knew for well over twenty of the last years of her life. I knew her both as a neighbour in North London and also as a prominent member of the International Brigade Association whose public events I regularly attended. Angela Jackson notes that when she met Patience Darton she was struck by her regal bearing and her imperious manner. I too remember that side of her which was visible as she traversed the pavements of our local high street in her motorised wheelchair clearly expecting the startled pedestrians to make way. My other memory was of her hard-line pro-Communist stance on all issues to do with the International Brigades, a position she shared with the secretary of the International Brigade Association, Bill Alexander. Angela Jackson was able to contrast these dimensions of the elderly Patience with the image of her as a deeply idealistic and emotional young woman.

That Dr Jackson was able to draw the in-depth portrait constituted by this book suggested something which also echoed some of my own professional experiences. I have written two biographies of English women who served in the medical services during the Spanish Civil War, one of Priscilla Scott-Ellis, the only British nurse who served with the Francoist military rebels and the other of Nan Green, a young Communist who served as medical administrator with the Republicans. I was reminded again reading Dr Jackson's beautifully well-rounded account of Patience just how difficult it is to write the biography of those with little public prominence. When writing biographies of major political figures, the chronicle of whose lives is shored up by a scaffolding of political information, speeches, public appearances and meetings with other politicians, the biographer can easily fill gaps in the personal life.

In the case of the unsung heroine or hero, the biographer might be lucky enough to locate their letters and/or diaries and even to have the ambiguous good fortune to be able to interview the subject. It is ambiguous because, in order to get the subject to speak honestly about his or her life, it is necessary to establish trust and therefore a relationship. This can then pose difficulties when it comes to confronting the value of memory and evaluating the extent to which the subject has re-written or moulded their own life-story. Angela Jackson had access both to the papers and letters of

Patience Darton and also to Patience herself, whom she was able to inter-view at length. As is demonstrated by the quotations in the book, Patience's letters were emotionally expressive, often with modern opinions but revealing her concern with the issues of the day and her finely tuned aware-ness of class differences. Given the sheer power of Patience's personality which was always evident in any conversation with her and the richness of her style of letter writing, Dr Jackson is to be commended for writing a deeply sensitive portrait without losing her own critical distance.

This makes the book all the more valuable. Patience Darton was a woman of a generation and a class that did not often speak openly of personal matters. Although not a public figure, the interest of her extraordinary life is undeniable. Precisely because she was not a public figure, the problem of whether there would be adequate material was only too evident. To the rare good fortune of Dr Jackson in finding sufficient source material to be able to write a full-length book, she had the even greater luck of being able to interview Patience. That she was able to do so, and so perceptively, reflects another advantage, or perhaps crucial precondition, enjoyed by Dr Jackson. This was her unique ability to place the life in its proper context being as she is the author of two major works on the role of British nurses in the Spanish Civil War: *British Women and the Spanish Civil War* (London: Routledge, 2002) and *Beyond the Battlefield: Testimony, Memory and Remembrance of a Cave Hospital in the Spanish Civil War* (Abersychan, Pontypool: Warren & Pell, 2005).

One of Angela Jackson's most recent publications was the novel *Warm Earth* (Cambridge: Pegasus, 2007) which movingly recounted the experi-ences of three British nurses who volunteered to serve in the Republican medical services during the Spanish Civil War. As befits a novelist, the present volume is beautifully and evocatively written and further enhanced by a remarkable collection of photographs. This is also a biography of many facets, offering a wealth of insight and textual content of particular rele-vance in the context of gender studies. It tells us much of the status of nurses in Britain in the 1930s. It is also an important contribution to the history of the International Brigades and the Republican medical services in the Spanish civil war and adds nuance to our knowledge of foreigners in China in a turbulent period of its history. The story of Patience will surely appeal to many general readers as well as to specialists in those fields.

PAUL PRESTON
Series Editor
London School of Economics

Acknowledgements

My thanks to all those who have helped to enrich this biography by responding so kindly to my requests for information and images and, in some cases, by adding constructive comments to draft chapters. Above all, I am grateful to Bob Edney for allowing me to use his mother's collection of papers, especially the letters from Spain that made it possible to offer a greater understanding of Patience as a young woman and draw on her own words to express her passion, grief and fortitude.

Picture Credits

The vast majority of illustrations were taken from Patience's personal collection in the Edney family papers. Other sources are as follows:

1.1, 12.6a, 12.6b, 12.6c: Portraits of Patience. *Courtesy of Diana Gurney.*

3.1: Father Roberts and Haile Selassie. *Courtesy of St George's Church, Bloomsbury.*

4.1: Tom Wintringham and Kitty Bowler. *Courtesy of Ben Wintringham.*

4.2: Kate Mangan and Jan Kurzke. *Courtesy of Charlotte Kurzke.*

5.1: Map of key locations. *Bernard Chandler.*

5.2: View of Poleñino and the river; 5.15: Patience in her bathing suit; 5.19: The hospital at Fraga. *Agnes Hodgson, courtesy of Judith Keene.*

6.1: Robert Aaquist aged six. *Courtesy of the Aaquist family.*

6.4: Nurses' residence at Valls as it is today. *Courtesy of Jordi Perez Molina.*

7.1: View of La Mola; 9.1: The River Ebro at Miravet. *Roger Jackson.*

7.3: Mas d'en Magrinyà interior; 7.4: Dr Jolly in the sterilising lorry. *Courtesy of the family of Fernando Iaffa..*

7.5: Winifred Bates with medical staff; 9.3: Cave hospital exterior; 9.8: Dr Reggie Saxton giving a blood transfusion; 9.9: Leah Manning in the cave. 9.11: Ada Hodson with a wounded prisoner; 9.12: Aurora Fernández with the wounded boy. *Imperial War Museum, London.*

8.1: Dr Reggie Saxton and Rosaleen Smythe. *National Museum of Labour History, Manchester.*

8.3: The XI Battalion march in Falset; 8.4: The Activists Congress; 8.5: The XI Battalion on manoeuvres; 8.6: The XI Battalion fiesta. *André Marty Archive, CHS du XXe siècle, Paris.*

9.10: Nan Green and Leah Manning; 11.1: Nan Green on the boat; 13.5: Nan Green and Ted Brake; 14.18: Nan Green, Ted Brake and Harry Pollitt. *Courtesy of Martin Green.*

11.2: Isabel Brown. *May Hill.*

11.4: The Mayor of Southport and Mr D. N. Pritt. *Arthur Clegg.*

12.1: Len Crome. *Courtesy of the Crome family.*

12.4: Frida Stewart and friends; 12.5: Newspaper article. *Papers of Frida Knight.*

13.9: Horo's gravestone. *United Synagogue. www.theus.org.*

16.1: Patience and the International Brigade Association committee. *Rosalind Miller.*

16.6: Obituary photo of Patience. *Peter Nicholls, The Times, NI Syndication..*

17.2: Patience unveiling a plaque. *Nigel Tanburn.*

17.3: Portrait of Patience. *Rosalind Miller.*

17.4: Plaque in the cave hospital. *Angela Jackson.*

List of Illustrations

In each chapter, illustrations begin on the second right-hand page.

Chapter 14: Falling in Love Again

Portraying Patience

As the winter light faded from the basement sitting room, Patience Edney and I finished drinking our cups of tea and she took up the threads of her story. The desperate, sad days in the last year of the Spanish civil war were still to be recounted, adding to the several hours of tape already completed. Though tired, she was stubbornly determined to continue till the bitter end, not only to tell of defeat, but also of the inspiration she found in Republican Spain – an experience that was to shape the beliefs she held for the remainder of her life. With a grim clarity, she had already explained how the appalling conditions in the slum tenements of 1930s London had given her an overwhelming sense of the need to bring about social change, 'to <u>do</u> something' to alleviate the suffering that went hand in hand with such poverty. When she heard that in Spain, people were indeed trying 'to do something about it', and that this aim was threatened by the outbreak of war, she knew that as a nurse she could be of help. Volunteering to join the medical services in Spain was the key moment of her life.[1]

When I met Patience Edney she was in her eighties, still strikingly regal in bearing and inclined, like many nurses, to issue imperious commands relating to practical matters. Even after almost sixty years, her emotions would surface from time to time at the memory of those she had seen die in Spain, soldiers of many nationalities, civilian adults and children. But as she told her story, her eyes were not seeing the room around her, strewn with books and festooned with memorabilia from far-away places. She was looking inwards, to distant times; to private spaces where no one could follow. Later I was to discover she had been remembering lost love and the days when crossing the River Ebro could be as deadly as passage over the River Styx. That day in 1994 with Patience Edney, the first woman I interviewed on the subject of women and the war in Spain, I unknowingly stepped onto a path of research that was to last years.

Most of those who knew Patience in her later life would think of her as remarkable, spirited, or perhaps even idiosyncratic, but few would have been aware of the passions that had burned so brightly in her youth. In some ways she had much in common with other women who had gone to Spain after civil war broke out in July 1936. Her extraordinary life illustrates not only these shared factors but also highlights the many differences between them – in their motivation, experiences and the impact of the war on their lives in the longer term. Through her narrative, wider themes can also be explored, such as the relationship between women and war, their political commitment, and certain aspects of the social and political attitudes of the times.

One of the key issues of the thirties was the rise of fascism, and as the Spanish civil war escalated into a struggle with an international dimension, over two thousand five hundred men from Britain volunteered to fight in the International Brigades, believing that fascism could be stopped in Spain. For much of the war, a total of over thirty-five thousand volunteers from more than fifty countries fought alongside the soldiers of the Republic against General Franco's insurgents and their allies from Fascist Italy and Nazi Germany.[2] The eventual defeat of the Republic has been largely attributed to the iniquities of the Non-intervention pact, instigated by Britain and France. In practice, while the Republican government was denied the right to buy arms, Franco's 'Nationalists' were able to make use of heavy armaments and troops sent by Mussolini, together with the air power of the Condor Legion, dispatched by Hitler to try out new tactics of aerial bombardment in readiness for the Second World War.[3]

The role of women during more than two and a half years of this devastating struggle between left and right was perhaps more complex and diverse than ever before in wartime. During the first weeks, Spanish women took up arms to help overcome what was essentially a right-wing rebellion against the elected Republican government. For women however, the choice to actually take up arms was brief indeed. As the fighting intensified, they were recalled from the front to take up more traditional roles, their presence in the male arena of battle seen as a distraction.[4] Only one British woman is known to have been involved in active combat at the front. Felicia Browne, a sculptor already in Barcelona at the outbreak of war, enlisted in the militias and was killed shortly afterwards at the front when trying to rescue a wounded comrade.[5] Soon, in the areas still controlled by government, Spanish women were working in munitions factories and public transport, while those in the countryside laboured longer in the fields, many of them carrying the double burden of work outside the home and caring for the family because the men were at the front. The heavy bombing of cities turned women and children into casualties of war on an unprecedented scale.

The rapidly expanding technology of international communications and media coverage also brought changes. Seeing newsreel footage of the

1.1 Portrait of Patience by Diana Gurney.

1.2 Photo portrait of Patience, *c.*1934.

bombing and action photographs from the front had a huge impact on ordinary people in other countries and caused some to become actively involved in the Republican cause. The majority of women volunteers who went to Spain from other countries, like Patience Edney – Patience Darton as she was called then – worked in the medical units within the Republic as nurses.[6] Others cared for refugees and orphans, often in centres and food kitchens run by 'Quakers'.[7] Women journalists and MPs also came for short visits, gathering first hand information to write reports and to make heartfelt speeches in parliament and in public meetings on their return.[8] In addition, there were countless others who were working abroad, as for example in Britain, where thousands of people participated in the tremendously successful 'Aid Spain' campaigns; forming committees to raise funds for medical supplies, caring for refugee children, collecting tins of food and condensed milk. Despite the fact that their backgrounds and beliefs ranged across a broad spectrum, they often managed to work together effectively.[9]

Patience was amongst dozens of British nurses who contacted the Spanish Medical Aid Committee in London to volunteer for work in Spain. She arrived early in March 1937 and was to remain until the withdrawal of the International Brigades in October 1938. What led her to make such a momentous decision? Aged 25, qualified in nursing and midwifery, and with, in the expression of the day, 'no shortage of admirers', her future could have been predicted with some confidence: a steady rise within the ranks of her profession, or perhaps marriage and children. Instead, she made the decision to go to Spain, a country at war and considered in those days by most people in Britain as 'a far away country of which we know nothing'.[10] After more than two and a half years of bitter fighting, the defeat of the Republic and the loss of comrades left deep emotional scars amongst those who had taken part. For many, the aftermath of war entailed coming to terms with grief and guilt, and in certain matters, disillusionment. However, their experiences had not been entirely negative. The sense of comradeship and shared purpose was never forgotten. Long afterwards, Patience and others of her generation who had been touched by this foreign war continued to think of it as the most important event in their lives.

This book explores why Patience Darton went to Spain, how her life was changed forever by her experiences there, and how she viewed her own past in retrospect. Although she did not keep a diary or write her memoirs, a wealth of other material has enabled this biography to be compiled. In addition to lengthy interviews recorded in her later years, much of her correspondence from her time in Spain has been preserved.[11] There are further letters and documents from the four years she spent working in China. Together with archival documents, testimonies of those who worked with her and contributions from members of her family and friends who knew her over the years, it has been possible to tell the story of a courageous woman who chose a road that would have daunted the faint-hearted.

2

Sniffing at Socialism

At first glance, Patience Darton's early years offer no clear motive that would explain her decision to go to Spain. Along with the majority of volunteers, Patience had never been there and knew nothing about the turbulent history within Spain that had led to the outbreak of civil war.[1] The scant few pages of her unfinished memoirs begin with the words, 'In 1911 the world I was born into was a fat and complacent one.'[2] Her family lived a life of comfort and privilege in Orpington, with maids, and a cook, and nursery staff to care for the children. Patience Mary Gertrude, the second child of four, clearly recalled moving to a larger house with a tennis court after the birth of her younger brother, a journey of about a mile which entailed transporting the furniture in horse-drawn carts.

> I stood beside the pram with the nurse and can still feel the jealous pang, almost rage, at seeing my elder brother sitting beside the removal man, high up on the seat, holding the whip, with two huge horses pulling, and the great wooden wheels creaking.[3]

In the new house, they had both a day nursery and a night nursery and the staff lived in. Her parents did not move in the intellectual circles of 'drawing-room socialists', and unlike the numerous volunteers who had grown up immersed in the working-class movement, she knew little of party politics.[4] Her father, Charles, a deeply religious man of the Anglican High Church persuasion, worked within the long-established familial tradition of book publishing.[5] Phillis, her mother, had been raised in the heartlands of southern England, the daughter of a prosperous country rector with minor county connections. She was very proud of her family, the Courtneys, believing her ancestors had come over with William the Conqueror. All were reputed to have had long, aquiline noses, hence the nickname in French for the contrary feature, 'court nez'.[6] Always conscious of her social position, Phillis did not view her own marriage as advantageous. Patience remembered her saying that publishing was all very well, but after all, you did sell things, and what was that but trade?[7] Phillis taught all her children to read, and the house was full of books produced by the family firm, 'lovely ones,' remembered Patience, 'with wood cuts and coloured illustrations and terrible stories about wicked children who came to a bad end, and good children with death bed scenes'.[8] Phillis instilled in her children a strong sense of morality based on High-Church precepts.[9] One of her strict tenets was that owing money was as bad as stealing. This led to a night of torment for Patience as a child, who succumbed to the temptation offered by the local shopkeeper to overspend her pocket money and be in debt to the tune of a halfpenny till the following week. In a 'state of tears and choked up misery', and fearful that 'the mark of Cain would show' thereby branding her a thief when the Ten Commandments were read in church, she confessed all to her mother. 'Dear me', Patience wrote in retrospect, 'what a moral child I was.'[10]

Like many of the women interviewed because of their involvement with the war in Spain, memories from her early childhood days included Zeppelins coming down in flames during the First World War, and wounded soldiers convalescing in a nearby hospital.[11] Canadian soldiers were invited to tea as 'mother had a thing about Canada'. Patience would sit enthralled, listening to the tales of her mother's adventures there as a young women. With true pioneering spirit she had arrived on a paddle steamer to spend three years keeping house for her two brothers. They lived far out on the prairies, surrounded by deep snow for six months of the year, only able to travel to the trading depot by sleigh. But in many respects, she had a good time. Patience remembered her mother telling her that as an English girl out in Canada in the 1870s, 'you had a tremendous whirl of chaps after you'.[12]

Life changed dramatically for Patience as a child when 'father went broke' and the publishing firm went into receivership. All that remained of his business was a tiny rented cubby hole in Ludgate Circus from which he ran a postal book-finding service. Phillis sold her jewellery to pay doctors' bills and, with a disinterest bordering on distaste, attempted to cook for the first time. 'Potatoes and peas', remembered Patience, 'could be mushy or hard – mother never knew why.'[13] She remained disinclined to learn. Despite the constant stream of unpaid bills, sufficient money was found to send the children to fee-paying schools. When aged eleven, Patience was sent to St Albans High School for Girls, a Church of England Day Schools' Trust, but disliked it intensely. This was in part due to the fact that for the first term she was in trouble every day for entering the infants' cloakroom to help her sister, Hilary, then aged seven. The family were seemingly unaware that Hilary's clumsiness and lack of ability to perform simple tasks, such as doing up her button boots, together with her failure to learn to read and write, was due to the fact that she was nearly blind. 'We thought "poor child – backward" so we just looked after her.'[14] When the school eventually realised Hilary's problem and she started to wear glasses, it was discovered she was actually very intelligent.

Patience soon began to notice the institutionalised humiliation of the scholarship girls.

> Every year at the beginning of the year, they used to say, 'Now girls, your fathers have all bought your school books, your own school books, but you see these girls – your fathers are paying for their books, and they have our second-hand books and they have to keep them very clean and look after them.' And I was horrified at this public business – anyway I thought they were clever girls to get there, which we weren't, we were there because our parents did pay, and I thought it was very un-Christian.[15]

This type of early awareness of social and class injustice frequently emerges in the narratives of women who have been interviewed because of their involvement with the Spanish war, or have left written memoirs in which the war plays an important part.[16] Possibly, this tendency reveals a predisposition to discern and deplore the sufferings of others. Certainly, the selection of particular early formative experiences made by each individual can help us gain insights into the pathways of retrospective memory. For all of us, choosing what to include and exclude for retelling to others is an essential factor in the ongoing process of 'composing' our life histories.[17]

An attraction to religious belief in childhood and adolescence featured strongly in the narratives of a number of British women who were later to become involved with the war in Spain.[18] In most cases, this early faith was subject to a rigorous re-evaluation due to the insistent questioning of an inquiring mind and an avid consumption of intellectually stimulating books. This was certainly so for Patience who, despite being 'very religious' as a young girl, was unable to suppress the 'terrible doubts, the appalling doubts' that arose in her mind. She was reluctant to even mention these 'wicked' thoughts that questioned the justice of God's laws and 'rules being made for you that weren't made by you'.

> I mean, it's rather mean to be put into the world and told you mustn't do this and you must do theat, but you didn't make those rules, and then you were blamed if you did wrong. The worst was about pain for people who hadn't deserved it or earned it, and children being in pain, and animals being in pain . . . forest fires started by lightning and things like that, which burnt the little birds and terrified things. Anyway, animals have a

2.2 Patience with her mother, Phillis, and brother, John.

2.4 Patience aged two.

2.1 Patience with her brother, John, and nurse.

2.3 Charles Clark Darton, 'Pop'.

2.5 Patience with her brothers, John and Tim, having a tea party in the garden.

2.6 Patience in the garden with her brothers, John and Tim, and sister, Hilary.

2.7 The Darton children out for a ride.

2.8 Patience aged about fifteen.

2.9 Patience as a young nurse at University College Hospital.

2.11 Patience's nursing certificate, 1935.

UNIVERSITY COLLEGE HOSPITAL, LONDON.
FOUNDED 1833.

This is to Certify that

Patience Mary Gertrude Darton

entered as a Probationer in this Hospital on the *Eighteenth* day
of *June 1932* and that she has received three years'
and ten weeks' training, including the period spent in the Preliminary
Training School, in nursing, Medical and Surgical cases, and has
successfully passed all the required Examinations.

Chairman of the Nursing Committee.

Kenneth E. Harris Physician.

Surgeon.

Matron.

August 30th 1935

2.10 Father William Corbett Roberts.

rather nasty life killing one another – I thought that didn't fit in with a loving God.[19]

Another problem related to one of the Ten Commandments.

Also, the 'Honour your father and your mother' annoyed me because I didn't honour either of them – I didn't think they were managing at all well [laughter]. I despised them in lots of ways, I was very fond of them, and I was a good daughter too, but I certainly didn't honour them. And one of the things that was a great relief to me was when I got Bernard Shaw out of the library, the public library – we used to get two books a head, twelve books a week from the library – I got Bernard Shaw out, mother didn't like it, and one of the prefaces, 'The Child is Father to the Man' I think, was all about how you didn't have necessarily to honour your parents. Parents were usually at fault – and there it was in print, and I thought well, there you are.[20]

Despite such agonising dilemmas relating to Christian principles, there is no doubt that the Church played a key part in the development of Patience's social and political attitudes. She was always full of praise for the education she received as a member of the Young People's Fellowship run by Canon Skelton at St. Albans Cathedral. She considered Skelton to be 'a very great leading socialist Christian', although 'the word "socialism" was never mentioned'. The classes included lectures on 'The Church and Social Order', covering themes such as Internationalism, Trades Unions, Imperialism, Poverty and Housing. These ideas fell on fertile ground in the minds of both Patience and her sister, though her brothers were less impressed. Her mother, although liking Canon Skelton, did not entirely approve of his doctrinal approach, 'she used to sniff about it', remembered Patience, and only accepted the socialist side on sufferance.[21] For Patience however, the ideas she was learning in the classes were made even more distressingly relevant by the sights she saw whenever she attended the early morning service at the cathedral. On her way there, she had to pass the refuge for homeless men who, a little before seven o'clock were all turned out into the street, come rain, sleet or snow, clothes in rags, holes in their shoes, where they would grub about in the rubbish, hoping to find cigarette butts.[22]

Aged fourteen, Patience left St Alban's High School, aware not only of the fact that she was learning very little there, but also knowing that her parents were finding it difficult to pay the fees. Although she had disliked school, and had hated the restraints of school discipline, she was rather regretful about having left so early when several years later it transpired that financial support would have been available for her to continue. One of the mistresses, keen for Hilary to go on to college, discovered that all the children in the family would have been eligible for grants to help with their education through their father's City Guild membership.[23]

After leaving school Patience was at first employed by a local family to help a daughter who was suffering from a 'reading block'. They had been living in India and the father remained there while his wife and children returned to England. When the boys were away attending public school, Patience went to the house every day to teach the seven-year-old girl to read. The general tenor of life in this High Church, Christian Socialist family was very different from home, where Patience's mother was a 'true blue Tory'. Exciting new influences came into Patience's life with the arrival of Gandhi who stayed with the family during a visit to England to see the Prime Minister. At first, Patience 'didn't think anything of it, he was just, you know, a little chap who was about the place'. Nevertheless, she soon heard of India's need to be free and was given the memorable task of helping to look after the Mahatma's goat.

> He had to have goat's milk, we had a lot of business getting hold of the goat and having it milked and things . . . that struck me very much, it was rather fun with all this goat business.[24]

Patience moved on to coach another child then, following a term as an emergency relief teacher at a prep school for Repton, she worked for a while in a tea shop, learning to cook and saving money to enable her to train as a nurse. Her choice of career was appropriate for more than the obvious humanitarian reasons. Reflecting in later life on her decision to enter the medical profession, she commented, 'If you feel you are oppressed, you look for work that will give you a certain degree of power. I'm sure many nurses and teachers choose their work for that reason. Of course, naturally, I wanted to help people too.'[25] Her dream of becoming a doctor was never worth mentioning as it was just so totally impossible. Even becoming a nurse was a challenging ambition in view of the initial costs of training and a uniform, then about £15, and the need to have the correct contacts. Mrs Skelton came to the rescue with a financial contribution and by arranging for Patience to have an interview at University College Hospital in London. She 'romped through the exam' for entry, thanks to all the essay writing she had done at the Young People's Fellowship.

Almost twenty-one, keen to help people and be useful, Patience began a career that brought her into contact with people suffering the extreme poverty prevalent in the thirties amongst the unemployed. Whilst training at University College Hospital, a major teaching establishment, she saw many cases 'too far gone' for treatment. Women especially couldn't afford medical care, 'they died on us', she remembered sadly. In interviews, she gave a detailed account of nursing patients with common illnesses such as tuberculosis and emphysema, bronchitis and of course, different types of cancer. On arrival, the patients were sometimes so dirty that it was a case of 'out with the ether bottle' to scour them clean. She remembered children being admitted for simple mastoids who fell victim to an epidemic of diarrhoea and vomiting, and died 'from coming into hospital'. With no antibiotics, the standards of hygiene expected to be maintained by the nurses was high, any case of wound infection was considered 'a disgrace' and everyone was horrified.[26]

Although Patience knew that the hospital was helping people who were unable to pay for treatment, she was not happy about the fact that private patients were treated differently, even down to the sheets and china they were allocated, and particularly, the bed pans. Whilst the poor were given 'horrible round metal bed pans which bit you terribly – ate into you – most uncomfortable', the private patients were given bed pans with a much more comfortable shape, a design in common use now.

This period was not without its problems as she became involved with a group of nurses who were intending to voice their grievances about the conditions of their training. Some, like Patience, who were amongst the most competent, were left in the same ward for weeks instead of being moved throughout the various departments to receive proper training in each. Patience remembered being kept on night duty for eleven weeks without having a night off. When rumours of trouble reached the ears of the Assistant Matron, the ring leaders were brought before her and told to drop the matter or it would 'kill Matron'. When each was asked separately if they were willing to kill Matron, Patience was the only one to answer in the affirmative. 'You can't believe how put down we were', recalled Patience. Senior nursing staff in those days saw complaining as 'very vulgar and horrid', 'a working class thing to do'.[27] Fortunately Matron did not die of horror when Patience presented their case.

In the little time she had off duty, sometimes Patience would attend St. George's Church in Bloomsbury, London, 'well known to be left wing'. It was here that she met the man who was to become a key influence in her way of thinking over the next few years, the Rector of St George's, Father Roberts. William Corbett Roberts followed his conscience rather than the views commonly held by the Church authorities of the day. This had led him to support the suffragists' campaign, even going as far as to contemplate the ordination of women. He was a pacifist, adding his voice to the movement that was increasingly active between the world wars.[28] As an intellectual who made great efforts to be both comprehensible and available to his parishioners, he was greatly loved. He and his unconventional wife, Ursula, better known as the writer, Susan Miles, filled the house with refugees and the homeless. He took on the Chaplaincy of a London County Council hospital for women and girls with venereal diseases, and for many years was the Chairman of the Association for Moral and Social Hygiene. However, the exceptional nature of his views and his compassion for the underdog can be judged from a remark he made when called to give evidence at a Committee dealing with Street Offences. With passionate conviction he affirmed, 'Legal action against classes of people on moral grounds is dangerous and to be avoided.'[29] Patience would sometimes be so exhausted after work that when she went to church, she would fall asleep. But Father Roberts, who was living quite near the hospital in Gower Street, became a great source of support and her confidant. 'I could go round there,' she explained, 'it was a home to go to, away from this very tiresome and very exhausting hospital. And I could talk.'[30]

Retrospectively, Patience was aware that the boundaries between religious and political belief amongst the people she encountered at St George's tended to be fluid, remembering that 'people sort of zoomed in, to and fro, from the Communist Party to it, and out again, mostly women, young girls'.[31] What could be regarded as a pattern of 'transference of faith' emerges quite frequently in the narratives of women who, at different times during their lives, had shown commitment to their church and to left-wing political parties.[32] At St. George's Patience learned about the persecution of the Jews, praying for them and for all the refugees, mainly from Germany, that were arriving in rapidly increasing numbers in Britain. When Italy invaded Abyssinia, Haile Selassie joined their congregation. Patience recalled that he seemed to her 'a funny little man with a bowler hat, little tiny creature, very gloomy – well naturally, who wouldn't be'.[33]

In 1935 Patience took her first small step into the world of politics by voting in the General Elections, 'quivering away – it was very exciting going to vote for the first time, voting Labour . . . The hospital was very much against it.' Her interest in politics grew after attending a speech given by Professor J.B.S. Haldane, a left-wing scientist from University College, London. The medical students handed out a notice saying that he would be giving a special lecture on the subject of the forthcoming election to the hospital staff.

We didn't know anything about J.B.S. Haldane, and two or three of us went from UCH, and one other person, a lad, a man – must have been either a porter or a male nurse – in a little hall, very near the hospital, off Euston Road. And J.B.S. Haldane completely lost his voice from lecturing and he came on the platform by himself to do it, and took one glance at the three of us cowering down the other end, and he came down and sat down, and said, 'turn your chairs round, and sit here in a ring,' and took off his collar and tie, which surprised us very much, you know, anyone doing that, and gave a marvellous lecture – he was a very nice person.[34]

His theories introduced Patience to new ideas about the social changes that were necessary for a healthy population; how certain illnesses, such as tuberculosis, could be overcome with the introduction of better food and living conditions for the poor.

Having decided that she wanted to become a midwife, Patience was aghast to find that she would have to find a fee of £30 for the training course. The only other alternative was to sign up for two years to work for the local authority after qualifying, a commitment she was loath to make. It was then that she discovered she would be eligible, as her sister had been, for a grant from the Cloth Workers' Guild. Due to traditions of patrimony, she had followed in her father's footsteps and become a member when she was twenty-one. However, there was still the problem of finding funds to pay for clothing and other essentials during her six months' training. Her first thought was to undertake some private nursing and save money, but the black mark she had earned during her protest about the nurses' training meant that she had been labelled as 'unsuitable for private nursing'. Without a recommendation from the hospital she had little chance of finding work in the private sector. Instead she found she could earn more, £5 a month plus board, by working in a cancer research hospital where the amount of radium in use was considered dangerous enough to warrant higher salaries. [35] She was scandalised to discover that while the doctors, medical students and supervisors were given a monthly blood test to monitor their radiation levels, it was not considered necessary to do so for the nurses.

> We nurses could accumulate any amount of radiation in our bodies because we were easy to replace. If we became ill, they would say, 'Poor thing. What a pity. We'll have to find another.' I never wanted to return to work in a place like that, not because of the radiation, but because I never would allow myself be treated in such away again.[36]

After three months she had saved £10, sufficient for her to begin midwifery training. Like many of those who went to Spain, the poverty and social injustice Patience was to see in her work laid the foundation stones for the construction of a subsequent commitment to socialism.[37]

3

The Road to Spain

By the time war broke out in Spain in July 1936, Patience was training in midwifery at the British Hospital for Mothers and Babies in Woolwich. She agreed wholeheartedly with the philosophy at this progressive institution, which advocated 'cooperative' childbirth and gave classes to prospective mothers so that they understood what was happening. When working 'on the district' in East London she frequently cared for women weakened by malnutrition and repeated pregnancies. The old tenements in which they lived were bug infested and squalid. Such unhealthy conditions in the cities of Britain had led to a substantial increase in maternal mortality over the previous decade.[1] Patience's memories of the poverty she saw were explicit. All but three of the fifty women she cared for during her training period were the wives of unemployed men, and as such, were subject to the indignities of the Means Test before receiving even the most paltry sums of financial help from the state.

> Of course, on the district there, particularly in the tenement houses, there were [several] families to a floor, with, if you were lucky, a cold tap on the floor, otherwise there'd be a cold tap downstairs, maybe four floors down. And each floor usually had a sink of some sort to throw water away in, it might have a lavatory, otherwise there'd be lavatories in the yard, but communal, very nasty – a long way too if you were on the third floor. There weren't any risers on the stairs, or banisters, they were taken off for wood – you had just the steps, but not the upright bits, and no banisters, no wood anywhere around – a family to a room on these floors, a gas stove with a penny in the slot, but unless you stood by your penny – your kettle that you'd put on, or got somebody to, somebody else would 'whup' out and get your penny's worth when you were back with the Mum, you see. And mostly people were out of work so there wasn't any money *at all*. You had to sell everything, and you were allowed to keep a table and a chair, a chair per person, and a table, and a cup and saucer and a plate – I don't know about the saucer, but a plate and a couple of pans and a kettle. Otherwise, anything else you had, had to be sold before you got your

eighteen bob a week per head. Anyone who was working had their pay deducted from that, working boys and girls had to leave home because otherwise, their money was taken – not enough anyway, you hadn't got anything left of your earnings. Oh! And people were putting up with it, they were absolute darlings, you see. Very nice being a midwife because you're longed for and you're loved you see, you're welcome, you're a king person – a queen person – in the house, it's absolutely lovely and anyway, you're doing a nice job. I loved it.[2]

Patience became accustomed to taking the most basic necessities with her to attend the women about to give birth.

Half the time the children were crammed on to the one mattress, and you had to park them around, get the neighbours up to get rid of the – to park the children out so that you didn't deliver the mother on top of the children in the bed. Usually there weren't sheets. There was quite often a blanket or sometimes coats and things on top. We used to take a sheet to deliver on, a draw sheet thing. And we used to take newspapers to put round us, to put our things on, to stand the chair on that you were going to sit on while you had to wait for it, because you could see the bugs on them then – on the newspaper, and you could hear them falling, 'tss, tss, you know, little cricky noise on the newspaper. There was one wretched woman whose husband was in a mental hospital, and he used to be sent out on holiday once a year and start a baby. That was dreadful because the neighbours didn't approve of her – she was a slumocky woman, I must say, poor thing – she was also a mental defective. But it was very difficult to get rid of the children – there were four or five then – they had to be parked round.

That was certainly the dirtiest place I've ever been in. Took a long while, she was so weak, she took a long while to have the baby. Goodness, was it buggy! Had a great, terrible double bed without a mattress on – on the springs. You couldn't reach her – I'd be lying right across on these bouncy springs. And on the Sunday, one of the days I was there all day and night, Sunday morning the Salvation Army came and played hymns outside because they looked after her you see. And that I found annoying – very loud. [Laughter][3]

In another interview, when referring to the same occasion, Patience explains her annoyance at hearing these hymns was due to more than just the volume of the music. Seemingly, it was due to the fact that the help the Salvation Army gave was of little practical use, given the severity of the woman's problems, and she was angered by the futility of singing hymns at such a time. 'HYMNS!', Patience repeated in exasperation, 'I never wanted to hear another hymn again.'[4] After the baby was born, small but perfect, Patience returned several times with clean baby clothes, always to find the infant covered with lice and the clothes gone, pawned or sold. 'There was no hope', said Patience sadly. 'How can a woman who can't even look after herself possibly look after five or six children?'[5]

Patience greatly admired the matron of the maternity hospital, 'an absolute darling, a real fighter', who had founded the hospital to improve conditions for women in childbirth at a time when Victorian ignorance and traditional superstitions were still prevalent. Matron was not, however, in favour of Patience's decision to go to Spain, calling it 'an emotional extravagance'.[6]

> I was very upset with this because I was very fond of her and it seemed to me quite straight forward . . . She thought it was an emotional thing on my part – which was probably true, it was – but it was quite a sensible emotion I thought. I was very downcast by that but it didn't stop me in the least.[7]

When reviewing the motivations of one's own youth in a retrospective light, all may be tinted by reflections from our later perceptions. After the Spanish civil war, Patience joined the Communist Party of Great Britain. When interviewed in the 1980s and 90s, with years of political activity behind her, she viewed her motives for going to Spain in the context of this later commitment.

> I was purely political. I was so terribly browned off with the state of England and nothing being done about it – and there were the Spaniards doing something about it . . . I realised that – I don't know how I had the sense, but I did.[8]

In another interview, she explains how before going to Spain she was not 'politically organised', thereby showing that in her mind there was a distinction between being 'political' in general terms, and being 'politically organised' by being a member of a specific political party.

> The hospital I was in, the midwifery, was doing good work, UCH was doing good work, but it wasn't getting anywhere, we weren't even touching the edge of the problem and I didn't know what organisations existed for this. It worried me very much. And then, I don't really know

3.1 Father Roberts and Haile Selassie.

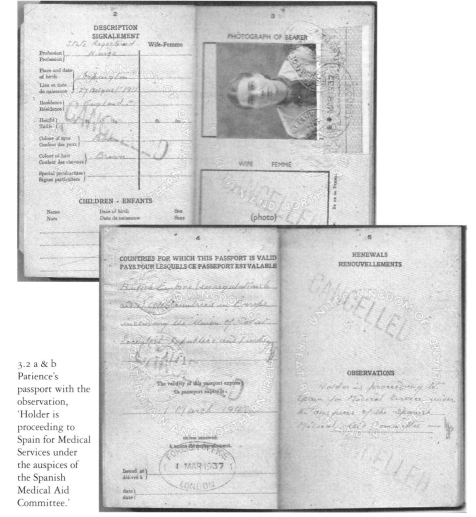

3.2 a & b Patience's passport with the observation, 'Holder is proceeding to Spain for Medical Services under the auspices of the Spanish Medical Aid Committee.'

how I had the sense – because I didn't read much in the newspaper, you couldn't afford to buy one, but if one of the patients had a paper they lent it to you, or gave it to you to take off in the evening – but I wasn't in the least politically organised, except touching with the church things, which of course, I'd lost when I got to Woolwich, a long way away from my dear St George's, which was political and knew about things and knew about Italy and took a dim view about Mussolini going in to Abyssinia. In that way I was organised, I knew there was something going on. But then when Spain started, I thought, they're doing something. They're just ordinary people there and they've risen and they're doing something, and I'm a nurse, I can do something too, because mostly women couldn't, you see. I didn't know how to get into it, but I knew perfectly well, this was the place, there they were doing something, and I was lucky, I could do something too.[9]

With a will to 'change things', not just within the framework of maternity care, but to assail the fundamental causes of the poverty she witnessed around her, Patience set off to volunteer. Having no idea how to get to Spain, she went firstly to inquire at the offices of the *Daily Herald*, knowing that it was a 'Labour paper'. There, the journalists, 'very nice young lads', ran round trying to help her. Someone remembered that the *News Chronicle* had been running an appeal for medical aid for Spain. With great enthusiasm, she was taken there in a taxi, and then to the Spanish Medical Aid Committee (SMAC) offices in Holborn. At the time, unlike some of the other nurses who went to Spain, she was not familiar with the Communist newspaper, the *Daily Worker*, which had been running an appeal for volunteer medical staff. After a brief interview at the SMAC office, she was accepted. She was contacted sooner than she had expected by the Secretary of the Committee. Urgent help was needed for the Commander of the British Battalion.

> I was rung up at the end of three days to say would I go out the next day to nurse Tom Wintringham, who was dying of typhoid. He had a wife in England, and he was dying of typhoid and the wife had only just got to know about it. And she went to the Committee and said, you know, one of your nurses must go. And I was rung up, we were on the phone then in St. Albans, and I was rung up by George Jeger who said would I go out the next day to nurse Tom Wintringham. So I demurred, I said I was really going out to nurse the Spanish people, the soldiers, and not a single foreigner. And he said well of course, you'll be going on to do this, but he had the sense to put Mrs Wintringham on to me and nothing much you

could do with the wife telling you about her husband dying of typhoid. So I agreed and went off.[10]

Mrs Wintringham, 'in a great state' of worry, gave Patience £3, a considerable amount in those days and within a week, a passport and visa had been obtained for her by the Committee. She was also provided with a uniform, but poured scorn on the Committee's choice of suitable clothing for service near the front line. She complained, justifiably, about the 'three silly little blue frocks with white collars and turned back cuffs', and of the problems of wearing the cross-over overalls that kept uncrossing and opening up. Particularly impractical were the all-in-one men's overalls. Few toilets were available at the front, only 'very low bushes, terribly low bushes, and if you wanted to get out to the loo for a pee, you had to take all your top off.' Furthermore, underwear, stockings, shoes, and sanitary towels were not supplied. As unpaid volunteers, sometimes with scarce resources of their own, the lack of these items could prove troublesome. Patience borrowed from other nurses until circumstances changed and she began to receive a soldier's pay.[11] She never wore the large white head dresses that had been included with the uniform. Apparently, the Committee was unaware of attitudes in the Republic regarding hats, where at the time, 'anyone who wore head-gear of any sort was considered a fascist'.[12]

Patience's parents knew nothing of her plan to go to Spain till after she had been accepted as a volunteer.

> And I went back and told mother, who gulped a bit. I must say, I was very hard hearted; it never occurred to me that she'd mind about it. . . . She certainly didn't like the idea very much but she swallowed and accepted the fact that I was going to do it anyway. . . . I didn't consider what my father thought about it, never occurred to me to ask him or discuss it.[13]

Oral and written testimonies reveal that many of the volunteers did not discuss their intentions beforehand with their families. When informed, the parents of these determined and independent individuals, like Patience's mother, often already knew the futility of attempting to change their minds.[14] Possibly, those who were less resolute discussed the matter with families and friends and were dissuaded from such a dangerous undertaking. Patience's mother had mixed emotions regarding her daughter's plans. She approved wholeheartedly of the idea of service to others, and could also feel some pride in the re-emergence of the pioneering spirit that had taken her to Canada in her own youth. For both parents however, their daughter's commitment to the cause of the Republic was a difficult pill to swallow. 'To the end of their days', recalled Patience, 'they did not think I could be any worse than a Socialist – that was bad enough.'[15]

At St. George's, Patience was given 'a good send off' shortly before her departure for Spain.

> . . . they had a great 'bidding' prayer from the Church. First of all it was mentioned in the service and then I was seen off down the steps, with all the congregation and Father Roberts, and there was Haile Selassie, but he didn't know quite what was going on [laughter] – anyway, he was dragged out to do it.[16]

The journey to Spain for Patience was unlike that of many other volunteers. Most crossed the channel by boat, then travelled mainly by train. In later years, Patience was amused to recall that her own journey to the front began from the prestigious Dorchester Hotel, the departure point for the bus to Croydon airport. A small plane took her to Paris. After travelling across France on the night train to Toulouse, she boarded another plane, delighted when it flew low over the Pyrenees and she could see the sun on the snow. She spent a short time in the airport at Barcelona, waiting for a flight to Valencia, still dressed in her uncomfortable uniform of blue dress, white stockings and typical nurses' headwear. She was charmed by her first encounter with a Spanish soldier, a small, smiling, young man with a rifle who, unable to say anything to her in English, rushed about to find flowers to give her instead.

On her arrival in Valencia in March 1937, while still tired from the journey, she wrote to Father Roberts at St George's, describing the flight and her first impressions of the city.

> My dear Father
> As you see I arrived safely and had a very easy journey indeed – everyone rallied to my assistance in quite an embarrassing way, not that I was embarrassed, now I come to think of it. It is lovely and hot here, and a beautiful place. The flight from Toulouse was absolutely heavenly . . . From Barcelona we flew over the sea – along the coast. It looked quite absurdly beautiful – blue sea, red country, pink mountains.
>
> The Spanish people are sweet – overfriendly and helpful. I have been journeying by tram today – the trams pack quite full, and you just cling on to the steps, but directly anyone saw my red cross they flew to get me in and give me a seat or talk and talk – all I can say is *Ingles Infirmaria* [sic], but it's quite enough for them. The job will be a tough one, but I don't mind.[17]

The letter also reveals that she had not been as confident about her adventure as her later interviews might suggest and gives an indication of the strength of her religious belief at the time. She tells Father Roberts that saying her prayers on the train from Toulouse the night before had helped calm her anxieties, leaving her feeling 'lovely and contented'.[18]

4

Patients and Politics in Valencia

A recurring theme in the narratives of the foreign volunteers is the vivid memory of their arrival in Republican Spain. Most had never been abroad before and were overwhelmed by the warmth of the climate and by the welcome they were given by local people. [1] Patience arrived in Valencia in March 1937, enchanted by the orange trees, the flowers and the vibrant life in the city. Her first impressions, given briefly in the letter she wrote to Father Roberts on her arrival, were still vivid decades later when she was interviewed in 1984.[2]

> And the trams were like – I'd never seen anything like it in England – the crowding, people jammed all the way round, holding on to the little rails round the outside, round the windows and jammed tight on to the back, all hanging on round the edges of things, not quite on top, but all but. And they put me on to this and said where I had to get off, and I couldn't hold on to anything, I held on to people. I got my feet on and I was held on and they took my bags. And when we got to the hospital, ever so many people got off the tram to help me across, they were terribly excited about this English nurse come to help Spain . . . And I thought this was very sweet and very welcoming.[3]

With some difficulty she found Tom Wintringham in the Pasionaria Hospital where he was in a room by himself. His nursing care was primarily being carried out by a young American woman, Kitty Bowler, with whom he was having an affair. They had met in Barcelona in September 1936 where both were working as journalists and had fallen in love. It was not a case of love at first sight. However, Wintringham, 'balding, bespectacled, and already married', had a gentle manner and sense of humour that soon captivated the petite and vivacious Kitty.[4] Shortly afterwards she began working for the propaganda department of the Catalan government, and Tom Wintringham asked to transfer to the International Brigades where his military experience in the First World War was considered very useful. He had taken command of the British Battalion on 6 February 1937 for a brief period until he was wounded in the leg during the Battle of Jarama.[5]

By the time of Patience's arrival Tom Wintringham had been in hospital for some time and was running a dangerously high temperature. Patience's memories of the hospital were not favourable. Standards of hygiene and asepsis were low at that time in Spain, and there was no tradition of nursing training comparable with that in Britain. When the Second Republic was established in 1931, initiatives had been introduced to set up nursing schools in some regions. The Catalan government began an ambitious project for training nurses, the first school having opened in Barcelona in 1933, but numbers of trained nurses were still minimal and nursing care of the patients was generally carried out by other family members or by nuns.[6] Despite Kitty's efforts to care for Tom, in Patience's opinion, his condition was as grave as the state of the hospital amenities.

> He was very wretched, and the place was filthy and the flies were awful, and there wasn't anything − nothing that you'd want − the sheets were dirty. I went to look at the loo − the loo was dreadful, it was open doors anyway, at the end of the passage, all open. And most of the people hadn't got there anyhow − not only on the floor, all shit, but up the walls − I still don't know how people do it so high up the walls. And the whole thing was blocked anyhow. I took a dim view of that.[7]

Fortunately, while at UCH, a teaching hospital, Patience had some training and experience of nursing typhoid cases.

> And I remembered quite well then that the old method for nursing typhoid was that you kept them on no food at all, sips of milk and thin bread and butter, nothingness, for six weeks, so they wouldn't perforate because that's what you do with typhoid if you get it badly, your intestines perforate and you get general intestinal poisoning and you die. And this was not considered a good thing. They had looked into it and the little 'Peyer's patches', the bits that get the infection in your intestines, give out in the second week of your infection. If you don't perforate in the second week, you're not going to perforate − that phase is over, and you'd better be fed, because people were taking a long time to recover from typhoid because they were starved. Now I remembered that and I thought 'Oh, well, thank goodness for UCH.'[8]

On learning more about Tom's illness from Kitty, Patience told her, 'Don't worry, if he's been ill that long, he's got over his typhoid, we'll have to feed him up.' While Kitty went to search for suitable food, Patience decided to 'tepid sponge' her patient to reduce his high temperature and make him more comfortable. 'He was so wretched you see, so dirty and prickly and horrible.' When the doctor arrived Patience welcomed him with smiles, but he responded with a furious tirade in Spanish. Patience could understand little of what he said but when Kitty returned, she explained the reason for his outburst. Apparently, he was firmly convinced that washing the patient was almost sure to be lethal. A form was produced for Patience to sign, taking complete responsibility for the likely death of her charge. She signed her acceptance when perhaps other, more timid young women, would not have dared to do so. This episode, occurring so soon after her arrival, was just a foretaste of the challenges and responsibilities that were to come.

The high temperature was, in fact, due to a wound infection beneath the sutures. Patience re-opened the wound and drained the abscesses. This intervention, in combination with good nursing and a diet of light foods, soon resulted in the patient's recovery. Visitors arrived, including Professor J.B.S. Haldane, who came several times and according to Patience, had heated arguments with Wintringham.[9] Now beginning to learn a little more about her patient, Patience realised that he was a Communist. However, when Harry Pollitt came to visit, she had no idea that this 'very nice' man was the leader of the Communist Party of Great Britain. 'Harry' she recalled later, 'was always an angel to everyone, particularly an angel to a nice young girl – all so "Harryish" but only in the nicest possible way.'[10] This assessment of Harry Pollitt's behaviour towards women is seemingly contradicted by his treatment of Kitty Bowler. Convinced that she was some sort of Trotskyist spy, he advised Wintringham to end the affair. The fact that Wintringham refused to do so, and went on to marry Kitty despite Pollitt's disapproval, soured relations between the two men and contributed to Wintringham's expulsion from the British Communist Party.[11]

On March 22 Patience wrote again to Father Roberts, thanking him for his letters. Those that were posted directly to her had only taken a week to arrive. She still had not received the letter he had tried to send through Spanish Medical Aid and already signs were evident of the tensions that were developing between Patience and the Committee. 'Don't take any notice of what they say,' she wrote, 'they're the world's biggest fools.' Tom Wintringham's health was improving rapidly so this gave her more time to enjoy herself. 'I'm having the time of my life here. Spoilt to death; taken out all the time.' Her letter then takes on a more serious note as she tries to assess attitudes in Spain towards the Church, finding it 'queer being here

4.1 Tom Wintringham and Kitty Bowler.

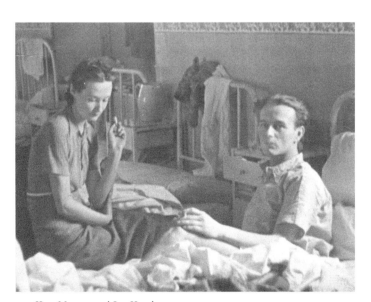

4.2 Kate Mangan and Jan Kurzke.

in Holy Week, but not so difficult as I expected'. She fears that the people are rejecting religion but writes that 'the tragic thing is that they know not what they do'.

> The anticlerical feeling here is very strong but I can't believe the people will lose Christ. There is no outward sign of this here though.[12]

One of the people Patience met during these first weeks in Valencia was the resourceful and determined Kate Mangan, who had come to Spain to find the German International Brigader, Jan Kurzke. In 1933, Jan Kurzke had fled Germany, where his commitment to Marxism and anti-fascism had led him to take part in street fights with the Nazis.[13] The following year he met Kate Mangan, a former student at the Slade School of Art.[14] When he joined the International Brigades, she followed him to Spain, arriving in October 1936. While searching with dogged determination for the man she loved, she turned her hand to various jobs, at first translating and interpreting then working for the press office in Valencia.[15] Kate wrote of Patience Darton's arrival in the city with her customary talent for observation.

> When the nurse arrived for Tom she caused a sensation. She was a lovely, earnest creature called Patience. She was tall, thin, angular and virginal. She had a mass of ash-blond hair done up in a bun, but usually covered by a white kerchief. Her face was pointed and eager, with a full mouth, rather large nose and very striking, very blue eyes . . . She looked like the kind of beautiful hospital nurse one dreams of . . .[16]

Kate persisted with her search for Jan Kurzke, and eventually found him, wounded and seriously ill. She managed to arrange for him to be transferred to Valencia.

> Though he reached the Pasionaria [hospital] by chance it was the best place for him. His operation was over, and to be in the same hospital as Tom [Wintringham], with Patience and Louise [Kitty Bowler] always in and out meant a lot of little extra comforts for him. The Spanish nurses were too modest to wash him but Patience did, and rubbed him with alcohol so he would not get sore from lying in bed.[17]

During her time in Valencia, Patience also became friendly with the foreign journalists working there, most of whom were staying at the Hotel Inglés. They supplied her with useful equipment in short supply, such as gauze and bed pans, and she took advantage of the friendship by bathing in the bathroom at the hotel. Kate Mangan, by this time working in the press office in Valencia, later recalled in her memoirs, 'She [Patience] used to come into the office in the afternoons to read the English papers and became popular with the journalists and British Embassy personnel.' On one occasion they were both invited to a dinner at the Embassy, which Patience attended in her nursing uniform due to the fact that she had no formal dress to wear. During the dinner Patience apparently became 'very earnest and rather shrill about Medical Aid in Spain', eliciting a polite but distant reply from her neighbour at the dinner table. They were not invited again.[18]

Patience's social life at this time included encounters with many of the writers and intellectuals either based in, or passing through, Valencia. She came into contact with Stephen Spender, 'a beautiful creature', who was visiting a friend from the International Brigades in hospital.[19] An English poet and middle-class intellectual, Spender was an ardent supporter of the Republic though his membership of the Communist Party was short lived. Whilst in Spain, he was attempting to help Tony Hyndman, his lover, who had been captured after deserting from the International Brigades. An undated note, accompanying Patience's letter to Father Roberts in March 1937, tells of her meeting with Spender and the well-known American writer, Ernest Hemingway, over a café cognac. Her description of them is refreshingly candid.

> Spender is tall – about 6'2" and too 'Great God' for words. He is perfectly sweet and very gentle and is torn in two between his pacifist nature – he couldn't kill anyone and hates war – and his mind, which sees this war as the only hope for Europe against fascist domination. He's got bright blue eyes, like a new kitten, with just the same groping expression of bewilderment against this bloody world. Hemingway is a great burly chap with a thick neck and a roll of flesh round the back of it. He is charming and humble – seems really so. He had a jaw wound in the Great War and has a hesitation in his speech.

She wrote that the conversation ranged over 'their own books and everyone else's books and life and love'. Stephen Spender lamented that he could only write of past things and not of reality. He wondered if he would find reality in Spain at war. Patience carefully noted Hemingway's reply.

> Hemingway said no – you think you find reality, because you think you're up against elemental things, but it's like squeezing a lemon on an oyster.

At first the oyster reacts and shrinks, but quickly it loses its power of reacting and the reality of the lemon ceases to be genuine.

Hemingway, she commented, 'can't say what he wants to say and he talks just like his books, in bursts'. She was amazed to find that they seemed prepared to listen to her opinions.

We were talking about books and I said how much I wanted the Oxford Book of English Verse. They both agreed and Stephen said he wanted to read right thru [sic.] the Bible. Hemingway said 'Have you ever done that? It's a hell of a good book – you find where all the others have pinched their titles from.' Spender said he'd lost his feeling of the necessity of keeping a moral standard, and civilisation and culture. He says the best thing for the world – the only hope for the world – was to fight it with its own weapons. I said I couldn't accept that, and they both agreed I was probably right. When I met them I was in a bad way, as living with Communists is very hard work. They live in such a different world, and are so sure that they are right and everyone else criminally wrong. However Hemingway and Spender were awfully kind and talked to me for a long while just as though I had as much sense as they had and I found I could speak their language and they spoke mine. Apart from that considerable comfort they were fascinating to listen to.[20]

Stephen Spender may well have heard from Patience about Father Roberts at some point during this meeting. On his return to England, Spender gave a talk about the civil war in Spain at one of the congregational lunches habitually organised by St George's church to hear the experiences of returning missionaries. Spender was apparently well aware of the reputation of St George's, knowing that 'three members of the congregation had gone as nurses with the International Brigades'.[21]

Patience, as is evident from her letter to Father Roberts, was still far from becoming committed to Communism, and later correspondence reveals that this continued to be a matter for much personal deliberation. Though her attitude towards Communists was to change radically as the war progressed, her own tolerant views on the sexuality of certain individuals she met remained basically unchanged. Subjects such as nurses' unwanted pregnancies or Stephen Spender's bisexuality were not mentioned in interviews. Years later, she still had reservations about the wisdom of making public any comments on the subject. When being questioned for an article about Spanish Medical Aid, she was prepared to criticise the organisation in certain respects but was nevertheless concerned that its reputation should be protected when it came to the sexual orientation of a Committee member, Viscount Churchill. She feared that her own attitudes, liberal for those days, might still not be shared by others, and that it would be better to omit information that could reflect badly on Spanish Medical Aid.[22]

> I didn't mention Peter Churchill derogatorily as a 'pansy'. In Valencia I had to beat off all the non-Spanish contingent and Churchill and his boy friend were a relief and a help. I wouldn't mention it as it might be regarded as bad for the Committee image.[23]

When Patience felt that Tom Wintringham no longer required a full-time trained nurse, her demands to be sent where her skills could be put to better use led her into conflict with the Spanish Medical Aid Committee. At first, she was sent to a fever hospital to nurse two Brigaders with typhoid. She was dismayed to find that quarantine was non-existent and that the doctors were nearly all pro-Franco. Patience soon joined forces with the medical students to bring about some desperately needed changes.

> (It was) a big convent, the whole place round a beautiful square, a nice medieval place, and with a sloping roof all the way round underneath, out of which they'd thrown all the dressings and things for some years, so if you opened the window, a rash thing to do, it used to 'woof' as the flies all flew up, just like a bee, you know, a real noise of the flies flying up. So we had a grand time sluicing this down with hoses and water, and having it taken away, with the students and me. I can't say it made the hospital people like me any more, the doctors, but anyway we had a very nice time doing this, feeling very revolutionary.

Kate Mangan's memoirs offer further details on Patience's work at the fever hospital, describing how she and Jan were drawn in to help with the work of making changes.

> Her crusading fervour was at its height and she had plenty of scope for it. The hospital was an ancient, insanitary building, rife with all the germs of ages, an antique lazaretto of a place. When Patience first got there she found that the sick men had never been undressed but were lying in dirty sheets in their filthy uniforms. The hospital had no change of linen and no soap. She said that every day she expected to find them all dead, but only one died. All infectious diseases were mixed together and all were allowed to receive their families, including children. Patience got us to write slogans in Spanish and set Jan to making posters representing

diabolical germs clinging to visitors' skirts or the dust on the ends of brooms.[24]

Life suddenly became more complicated for Patience when she became embroiled in events surrounding the fate of Basil Murray, an episode which was to have far-reaching implications for her. Basil, the son of Professor Gilbert Murray, the Oxford classicist, was one of the idiosyncratic characters drawn to the Republican cause. In retrospect, Kate Mangan thought they had all tended to treat him rather heartlessly, failing to take him seriously and even avoiding him when he tried to waylay them for a chat in the hotel corridor where they both were staying. She described him as clearly 'the désorienté intellectual', 'around forty and, I think, a bit of a failure'.

> He wore his hair long at the back, like Lloyd George, and was very sensitive. He had bright, dewy eyes like a stricken deer.[25]

He worked in the press office for a while and then for the International News Service, but was given the sack. He thought of joining the International Brigades but was discouraged by Tom Wintringham who told him, 'You can do far more good by getting your father to use his influence for the Republican cause.' Lonely and depressed, he nevertheless refused to consider going home. By this time he was drinking heavily and, as Kate Mangan recalled in her memoirs, his behaviour was becoming bizarre.

> He bought a monkey with sad brown eyes a bit like his own. The management [of the hotel] protested but he said, 'What about all the other monkeys who live here?' and they gave way. It was not a nice monkey; it was too big for a pet and very ill-tempered. It had a habit of snatching at one through the open door as one passed as if conniving with its master to drag visitors in. He named it after a girl he had been in love with.[26]

One evening shortly afterwards, Kate Mangan was told that Basil was ill and went up to his room to see him. By this time, the monkey had disappeared. Basil was sallow and waxen, his eyes luminously bright. He had been vomiting and complained of pain in the diaphragm and difficulty in breathing. Kate stayed to translate when the doctor was called. The diagnosis was 'internal inflammation', most probably a gastric ulcer. Kate dismissed Basil's excitable behaviour and the dramatic presentation of his symptoms as attention seeking, but the next day she began to realise that she had been mistaken.

When Patience came to the hotel I told her Basil was in bed and suggested she might go up and have a look at him. When she came back she scolded me for my indifference.

'He's a very sick man,' she said. 'If it's a gastric ulcer it's dangerous, but I don't think it's that. He's much too ill to be left to what attention the hotel can give him.'

She fetched a few things from the hospital and stayed all night with Basil. She contacted the consul, and arranged an ambulance to take him to Alicante the next day.[27]

His parents, who had high connections in the Foreign Office, arranged for his return to England. Patience accompanied him in an ambulance to Alicante and took him on board a British Navy hospital ship. According to Kate Mangan, when Patience came back she said, 'It's pneumonia. I suspected it from the peculiar way his nostrils dilated, and the ship's doctor confirmed it. They are giving him oxygen and doing all they can.'[28] Various suggestions have surfaced as to the original cause of the pneumonia. Patience thought he had attempted suicide as a result of unrequited love. Vomiting whatever he had deliberately ingested and spending several days semi-conscious had led to pneumonia.[29] Basil himself told Kate that he had started to be violently sick after a lunch of shrimps and beer.[30] Others believed that he had caught something virulent from the monkey. Those who disliked him made various lewd suggestions as to how this might have happened.[31]

Unfortunately for Patience, this was not the end of the story. Basil had fallen madly in love with her during the 36 hours she had nursed him. On the hospital ship, Basil had changed his will in her favour, and had demanded from his death bed that he be taken back to Valencia to see her again. Patience was ordered by the Foreign Office, via the Consulate, to visit him on board ship, anchored at sea. The port of Valencia was being shelled by the German ship, the *Deutschland* but, after some delay, she was taken in a small boat to see him. Knowing he was dying, Patience tried to be kind to him but, fully aware of the frequency with which sick men fall for their nurses, she asked the Captain to destroy the will. Presumably he complied, then invited her to lunch, wanting to know what a nice girl was doing there, working with the Reds?[32] Patience retorted by asking why he wasn't doing anything to stop the shelling of Valencia by the Germans. Although unwilling to believe this was actually happening, and certainly not in agreement with her support of the Republic, he was not without sympathy for her humanitarian work. He subsequently sent her, via Wintringham's address, 'crates and crates' of supplies, 'butter and cigarettes and drink, and lots of lovely medical supplies, glorious things, bedpans and things – a very

good lot of stuff'. She was very pleased about this and passed almost everything on to the Committee, having to admit, 'I had some of the cigarettes
– well obviously, I had some of the cigarettes.'[33]

Tom Wintringham, often amused by Patience's escapades to evade
admirers, knew that such a windfall of supplies would not go un-noticed.
Patience naïvely had not foreseen that there might be questions asked
regarding goods sent by the British Navy to those working in the Republic.
'It never occurred to me', she said, thinking just that they were 'fine things,
I thought it was very nice.'[34] She had also angered the Spanish Medical Aid
Committee by her 'collaboration' with the Scottish Ambulance Unit in
transporting Basil Murray to Alicante. The Unit had a dubious reputation,
and was known to have been involved in smuggling Franco supporters
across the border. Her lack of awareness of the complex dynamics at play
behind the scenes resulted in various detrimental reports being written
about her. Throughout the remainder of her time in Spain, she would never
risk asking for leave in England in case the Spanish Medical Aid Committee
refused to allow her to return.

A report from the Moscow archives contains a profile of Patience Darton.
Written by Winifred Bates, who had been appointed by the Spanish
Medical Aid Committee as a personnel officer in Spain to check on the well-
being of the English speaking medical staff, it mentions the problems that
Patience encountered while in Valencia, though exactly what she was
supposed to have done remains undefined.

> Patience Darton was sent out in February 1937 and worked in the isola-
> tion hospital in Valencia. She got into difficulties because she associated
> with members of the British Embassy. She asserts that Lord Churchill sent
> her first to get cigarettes and being quite without political knowledge
> (and one might add for her, being attractive and young) she did not know
> that she was doing any wrong. The truth of her story in Valencia will
> always be difficult to get at. I have questioned numbers of persons,
> including members of the Spanish Medical Aid Committee, and I person-
> ally believe that whatever she did was done in innocence.[35]

Basil died at sea, floating between Alicante and Marseilles, and Patience
believed that she would hear no more about him. She was therefore surprised
to learn that his parents had contacted her own mother and father with the
intention of treating her as a daughter-in-law. Basil had written home to
say that after meeting her, he was a new person and was going to join the
International Brigades on his recovery. 'And the poor, wretched parents
wanted to believe this. It was terrible for them.'

Patience must have related this sad saga to Father Roberts in a letter, unfortunately not amongst the collection that has survived the years. In a later post script she refers to the custom of reading out letters received from those who had gone abroad as missionaries, or who were connected with St George's in some way, at 'Mish' teas. These were monthly events to which people would bring any letters they had from overseas and read them aloud. Patience learned that Father Roberts had read out one of her letters to the congregation. She wrote crossly, 'Which one for goodness sake? They're not suitable – I hope not the one about Murray.' [36]

By now thoroughly angry by the lack of action from the Spanish Medical Aid Committee to send her where she could be of more practical use, Patience even threatened to write to the press. The Committee members, suspicious of her political affiliation and doubtless somewhat irked by her increasingly abusive demands for a more active posting, decided to send her to Poleñino, on the Aragon front.

5

A Modern Woman Making Waves

Patience had experienced an atypical introduction to nursing in Spain, but from this point onwards, like the majority of nurses, she was usually working as part of a medical team with other foreign volunteers.[1] She was not happy to find that she had been posted to a small hospital staffed mainly by trained British nurses, located at Poleñino on the Aragon front.[2] Earlier in the war, the front had been very active, but by this time the fighting had moved elsewhere. 'It was nice to be with some English nurses again, but we hadn't got anything to do – it worried me frightfully,' remembered Patience. The report by Winifred Bates gives a rather less positive perspective on Patience's response to her new posting.

> At the end of April Lord Churchill transferred her without explanation and in very un-comradely way to Poleñino where other members of the B.M.U. [British Medical Unit] were working. She was told it was for a few days and when she found that she had been tricked she behaved in a bad-tempered, high-handed way and quarrelled with a number of comrades.[3]

At this stage of the war, the Republican forces had begun to undergo a process of centralisation as the many autonomous militia groups were brought into the new Republican army. This particular hospital at Poleñino was attached to the Carlos Marx Division, linked to the Partido Socialista Unificado de Cataluña, and although some villagers were sympathetic to this Catalan left party, which included both socialists and communists, much of the area was strongly anarchist. The hospital was housed in a wing of the village community centre, the *Casa del Pueblo*, also used as the headquarters of the Poleñino village committee.[4] The diary of one of the other nurses working there, Agnes Hodgson, includes more detailed information about daily life at the hospital and various references to Patience. Agnes Hodgson was one of the four nurses who came from Australia to Spain during the civil war. As the least politically committed of the group, tensions arose between them on the journey to Spain, and on their arrival, while the others were sent closer to the front, Agnes was left in Barcelona. She was assigned to the hospital in Grañen, originally set up by the first British Medical Aid unit. Then, when that hospital was handed over to the Spanish, she, along with other members of the unit, moved to Poleñino in March 1937.

Agnes found Poleñino much prettier and cleaner than Grañen.[5] She was enchanted by the surrounding countryside; the river near the village winding round below high banks and rocks, the poplar trees in blossom and the hills in the distance strikingly clear.[6] After her first walk outside the village, she wrote in her diary, 'The Pyrenees looked magnificent beyond the coloured spring loveliness; a lovely curve of snow was on the highest peak. It took away my bad feelings.'[7] It seems that when Patience arrived a little later on, they were generally on good terms. A photograph shows them playing handball together on the terrace outside the hospital, and Agnes speaks of going for walks together in the evenings, sharing an enjoyment in the colours of the scenery.[8]

Another nurse Patience met at the Poleñino hospital was the twenty four year-old Margaret Powell, from Wales. Like Patience, she had trained as a midwife after qualifying as a nurse. She had arrived in Barcelona in early April and was soon posted to Poleñino, arriving at night after a twelve hour train journey and a walk of three miles. In a short memoir, she gives her first impressions of the hospital building, 'large and of stone', with walls that were several feet thick. The nurses' accommodation was very basic.

> I was shown our communal bedroom, six beds and a shelf and a hook for our few clothes and a washstand with bowl and jug. No room except for a sideways footstep. Luckily none of us snored. The one lavatory, a hole in the thick stone floor, was on the same first floor as our bedroom and how we knew it as the weather got hotter.[9]

Margaret Powell's memoir also provides vignettes of some of the characters that Patience was to be working with during the following months. The chief surgeon at the hospital was Dr Aguiló from Majorca, whose skill in the operating theatre was praised by many of the nurses who worked with him. He could operate for long stretches of time, sometimes for two days without sleeping. Margaret believed him to be an 'undeviating Republican but otherwise non-political', and 'no lover of Communism'.

> He could speak English and French perfectly. If we talked politics, as we

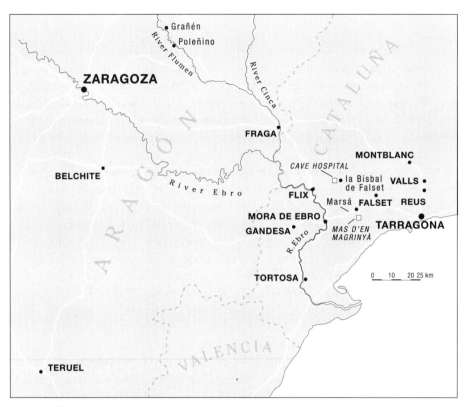

5.1 Map of key locations.

5.2 View of Poleñino and the river.

5.4 PD notes: 'This is the big farm yard at the back of the hospital at Poleñino. The steps lead up to the kitchen. The windows on the right are of the theatre.'

5.6 PD notes: 'The big ambulance, the small ambulance, the doctors' car and the food truck.'

5.3 Entrance to the hospital in Poleñino at the Casa del Pueblo (According to Agnes Hodgson, the house of the family Torres-Solanot). PD notes: 'The front of the hospital. See the "Casa del Pueblo". The village originally feudally owned – is now collectivised by the anarchists and the FAI (recently disbanded in Barcelona). The house was owned by an absentee landlord and the Village Committee use half of it and we the rest.'

5.5 The farm buildings in the courtyard at Poleñino.

5.7 A stretcher patient being unloaded from an ambulance at Poleñino.

5.9 The kitchen and staff at Poleñino.

5.8 Agnes Hodgson in the theatre (dated by Agnes 31 March 1937). PD notes: 'The theatre – originally two rooms – now painted white and kept clean. The equipment is from England.'

5.10 The 'Red Corner'.

5.11 Nurses sleeping quarters. PD notes: 'One of the few times we had a room to sleep in – usually we slept in the ward or just put our mattresses under a tree. Here's my bed and Joan Purser's.'

5.12a Staff at Poleñino: Front row: Rosita Davson, Mary Slater, Anne Murray, Dr Aguiló, Agnes Hodgson, second row: Margaret Powell, Roy Poole, Patience Darton, Susan Sutor.

5.12b Staff at Poleñino: Seated: Agnes Hodgson and Mary Slater, standing (left to right): Margaret Powell, Susan Sutor, Anne Murray and Patience Darton.

5.13 Patience and Agnes Hodgson playing handball on the terrace at Poleñino. PD notes: 'This is the terrace outside the main ward. Those are convalescent patients in the background. That is me looking exactly like mother playing deck tennis. The long building in the back is the church. I made the handsome deck tennis net.'

5.14 Sitting on a stretcher on the terrace at Poleñino from left to right, Patience, Doctor Massons, Agnes Hodgson and a medical student, Ramon Santesteban.

5.15 Patience in her bathing suit, supposedly 'frightening the mules'.

5.18 The Spanish 'chicas' at Poleñino.

5.16 Aurora Fernández (left) and Spanish nurses.

5.17 Patience (right), Isabella and Agnes Hodgson.

5.19 The hospital at Fraga.

ignorantly and frequently did, he would go to sleep until we'd finished. We once asked him how he knew when to wake up and he said, 'The noise is different.'[10]

His bedroom was also the pharmacy where the staff would sometimes congregate to play an ancient gramophone. There was only one record, 'Smoke gets in your eyes'. Eventually, he married one of the British nurses, Edinburgh-trained Susan Sutor, remembered in Margaret's memoir as 'the least political and most sophisticated of us'. Mary Slater was from a very different background. She had worked in a Lancashire cotton mill, winning a trade union scholarship to improve her education, then qualifying as a nurse when aged almost thirty. As an ardent Communist supporter, she was keen to work in Spain though never learned any Spanish. Margaret thought Mary must have been lonely, as despite being a hard worker, she had little in common with the other, younger, nurses at Poleñino. One of the senior nurses was Ann Murray from Scotland whose two brothers were fighting in the International Brigades. She had become a member of the Communist Party before coming out to Spain.

Margaret also wrote at some length about the Spanish staff, particularly the gravedigger, nicknamed Pies Tranquilos (Quiet Feet), saying it was 'impossible not to love him', despite his drinking problems.

His wife and children had been killed in the war and he'd never been sober since. He had rigged up a Heath Robinson contraption so he could take another drink by moving the big toe of his right foot. He frequently had DTs and sometimes it was necessary to tie him up.[11]

Another key person in the team was Angel, the driver, who 'loved and cherished' his ambulance so that it never once let them down. There was also a young Catalan 'who was always making mischief and was not a good cook'. Margaret described Patience as a 'wonderfully good nurse' who, on the day after her arrival, fly-proofed the hospital. Fortunately supplies of gauze were always plentiful.

During these relatively quiet days in Aragon, Patience became aware of the political discords plaguing the Republic, struggled against professional elitism and began to notice instances of gender prejudice. Before coming to Spain, she had known nothing about the political divisions within the Republic, but soon began to discover more. Problems came to a head in May 1937. The Carlos Marx Division had Anarchists on the right flank and the Trotskyist POUM, the Partido Obrero de Unificación Marxista in which George Orwell was serving, was on the left. Patience was totally convinced, as were many of her contemporaries, that the soldiers of the POUM abandoned their posts on the nearby front to join in the conflict taking place in Barcelona between different factions of the Left.

> Orwell and friends used to come over on Sundays to see the local English 'talent' – normal thing to do. I didn't know who he was, quite pleasant – there were five of them, quite pleasant people. So we brushed them off mostly, because of course we weren't on that side, we were in the Carlos Marx, we weren't in the POUM, but nothing much you can do about English chaps coming over, you see, intelligent people. Anyway, off they went again, on Sundays, just calling in on Sundays. But next thing we knew, when they were rising in Barcelona – the POUM left our left flank and marched to Barcelona, leaving the flank open. Well, we hadn't really got enough to cover it – we couldn't expect the Anarchists to come because they were very badly organised, the Anarchists, that's part of being Anarchist. So we had to spread over and cover that – and I still take a dim view – because it might have been an active front, and I thought the war was more important than having nice little revolutions in Barcelona, and in any case, we mightn't have been able to cover it and we would have let them through. I've never forgiven the POUM for that.[12]

Her vexation at this alleged mass desertion echoed down through the years, though no clear evidence has since emerged to support her testimony. When the film *Land and Freedom*, directed by Ken Loach, was released in the 1990s, she was moved to restate her case, joining with others from the International Brigades who voiced their objections. The film gave the Orwellian perspective on the May events in Barcelona, a view which decried the actions of the Communists and the International Brigades. In an angry letter to her friend Frida Stewart, Patience complains, 'This damned film is a bit much – I feel particularly angry with it, as I was in Aragon, in the Carlos Marx Division on the same front as the POUM.' She writes of how angry they all were on hearing that the POUM section had left the front 'to go down to bugger about in Barcelona. We felt strongly that the obvious fight was with Franco.'[13]

While at Poleñino, Patience found herself in open disagreement with some of the other nurses on a professional level as a result of their attitudes to Spanish girls, the *chicas*, who were working in the hospital.

> And there were seven of us (British nurses) by the time I got there, all trained, and we weren't training Spanish girls who wanted to come in

and help – which was a very brave thing to do because it wasn't the thing for a good Spanish girl of any sort, to go and work in a hospital with men, it wasn't at all proper. And we were letting them do the skivvying, which was a thing I disagreed with profoundly. I thought we should train them. I mean, this was our chance to train them to do the things we could do.[14]

Subsequently, Patience worked with many qualified nurses in Spain who recognised the practical importance of training local women volunteers, and shared her awareness of the social implications in doing so. Coming into contact with professional foreign nurses could be an eye-opening experience for some of the Spanish women who had been brought up within the constraints of strict traditions.

And to them it was an enormous thing – we were modern women that they hadn't ever come across, you see. We didn't mind talking to men, we didn't mind throwing our weight around either, which we did a good deal, because you know what nurses are! And without thinking much about it, you see, but a Spanish woman couldn't have done that, and she couldn't have nursed a stranger – she couldn't have touched a strange man, let alone washed him or looked after him. For them it was a tremendous thing they were doing, to accept it, you see.[15]

Aurora Fernández, one of the Spanish girls who worked with Patience, found it of 'political significance' that rather than being ordered to do some-thing by the British nurses, the Spanish women trainees were asked politely if they could 'help' them to carry out a task.[16] However, there were few British nurses who, at the time, would have thought of themselves as in any way 'feminist'. Even those who were more politically active would not have considered progressive attitudes towards sexual equality as a separate issue, but as part of the left-wing political agenda, although often unfulfilled in practice. The development in the 70s of a more gendered analysis perhaps resulted in a shift of emphasis in the later narratives of Patience and others. In 1983, Patience wrote that before the war, Spanish girls had traditionally had a 'lousy time', and using the terminology of the 'Women's Lib' move-ment added, 'I was all for freeing them and showing that they too could be liberated people.' The impact of this attitude on the young Spanish women she trained is evident in her description of a chance encounter with one of the *chicas*. In a letter written later on in the war, Patience wrote of how the girl saw her in the street, 'and the next thing I knew she was hugging and kissing me and crying like hell, and saying how much she missed me and the comradeship and everything; all the things you like to feel that we had there'.[17]

As spring turned to summer, there was time to relax, both for the staff at the hospital and for the local inhabitants. Agnes Hodgson described a typical village scene.

> All the village women sit in the street at the doors of their houses, knitting and sewing or feeding their infants . . . There are low doors and mules disappear through the entrance hall and one almost expects them to mount the stairs to the *primer piso* (first floor). The restless sheep and their tinkling bells go by, goats with them.[18]

But the war was not far away. In a letter to Father Roberts in June, Patience mentions the fact that there is a 'big push' going on, saying 'The noise of the guns has been much louder and last night we heard bombing – quite a different noise.'[19] Agnes wrote in her diary that the Catalan coastal villages had also been attacked, and records a conversation with Patience about the possibility that the bombardment had been perpetrated by the heavy cruiser, the *Canarias*.

> I was talking to Patience about the Catalan village bombings. She tells me that the British Embassy at Valencia has had adequate proof that Germans were bombing these small villages and it was announced that they were bombed from the *Canarias*. But the *Canarias* was in several other places at the same time. The British Embassy cook was killed. Now the English staff sleep down the coast and see the Embassy only as an office.[20]

Soon they were hearing that Republican troops had surrounded Huesca and were advancing on Zaragoza. In high spirits when the team with the blood transfusion ambulance arrived, there was a chance to socialise. 'We made fairly merry after supper waltzing to the radio,' writes Agnes, though she also records that the news from Bilbao was not good.[21] During the following week, they began to receive wounded from a nearby village. 'Apparently,' Agnes noted, 'there was a military parade in Alcubierre and the fascists must have known. Several houses were destroyed and people buried under them.'[22]

But in the heat of June, Patience and the other nurses had time for swimming in the river and sunbathing. In the afternoon when the breeze freshened, Agnes would sit by the water, 'looking down at waving silver trees like birches and the green gardens on the other bank', feeling bored and homesick.[23] Patience seemed to enjoy the sun, and wrote to tell Father

Roberts that she was getting very fat and 'was a marvellous brown all over'. His latest letter had contained the news that he was leaving St George's. Now aged almost 65, his health was deteriorating and he was no longer well enough to continue fulfilling all his commitments. Patience was concerned to hear of his intended move to a quieter parish, though partly for selfish reasons, remembering her troubles in Valencia.

> I hope you're alright. I feel a little pang when I think of St Georges without you: Where are you going to? Not too inaccessible a place I hope or what shall I do when I get in a jam? You may have gathered from my last letter, if you got it, that I had been in a considerable jam – out of it now. I seem to be getting better and better at bobbing in and out.[24]

Unfortunately, the nurses' enjoyment of swimming in the river became the subject of a cultural clash with the locals. Although legislation had been introduced by the Republican government to bring equal rights to women, at grass roots' level the traditional current of 'machismo' often continued to prevail. With a mixture of annoyance and amusement, Patience spoke of the male chauvinism she encountered in Aragon.

> We were in an anarchist village that didn't care at all for having us any-way – Carlos Marx Hospital – and they didn't like foreign nurses either, we were very 'uppish'. And the anarchists are, on the whole, rather back-ward about women, they weren't at all sure women should learn to read and write. Spain was, on the whole – ninety per cent of the country was analphabetic as a matter of course. There were no schools anyway and it wasn't the thing – it wasn't considered a good thing for people to learn to read and write, very dangerous. And how, it's true! And the anarchists didn't like us at all. I'm still annoyed with them because we used to go and bathe in the river in perfectly respectable bathing dresses, proper built up tops and things, well away from the village – very hot summer – and they didn't like this because they didn't approve of it – so they stopped us doing it. They said we frightened the mules – and I haven't forgiven them yet![25]

Boredom really set in during early July when there was little work to do. The hospital received the occasional surgical case, mainly as a result of injuries sustained during bombardments. Margaret Powell delivered babies in the villages and on one occasion, twenty casualties were brought in when a lorry overturned taking a band to play at a local dance.[26] Meanwhile, the congregation at St George's continued to send packages of cigarettes out to

Patience, though not all reached their destination intact. In reply to a letter from Father Roberts, she wrote about shortages.

> Of course we lack most of the necessities, but I didn't want to write and say so every time. What I do miss dreadfully are cigarettes and butter and books and newspapers – cigarettes first. Naturally the nurses' quarters and the equipment are more rudimentary than you can imagine and if I once begin to describe it I should never stop. However, I'm very content though there are heaps of things I should like to be different. But when I came out to a country which was primitive anyway, and in a state of war on top of that, I took it for granted that I should have to put up with things.
>
> This letter is not meant to be peevish, but it's very hot today and the flies are an absolute curse.[27]

When plans were being made for a new attack, Poleñino became suddenly busier with the arrival of the *Estado Mayor* (HQ) staff and vehicles.[28] Despite the fact that for a short period, there was an influx of wounded, the diary entry written by Agnes on 25 July shows that some leisure activities continued.

> Very hot. *Estado Mayor* arranged a football match in aid of the hospital. I didn't see it. Patience kicked off amid cheers and afterwards there was dancing in one of the *plazas del pueblo* [village squares].[29]

At the beginning of August, Patience was on leave in Barcelona. Staff on leave from the medical units or in transit usually stayed at the flat run by Spanish Medical Aid at 167 Balmes.[30] Father Roberts received a letter soon afterwards from her saying, 'I have had a most diverting time and have been too lazy to pull myself together and write.'[31] Meanwhile, changes were taking place at higher levels. Despite the objections of some of the Committee members, who Patience described as being 'tied up inside themselves with not being political', the medical units serving the army were soon to be affected by the militarisation of the Aragon militia and their incorporation into the Republican army. The Spanish Medical Aid Committee had agreed that all personnel and resources supplied by their organisation would henceforth be under the authority of the Spanish government.[32]

By the time Patience had to return to work, the unit had moved to Fraga.[33] In a letter to Father Roberts she describes her new surroundings.

> I've just been on leave in Barcelona and now we are in Fraga – it's on a

large map of Spain. It's a marvellous little town – very old and beautiful. It's right in the mountains, on the steep sides of a valley with a river. The mountains are quite bare and barren – a sort of pinky brown, and they go all colours as the light changes and the valley is green as green, full of trees – almonds and figs and olives, with a wide river that always shines bright blue by day and green at night in the moonlight. The town is built in the side of the valley – the houses are tall and thin and huddled together with very narrow cobbled streets – so steep that they are in wide steps.[34]

She also tells Father Roberts that her Spanish is much improved. Her early efforts to learn the language had caused some amusement amongst the patients on the wards, especially when she had confused the word for 'married', *casada*, with 'tired', *cansada.* Each time a new arrival asked if she was married, they all laughed uproariously when she replied, 'not this morning, thank you' or 'a bit'.[35] Now she was able to write, 'I don't find it an effort to understand and talk now; before it was terribly tiring.' Her progress could well have been due in part to the conversation practice with numerous male admirers. With her customary frankness when writing to Father Roberts, she informed him,

> It is half past one in the morning and I have just come in from a concert to which I was taken by four passionate Spaniards. Gosh, are they quick workers or are they? You'll be glad to hear I came away early.

Already in this letter, there are indications that she knows it will be difficult to resume her old life after the war.

> It will be terrible coming back to England again after having such an extraordinarily satisfying life here. I can't imagine what I am going to do afterwards.[36]

Most probably, she was referring to her religious beliefs when she wrote in the same letter, 'I'm afraid I'm letting a lot of things slide.'

The tensions within the medical unit continued to be exacerbated by the fact that there were, according to Patience, 'too many of us doing nothing'. She therefore welcomed the opportunity to go to the front in an ambulance that had been converted for use as a mobile operating theatre. As an experienced camper with the Girl Guides and Wolf Cub leader, she advised the two doctors on the team about some of the equipment that would be needed for sterilising instruments for surgery and dressings. Overlooking the city of Zaragoza, two tents were set up for the wounded, the majority of patients only remaining for a few hours before being moved elsewhere. She lacked many things that a nurse would normally take for granted, such as pillows, feeding cups and adequate lighting. 'Of course, we hadn't got any lights, it was a long while before I learned how to use little tins with oil in them and a wick for a light.' Amongst the patients treated were two with self-inflicted wounds.

> You had to operate on them without an anaesthetic, it was the rule – to 'learn' them, but anyway we just made them drunk, totally drunk. One was a finger and one was a foot, and they were sent back.[37]

In the distance they could see some of the activities going on around Zaragoza, held by the Nationalists.

> We saw a procession coming out, we could see the priests and the little white clothes and gold, all sort of gold bits on them, and crosses and statues – terribly small – it was exactly like watching a film, only a film of toys – little tiny things down in this hot plain.[38]

One morning the city was subjected to an aerial attack, though the scale of the bombing being carried out by the Republican air force did not compare with that being carried out by German and Italian planes in support of Franco.[39] Patience saw four small planes circling the city from which were thrown 'hand grenade sized bombs'. This provoked protests from the Republican soldiers in the trenches and fox-holes nearby who were being held in reserve. Patience was struck by their strong objections.

> They had meetings, you see, which I wanted to know all about, and that was what it was, it was beneath the honour of a Spaniard, Spanish revolutionary people, to bomb open cities.[40]

Once more back with the main body of the medical unit attached to the Carlos Marx Division, Patience was at last able to seize an opportunity to move on.

> And one day, a couple of doctors came over from the International Brigade, on the scrounge – they'd heard about the nurses and they came and took two of us. We didn't mind, we were all ready to be abducted . . . They had a better organisation and they needed nurses, and we obviously, I mean I was still fed up about this – there were <u>nine</u> of us – doing nothing. All English, all trained, I found it outrageous. So I was all for it, and off I

went. And then it was quite different of course, we were all properly organised, and it was a great boon and a blessing to everybody.[41]

Margaret Powell's version gives a rather different slant on the events
leading up to this transfer.

> Patience was not diplomatic, nor did she approve of our free and easy way
> of eating and living together. We all had our main meal together at a
> round snow-white bare deal table. And we stretched for what we wanted.
> And at first the food was good and sufficient if not plentiful. It was too
> late to change this custom which we all enjoyed, so she set about mending
> our manners, especially those of 'Pies' [the gravedigger] and Angel [the
> ambulance driver]. We must ask to be excused if we stretched, so that meal
> time became an ordeal. Then she had a row (she knew no Spanish) with
> the young and lazy cook and she was probably in the right though she
> shouldn't have slapped him. That was the end, and Antonio said, 'It's her
> or me.' She was worth 20 of him but of course she had to go. Luckily there
> was a small group of International Brigades close by and they took her
> with alacrity. I was sad – we were not to find another as good.[42]

Patience vividly recalled the response of the Spanish Medical Aid
Committee when she left Poleñino to work with the International Brigades.

> They threw me out for going into the Brigade. They dispensed with my
> services as far as they were concerned. They took me back later, they took
> us all back. They threw us over because we were not meant to be as polit-
> ical as that you see. Silly – as if you could be non-political. But not all the
> nurses did, we were the lucky ones, to get into the Brigades, not all of
> them got the chance.[43]

At the beginning of October, she wrote to tell Father Roberts of the
move.

> Life has been very hectic and changeable just lately. I've had a quarrel with
> the London Committee and have transferred myself to another division
> where I am much happier.[44]

She informed him that she was working as part of a team led by the
Catalan surgeon, Dr Moisés Broggi, together with the American nurse,
Esther Silverstein. Also on the team was Joan Purser, another nurse who had
trained at UCH in London.[45] At the time of writing the letter, Patience was

recovering from pleurisy, apparently resulting from having had to spend time in bed after somehow burning her foot. The three short postscripts to the letter convey her concerns, firstly to reassure him that she is 'OK really, but in a bit of a whirl', secondly to ask him not to mention the fact she has been ill to her family, and lastly to ask him to write again to tell her about his own state of health.[46]

Patience now began to receive 10 pesetas a day; the equivalent of an ordinary soldier's pay. American nurses with equivalent or lesser qualifications were classed as officers, and paid more, a seemingly inexplicable bureaucratic anomaly that irritated Patience somewhat.[47] Nevertheless, her soldier's pay book remained a treasured possession for the remainder of her life. She was pleased to be able to request trousers and shirts from the Brigade stores and to be able to buy *alpargatas*, the rope-soled sandals widely worn in Spain.

Patience was now meeting volunteers of many nationalities and was particularly impressed by the dedication of the German Brigaders. Working practices in the Brigade medical units met with her full approval. The new system of 'triage', the rapid risk assessment of casualties later adopted by the American MASH units, functioned efficiently.[48] Incoming wounded were sorted into categories: those that needed immediate attention, those that could wait a few hours, and the remainder, such as simple fractures, who could be given initial treatment then evacuated to hospitals further away from the front.[49] Although full of admiration for the skills of many of the Spanish surgeons, she commented on the fact that the foreign doctors in the Brigades, accustomed to working with trained nurses, were much more aware of the importance of aftercare than the Spanish medics. Despite the lack of antibiotics, still to be brought into general use, and with even the sulphanilamides a rarity, advances were made that greatly increased the survival rate. Blood transfusion was carried out on a large scale for the first time, and new techniques for the thorough excision of all dead, damaged or contaminated tissue in wounds – a procedure known as 'débridement' – prevented the onset of gas gangrene.[50] Methods for putting open fractures into plaster casts had been introduced by the Catalan surgeon, Dr Josep Trueta, and were proving highly successful.[51]

However, she found that not only the Anarchists had old-fashioned ideas about women's equality. She soon locked horns with a Spanish Political Commissar who discriminated against women in the vital matter of cigarette quotas.

> I had a terrible quarrel always with the commissar who gave out cigarettes
> at the hospitals, and to the medical staff, because he was under the strong

impression that women shouldn't smoke because it deprived the men, and I was under the impression that women should have as much right to smoke as the men. So we had a permanent quarrel about this, challenging him on feminine rights. The chaps supported us even though it did mean one less for them, one packet less for them, they supported us on principle – it was just a rather old fashioned Spaniard.[52]

   The only good thing was, when we had visitors coming round, Generals and people, they always gave the women cigarettes [laughter]. Otherwise we'd be picking up tabs off the ground, same as the soldiers, you know, rolling the butts – re-rolling, seven butts would make a cigarette and you could re-roll the bit after that.[53]

The nurses were working in a predominantly male environment; some men posed more of a problem than others. It was difficult for Spanish men to place the 'modern' British nurses like Patience within their customary binary categories of either 'tart' or 'good girl'. Nevertheless, unlike men of certain other nationalities, she found that they usually treated her with respect.

The Spanish men you see, thought we were modern women, we were different. Fortunately for lots of us, they put us up on pedestals, pedestals we didn't deserve just for being different you see. And of course the International Brigaders knew perfectly well what nurses were [laughter]. That was another matter altogether. You learned quickly not to have much to do with the French or the Poles – they weren't in the least safe. The Austrians, the Germans and the Dutch, the Belgians, you could cope with, but the French and the Poles were devils, you couldn't trust them at all, not an atom. You see, they couldn't have Spanish girls, Spanish girls were either tarts – real tarts you had to pay – or untouchable, so poor things – good English nurses, you see, or other foreign nurses . . . The Poles in the end, you could beat off, but they were much more tiresome than the others.[54]

Now Patience was living and working in a much more politically orientated environment. Education, both general and political, was high on the agenda.

They were very keen – wherever we were, every time we moved, we set up another school, we began teaching reading and writing, always. And we wanted the women in, too. And we used to have a 'Red Corner' with cut out things from newspapers and things, and little talks about it. Oh, no, this was part of being a soldier or a hospital or anything else, you had everything going at once.[55]

In the early autumn, when the Republicans were planning a new attack on the Aragon front, she was part of a medical team stationed not far from Huesca. 'We were all living loose on the countryside, in three huts, by the side of a river,' remembered Patience. Unfortunately, the seasonal heavy rains came early that year and with them, a terrible outbreak of typhoid fever. Most of the Spanish soldiers were resistant due to previous exposure, but the foreign International Brigaders suffered badly. According to Patience, differential diagnosis was made more difficult due to the simultaneous presence of malaria and endemic dysentery. With the sudden influx of typhoid cases, there were not enough beds for the patients, or sufficient bedding.

A detailed account of this terrible time appeared in the Bulletin for the Spanish Medical Aid Committee.[56] Amongst the extracts published from diaries written by British medical staff in Spain was one from Rosaleen Smythe, who was working as an administrator in the same unit as Patience, keeping records and carrying out many other general tasks. Rosaleen, originally from Bedfordshire, had gone to London aged seventeen, where she met Ralph and Winifred Bates. Through them, she became a member of the Communist Party, joining in demonstrations against Oswald Mosley and the British Union of Fascists. In the first weeks of the war, she worked for a newspaper in Barcelona with Winifred before moving to the first British Medical Unit hospital in Grañen.[57] Later, she and Patience sometimes worked in the same unit, as was the case during this particular typhoid epidemic. A harrowing picture of their situation emerges from her diary entries written at this time.

– It has been raining for days and days. This prevents attacks. The river is rising hourly; it has reached the door of the hospital, which is only a wooden hut. Operating room and triage are divided from the wards by sheets. My office is in triage.
– We had orders to pack up and move off, but the floods have prevented the lorries from coming up. For two and a half weeks we have been in a state of package. We have scarcely any food and what there is, is bad . . . Dr Saxton has to chlorinate the water every morning.
– The cases are increasing. We have no clean water, no fires, no heating, no lavatories.
– Existence is a misery. Rain is coming in. Rats run across the floor.
– We have no milk, eggs or potatoes for the typhoid patients (yet owing

to good nursing only 8 per cent died.) I cannot say enough about the splendid way Ada Hodson, Patience Darton and Lillian Urmston are working. How Ada makes us laugh when she tries to drink the peculiar liquid which is neither tea, coffee nor cocoa, but a mixture of all. In the evenings, by the light of a few candles we put on a gramophone. The records we have are Beethoven's Fifth Symphony, one movement of Schubert's Unfinished and one Haydn. We play them over and over again to the drip, drip of the incessant rain. We put on extra pullovers to go to bed in, we have given our blankets to the patients.
– A bitter cold wind and a frost has set in. Those poor *chicas* have to clean the few bed pans in the icy river water.[58]

Attempts were made to improve the levels of hygiene so that the typhoid did not continue to be passed through the kitchens, but as the river was used for washing up as well as for purposes mentioned in Rosaleen's diary, this was difficult to implement.

When the presence of the hospital was discovered by Franco's forces, Patience remembered how they became a target for aerial attack.

Queipo de Llano, the mad old general who used to broadcast, said that he'd got the Brigade hospitals – he was rather proud of that. He did chase us around. And the poor people in the village got bombed of course, but we did take them in – obviously we looked after them.[59]

Rosaleen's account gives further information about the sudden flurry of wounded.

The village has been bombed, the hospital, garage and one or two houses. We had fourteen patients in the hospital. One of them died. A cavalry man had to have his leg amputated. They have been bringing his horse to the door of the ward to see him.[60]

Due to shortages of supplies of preserved blood for the injured villagers, Patience gave her blood directly in an arm to arm transfusion. Using this method it was easy to donate rather too much and Patience 'puffed for a day' afterwards. Her blood had actually not been a good match for the injured man and had made him rather ill, nevertheless, he and his family were full of gratitude and excitement, thinking that this now made them blood brothers and sisters. Patience recalled that it all seemed 'very dramatic and lovely' for them.[61]

Eventually, the epidemic began to burn itself out. Recovering patients were evacuated to a convalescent hospital closer to the Catalan coast. The Spanish Medical Aid Committee Bulletin contains a report from an unnamed source about the move.

> Rosaleen Smythe arrived with a Spanish doctor, two cooks (Manuel and Pepe) and Jeronimo, a stretcher-bearer. With the help of one *chica* from the village they cleaned the house and prepared the beds. They had no sheets. Two days later, Patience Darton, Carmen and Maruja (*two chicas*) arrived with 25 patients at midnight. There was no food but rice and salt and garlic, and these were post-typhoid cases . . . They had no electric light for three nights . . . Then the drains became stopped up.[62]

These appalling conditions made it necessary to find better accommodation. The typhoid cases were moved to a hospital in Valls, and the local Mayor allocated a lovely mansion as accommodation for the nursing staff.

For Patience Darton, the following year proved to be one of momentous importance in her life.

6

Blossoming Spring to Bitter Winter

7 February 1938
Father, Mother, Happy Birthday Father. Once again I am in the hospital
where I was not too long ago, but something good came out of it too. I
met Patience, the most wonderful girl I've ever met. We take walks
together everyday, all the trees are in bloom. It would be wonderful if we
could all meet somewhere . . .
My regards to everyone. Robert.[1]

Robert Aaquist was a young International Brigader of German Jewish
origin. He had emigrated with his parents and sisters from Hamburg to
Palestine in 1934. As a Communist, he had been arrested and gaoled by the
British, then expelled from the country on his release. Along with approx-
imately 300 others from Palestine, he had volunteered to fight in Spain,
arriving in February 1937.[2] At first he was in the Tchapaiev Battalion, but
by August he was serving as a lieutenant in the Machine Gun Company of
the Edgar-André Battalion.[3] He was wounded several times during the year,
and on one occasion, had jumped onto an ambulance to return to his
battalion before being officially discharged as fit for duty. This was a fairly
frequent occurrence amongst the less seriously wounded patients, a practice
often referred to by Patience as 'deserting to the front'. In November,
Robert wrote to his parents to let them know that he was in hospital again.[4]

Sometime during the last months of 1937 Patience had been posted to
the *Casa de Reposo*, a convalescent hospital in Valls, a small town in the
mountains inland from the Catalan port of Tarragona. It was here that she
first met Robert who had been sent there to recover from typhoid fever. In
a lengthy letter to Father Roberts, Patience described how she and Robert
got to know each other.

He was a patient in a convalescent home where I was working, and when
he got better – he had been very ill – he was elected political delegate. He

is very young, only 23, but a natural leader of men, and everyone loved him. We used to get on very well and argue a lot, and work together very well, and became used to depending on one another without realizing it.[5]

Meeting Robert was to change Patience's life in many ways, and certainly exerted a strong influence on her level of political commitment. The impact of their relationship was noted in the early days by Winifred Bates, responsible for checking the welfare of the English-speaking nurses for the Spanish Medical Aid Committee. Winifred had certainly heard rumours about the troubles surrounding Patience in Valencia. As a stalwart member of the Communist Party, she was probably expecting to have to write an unfavourable report on Patience when she visited Valls, but much had changed.

I first met her at Valls' *Casa de Reposo* in January 1938, and was surprised to find an agreeable woman, reading left-wing books, asking intelligent political questions and seeking the company of Communists. I have seen her frequently since, discussed political questions with her, and have found her anxious to learn.[6]

Many of the patients at Valls were German International Brigaders, and Patience was starting to learn German as well as Spanish. In this she was helped by Rosaleen Smythe, who was working as an administrator in the hospital, responsible for admissions, record keeping and general organisational matters.

[Rosaleen] knew quite a lot of Spanish and German, and I heard her asking, 'you know, when were you wounded, how long have you been wounded, are you sick or ill, where do you come from, what is your address, who do you want people to write to and so on.'[7]

By the time Robert was fit to return to take part in the battle being fought for Teruel, Patience's admiration for him was changing to something deeper.

When he went after nine weeks I missed him very much, but I was working hard and was used to my good comrades being moved, and though I missed him a great deal, and constantly found myself wanting to consult him or tell him something amusing that had happened, I wasn't in love with him. I knew we should meet again, unless he got killed, and I looked forward to seeing him, and hearing from him. I was quite conscious that we had a very real and genuine companionship but I didn't think it was anything else. The reason I liked him so much was that I respected him in every way. He has a very fine character and a very fine brain, and he had a very hard life and I could realize all this quite dispassionately. He is quite well known out here. This isn't just the maunderings of a girl who is very much in love.[8]

After Robert's departure Patience stayed on in Valls, and when the doctor at the hospital was called to the front, he left Patience in charge as medical officer. She would take the daily sick parade, only calling for another doctor if she felt there was a problem beyond her capabilities.[9] According to a Spanish Medical Aid Committee Bulletin, the cousin of the hospital doctor had offered to come everyday, walking over the hills from the village, but Rosaleen Smythe accepted his offer for just three times a week; all his services being, as the article points out, offered free of charge.[10]

When the fighting near Teruel intensified in January 1938, Patience was called up to the front. Once again, her path was to cross that of Robert Aaquist. Her letter to Father Roberts continues the story of their developing relationship. Her sentences take the form of a stream of consciousness; minimally punctuated but transparently honest.

> On the way up [to Teruel] I passed through a town where there were a lot of convalescent Internationals and saw some old patients who said did I know Robert was here wounded. So I said no, was he bad and they said no, in fact there he is walking along, so I rushed over and we were terribly glad to see one another again, ever so much more than I realised I would be. He was lucky and had a slight wound in his left arm. He and I were always quite natural and unreserved with one another so we quite automatically showed how tremendously glad we were to see one another. He asked me what I was doing and I said going up to Teruel at which his face fell rather and he said that he had tried to get a transfer to the convalescent home but that he wouldn't if I wasn't going to be there and then immediately he forgot about that and was glad with me that I was going up because I had been longing to go up, but couldn't be spared.
>
> So I saw that his arm would take about a month and I should be back before that as they couldn't really spare me from the convalescent home and I was only going to relieve the nurses who were tired out, and after ten days I would be back and pick him up and would go back together. So we said goodbye very gladly and I went on in the ambulance. Curiously enough I found I was sitting gazing out of the window, seeing nothing and singing loudly, happy as hell, and I couldn't think why. I'm

6.1 Robert Aaquist aged six.

6.4 Nurses' home at Valls as it is today.

6.5 Patience and others by the windows in Valls hospital.

6.2 Robert Aaquist (back row, 3rd from right) and comrades.

6.3 A postcard of Valls Hospital.

6.6 Patience picking flowers.

6.7 The laboratory at Valls (Ramon Maurí in the centre).

6.8 Patience and Rosaleen Smythe with Robert Aaquist (right) at Valls hospital.

6.9 Patience reading at Valls.

6.10a & 6.10b Valls currency, 1937.

happy, anyway, in Spain, except that always I worry about the war and the international situation and the fascists being so apparently powerful, but it is wonderful having a job against them – but this was quite a different thing. I was just absurdly happy, I didn't know what about, till I remembered that Robert had said he wouldn't go to the *Casa de Reposo* unless I were there. You don't know how moral and high minded and conscientious and how unlike him it was to let any personal consideration count at all. There are a lot of people here like that. It is a wonderful spirit to work amongst. However I got quite a shock when I realized what a lot it meant to me and gave myself a good lecture on the subject. I realized then that I'd fallen hopelessly in love with him but thought that it wasn't any good, I wasn't nearly good enough for him, but all the same I went on singing loudly.[11]

In a letter to his parents, Robert told them how he had been wounded on this occasion. Only three days after returning to the front on 17 January 1938, he had been hit in the left arm, though the bone was fortunately not badly damaged. The cigarette lighter in his left breast pocket was also shredded and splinters of metal went in under his arm.[12] While he was evacuated to convalesce at Benicasim, Patience went on to the front.

The town of Teruel, clustered tightly around its Moorish towers and surrounded by a deep gorge, is an isolated place, the bleak plains stretching for miles around. When Patience first saw it, in the grip of a severe winter and with all the colour in the landscape covered by a blanket of snow, it would have seemed even more remote and lonely than usual. Franco's planes flew overhead like black birds of prey. Sometimes, when fortune favoured the Republicans, the bombs being dropped on them landed in deep snow, raising only faint white flurries. Patience went on to the small village of Cuevas Labradas, where poverty was rife, war or no war.[13] Many villagers lived in houses cut into the rock with no windows and only a barricade at the entrance. The children and most of the women had bare legs and feet. Despite their own deprivations, they wanted to share what little they had and were keen to help with the wounded.[14]

Franco's counter-offensive had begun. The situation was grim. Temperatures were often as low as −20°C, placing wounded soldiers in mortal danger and making the task of nursing even more difficult than usual. The hospital was located in a large, draughty old building with no electricity; the only lighting available in the improvised operating theatre was generated by car batteries. In the wards, conditions were primitive.

We had little milk tins, sweetened condensed milk tins, which were the

ordinary issue for milk for the hospitals, you hammered down the edges
so they weren't rough, because we only had those awful tin openers that
chew around leaving great jags, and you put oil in that, and a wick, very
primitive. You carried it around just to where you were exactly, at night
. . . We used to burn alcohol in the ward and in the theatre, to try and
keep the temperature from freezing. But of course it didn't last – phut –
it went up in a flare you see, and it was very hot while it lasted, but it
didn't really warm . . . [15]

Severe frostbite was common, resulting in numerous amputations. There
were occasions, as Margaret Powell remembered, when anaesthesia was not
available, even for major operations. She told of how one soldier insisted
that he could bear the pain of having his leg amputated. To her surprise he
bore the whole procedure well, his only complaint being that he would no
longer be able to fight.[16] Lillian Urmston, also working with Patience,
explained how the casualties they received there differed from others they
had seen previously. Apart from the high incidence of frostbite, they were
seeing wounds of a different type.

It was snowbound, hard, rocky, and no one could dig trenches deep enough
so instead of just getting head and chest wounds which were typical of the
Spanish war, we were also getting abdominal wounds galore and also what
was terribly sad, wounds in the groin. That was one kind of injury that
the Spaniard just couldn't take, his manhood was taken away. You never
had to break the news gently to them when they came out of the anaes-
thetic because they would fumble around with their bandages and guess
something was wrong and they had tubes in the bladders, or what was left
of their bladders and urethras and there would be that ghastly shout,
'¡Madre mia! I'm not a man any more.' I had to go and sedate them and
talk to them. We used to stay with them and hope that they wouldn't be
tempted to commit suicide.[17]

Lice tortured the wounded and nurses alike. Aurora Fernández, the
Spanish girl who worked with Patience for most of the war, resorted to
extreme measures.

Lice had bothered us in the summer and autumn, but now the opportunity of having a wash was very small due to the cold weather so we
scratched and scratched day and night. Sometimes it was impossible to
sleep and I had the idea to pinch a little ether used for anaesthetics and
pour a little on me so the lice slept and also myself. I think it was Lillian

Urmston who told me, 'Everyone is smoking here and you could go up in flames.[18]

The black slate mountains, the snow and the cold, but above all, the poverty of the people remained indelibly printed on Patience's memory. As usual, the hospital staff set up a reading corner to try to teach local people to read. The nurses were surprised when this time, nobody came. But in this village, it seemed that the idea of literacy was closely associated with fear. Patience discovered the reason from one of the local women volunteers in the hospital. Some years previously, the villagers had chosen two young men to go to the town and make a request for a school. On the following Sunday, the priest, who came once a month to say Mass, refused to open the church. He told them that they had no reason to learn to read and write. The two young men never returned.[19] Hearing this sad story must have confirmed Patience's belief that she was helping to 'do something' to overcome the inequality and ignorance that had traditionally been so prevalent in Spain before the coming of the Republic.

The noise of the bombardment of Teruel was constantly in the background as they struggled to deal with the wounded, and once again, the village where the hospital was located was hit, causing casualties amongst the locals. Patience felt a mixture of guilt and resignation.

> And we had three people in, one of whom died, and it felt terrible – you'd brought this to them. And the people still welcomed us and were grateful, you know, were very proud to have us. It seemed terrible that we'd brought this one death and two badly injured. Nothing you could do about it.[20]

The day following their chance meeting, Robert wrote to Patience from the *Villa Dakovic* at the convalescent home in Benicasim; a short, comradely letter, written with a reasonably good command of English. He says how surprised he had been to see her the previous day and asks if her journey to the front had been 'comfortable'. Mostly, however, he is offering her advice. It seems that she had been complaining about being kept for much of the time at a hospital so far behind the lines when she was longing to spend more time at the front. Perhaps his election as 'political delegate' at Valls had fostered an inclination to dispense guidance with a rather heavy hand. He recommends that she should change her attitude and curb her feelings.

> Don't tell yourself and others that they'll run the work without you as well. What would happen if everybody would act only out of emotions?! Taking you as an example, there would be created a situation of complete

disorganisation. Without everyone fulfilling his duty on the spot where
he was put, it is impossible to run this Spanish job. As to yourself, get rid
of all emotional acting, that's the first thing, to get clear with yourself. It
is more difficult, but it makes you stronger and more content.[21]

He ends the letter by saying 'I really hope to meet you again' and with
a 'hearty handshake'.

Patience's work at the front was curtailed when her arm became infected,
she believed resulting from a scratch of some sort. As it was not advisable
for her to continue nursing surgical cases with a septic arm, it was decided
to send her back to Valls where she could care for the convalescent typhoid
cases without endangering the health of her patients. The journey took place
on 20 February 1938, just as Teruel was falling once again into the hands
of the insurgents.

> And I went through Teruel by chance, and it fell. The ambulance driver,
> an English chap, had this little tiny, rather rickety ambulance, small one,
> and he had to take some message in, he was being a courier. So he left me
> while he went to find the place with this message – sitting in the square
> in Teruel in the dark in this ambulance – felt terribly thin, because the
> place was under an awful lot of fire. Lots of machine gun stuff simply
> whipping around the place, ricocheting everywhere, mortars – and I never
> have liked mortars – and nowhere to go to. I mean, I couldn't get out of
> this damn thing, I was sitting crouched in the ambulance and it felt very,
> very thin indeed, and of course, terribly cold.[22]

By this time she had received another short note from Robert, who had
heard about the bombing of the hospital where she was working. As he ends
with no more than a comradely, 'Rot Front! Robert', she convinced herself
that the attraction she felt for him was not reciprocated.[23] Patience
managed to persuade the driver who was taking her back to Valls to make
a detour via the hospital at Benicasim where she hoped to see Robert.
Arriving at Benicasim, she went directly to Dr Fritz Jensen, the well-known
Viennese doctor in charge of the hospital, who now began to play his part
in Patience's life by agreeing to her request to transfer Robert to the hospital
at Valls. Patience was sure that Jensen thought she was asking for Robert
to be moved to Valls because she was pregnant. For whatever reason, Jensen
was willing to rush through the formalities for the necessary paperwork.[24]
Patience's letter to Father Roberts continues the story for a further two
pages, the thin paper written on both sides without margins in small,
tightly-spaced script. There are many examples amongst the correspon-

dence written in Spain by International Brigaders that convey what it was like to be in Spain fighting for a cause in which you believed, but few letters express so clearly exactly how it felt to be there when young and falling in love.

And then sure enough, I went back via the last place I'd seen him. By that time I'd got myself quite under control, and still liked and respected him as a comrade and expected to go back again on that footing. You see my work at the *Casa de Reposo* wasn't only nursing, it was cultural and moral and political as well, and we worked together perfectly and I thought would do so again. Anyway, to go on with the story. It was dark when I got to Robert's hospital and he wasn't in his ward, so I went out to look for him in the *Sala de Cultura* and in the dark met him. I couldn't see him but I just knew it was him and said hallo Robert and he said hallo Patience – he talks English by the way and I talk a bit of German now, and we both speak good Spanish, and he said come in, we've got to hurry, so we rushed off. I didn't know where. I found myself going round Commissar's offices, and *Estado Mayor* arranging a transfer p.d.q. for him to come to my hospital. We talked all the time, I don't know what about, like a couple of kids home for the holidays, not saying anything that mattered, in fact both of us keeping off anything that mattered but holding hands and carefully avoiding noticing the fact. Absurd isn't it? However, Robert by that time was well known to everyone and apparently had been talking all the time about me so everyone said and this is Patience isn't it, yes, yes, we quite see you have to get a transfer. It was like a play or a dream or something and still we didn't say anything to one another as we were both frightened of the other and neither thought we would have a chance. We both had such a respect for the other.

However he got leave to go, but he couldn't come that night and so I went in the ambulance. When we said goodbye we found we were kissing and I said oh Robert, he said you angel both in such surprise and then the ambulance went on with me struck all of a heap. Actually I was rather ill. I had *grippe* and a septic arm and was dead tired, it was 2 a.m. and I hadn't had any sleep for nights and nights, but was I tired – I was just in a dream, but still I assured myself that it was just his comradeship and naturalness and he's very pure, really pure, and I thought would probably think nothing of it except a real friendship.

Gosh this letter's going to be a long one. I can talk about Robert for hours though so you'd better prepare for the worst and just settle down to listen. I hope the censor's enjoying himself poor dear. Well, anyway I got to the home and slept till late and had my arm fomented and felt better and waited and waited for Robert to come. He didn't come till the evening and by then I had quite reconciled myself to be on the same terms and I was in a ward anyway with lots of people talking to me when he came. He said he had had a lousy journey via *camiones*, that is lorries, and had walked the last fifteen kilometres and grinned at me when everyone said why didn't he wait for transport and we opened up some long cherished jam and ate, all of us, just as it always was. However in the morning, bright and early he said come for a walk so off we went. I don't know what we said. I found out ages afterwards that apparently I'd said that I'd live with him for ever and that I loved him and I expect he said the same thing but we came out of a trance about half past six that evening and found we were starving. I think we'd kissed once, but we each treated the other as though we would break and scorned such earthly things as kissing. However, we hadn't any wish to go back to the home where mere ordinary people lived so we walked down to the village, six kilometres each way – remember we were both ill – and I ate 11 eggs and he ate 16, not to mention *ensalada*, and *mistela*, a rather good drink.

We floated or flew back I don't remember how and found a fiesta going on, which seemed too commonplace and *mundial* so we sat outside in the dark and laughed and talked and kissed. By that time we were rather convinced that the other one wasn't disgusted at mere kissing. I think it must have been the eggs we had eaten. No angel could eat 16 eggs, I thought. You'd be surprised at the amount of things we discovered for the first time – why poets write poetry and the birds sing, and the world was beautiful, and god made men and women and little oddments like that. It was just like being at the beginning of the world, and still is. Well we were together for 14 days and it didn't occur to us not to sleep together. We were staggered when someone put forward the view that we were immoral. It just seemed funny, like someone speaking another language. In fact they were speaking another language, and we were inexpressibly shocked at the wickedness of the world. We were made for one another, two parts of the same whole so what the hell.[25]

Those early spring days in Valls remained indelibly imprinted in Patience's mind and would re-emerge years later.

The peach trees all came out, all these acres of pink peach trees over the bare ground, and lots of little bulbs, lovely little bulbs, little daffodils and things, and squirrels.[26]

Until 1996, in the many interviews she gave over the years, Patience

never mentioned Robert. Although saying nothing about their relationship, she always spoke highly of the German volunteers and stressed how
much she had learned from them.

> There was a marvellous crowd there, German International Brigaders who
> were some of the finest there were, because they knew exactly what was
> going on. And it was from those Germans that I really did learn every-
> thing that I learnt in Spain, all that I didn't learn from the Spaniards,
> which was plenty, but from those Germans about the international situa-
> tion . . . They were very surprised about how little I knew about the
> international situation. I really hadn't got much further on than thinking
> that Italy was a bad show with Mussolini. I thought I was a socialist but
> I was not in any way organised. I knew Hitler had put Jews in concentra-
> tion camps. I didn't know the real emphasis of Hitler – starting off with
> the trade unions and the others, and I didn't know the horrors of Fascism
> until they said what had happened to them and their families.[27]

The memory of those days would change the mood of her narrative. In
the recorded interviews, lengthy pauses and sighs indicate unvoiced
emotions when she speaks about the German International Brigaders.

> [They were] the first people who would talk to me, you see. [Pause] I mean,
> they would take a lot of time to talk to all of us, but they certainly talked
> a lot to me. [Sigh, pause] And they took such a lot of things for granted –
> that you had to fight Fascism; that you had to do it – I mean, there was a
> compulsion with them. They were awfully good with the Spaniards; they
> had a very nice attitude to life and people; they were good about women.
> I mean, they were an example to others about the whole attitude. They
> were marvellous. [Sigh] And they were all very – I mean, they had no
> future; they didn't know what would happen to them after Spain.[28]

Her tone of voice at this point in the recorded interview leaves no room
for doubt about the depth of her feelings relating to this brief but crucial
period of her life in Spain. She must have been thinking of Robert when in
1994, she said that to her, the German Brigaders had seemed 'marvellous,
wonderful and young and full of zeal and glory'.[29] There can be no doubt
that the day she and Robert had discovered they loved each other was in her
mind when she said that one of the German Brigaders had eaten 16 eggs in
an omelette, described in such detail in her letter to Father Roberts.[30] But
these happy days in Valls were to be no more than a brief interlude before
the war intruded upon their lives once again.

7

Retreat and Recovery

On 7 March 1938, the Republican forces on the Aragon front were forced into a desperate retreat under the pressure of a massive attack, preceded by a heavy artillery and aerial barrage. The troops were weary after the Battle of Teruel and equipment was so short that many of the men were lacking rifles.[1] Robert wrote from the front, sending the letters and photographs he had received from his family to Patience for safe keeping. In this pencil note written on a rough sheet of lined paper, he writes, 'I tell you it's more help-less than ever, but not hopeless.'[2] This time he ends the letter with 'Have all love, your Robert.'

Patience too was posted closer to the front.

> We have moved, as you probably know, and I am sitting in a little dugout I have made for myself – very nice it is. There is a lot of aviation. The dirty dogs woke us up at 6 or so this morning.[3]

She describes her surroundings from the perspective of a person suffering from dysentery. 'There's plenty of open country here, nice and near.' Just when she wants to go and 'find a nice bush' for the fifth time that morning, she hears the sound of approaching aviation, though from the engine note, she identifies it as possibly a *chato*, 'one of ours'.[4]

But soon there was no time to write letters as Franco's forces advanced rapidly through Republican lines.

> We had a terrible breakthrough, and that was really horrible, terrible, because you didn't know what was happening – everything went wrong, and we hadn't got enough transport to take us all in one go, so we were leap-frogged. One lot went right back and set up somewhere and then they would come back for us. And we didn't know whether we were going to be surrounded, or whether Franco had got there, or what was going on. It seemed to be years and years and hours of the day before they came back for us.[5]

Streams of refugees began to flood the roads, complicating the evacuation of the hospital staff and the wounded. The scene reminded Patience of the biblical flight into Egypt, 'the woman on the donkey holding a baby and the man walking alongside, one after the other'. Only the fortunate refugees had beasts of burden, others were just carrying their pitiful few possessions. As they fled, they were repeatedly machine gunned from small aircraft. Attempts to take cover at the side of the road were not always successful.

> One of the times we were machine gunned, we'd got quite a lot of refugees in the truck with us. Obviously, we picked them up, and one woman with a little baby – small child, must have been about two – and the baby was killed, machine gunned, and she wouldn't believe it – it was all so quick. We got out and we ran and they machine gunned us and the baby was killed, and she got back in the truck with this dead baby – it took about three quarters of an hour the machine gunning – and she wouldn't believe it, she couldn't believe it, that one moment she was holding her live child and the next moment there was a dead baby in her arms. And she didn't know what to do – how can you bury someone when you're away from your village with nothing – and she didn't know where her husband was. Machine gunning refugees is terrible, terrible.[6]

When interviewed almost ten years later this story was retold with great anguish, ending with the words, 'I've never forgotten, I've never forgotten her.'[7] Amongst the hundreds of wounded people she cared for, Patience remembered certain patients as individuals. The names of the men might not be remembered but their suffering is recalled in great detail. One such example occurred during the retreat. The hospital was set up several times along the way while a rearguard action was fought. A safe temporary site was found on one occasion in a disused railway tunnel. It was 'lovely' said Patience, because you couldn't get bombed. While there, working 'at top speed' in the midst of the chaos and carnage of war, a letter and yet another package from St George's, arrived like 'a fresh breeze on a hot day'. [8] Sometimes the nurses would sit in the sunshine at the mouth of the tunnel, exhausted and not knowing what was happening – but when an ambulance arrived, they ran inside quickly in case it was being followed by a plane with a machine gunner. Patience was caring for three Spanish soldiers who had been picked up from an abandoned hospital during the retreat. They were dying from gas gangrene, an appalling problem that had been almost totally eradicated in the Brigade medical units due to the improved techniques in dealing with wounds. These unfortunate men became imprinted on her memory, 'an absolute nightmare – they wouldn't die. We filled them up with morphia, there was no treatment.' The four days they took to die seemed interminable to Patience, who could do little to relieve their 'great wretchedness'.[9]

As the front moved inexorably towards the coast and Franco's troops came ever closer, Patience had little idea of where she was each time a halt was called to set up a temporary hospital.[10] The feeling of shock was immense when she awoke one morning in yet another strange location, and on opening the shutters saw the Mediterranean sparkling in the sunshine. The area held by the Republicans was now, in April 1938, divided in two. Under the calm command of Len Crome, the Chief Medical Officer, the unit re-organised. Some of the retreating soldiers had been forced to swim across the Ebro to avoid capture. Wet, cold and starving, they had succumbed to pneumonia. Patience worked hard to care for them, her spirits lifting a little with the arrival of good news.

> Some of the British I knew well . . . ran into my particular lot of Germans from Valls – because we kept trying to send messages as to whether any of us existed or not you see, or were alive or captured or what. And I suddenly heard news of them [sigh], doing marvellously as I knew they would, and they got news of me.[11]

Any such news was a welcome relief, but always tinged with doubt. No one knew what could have happened since then. Anxious days and weeks could pass, hoping, sometimes in vain, that a loved one was safe and well.[12] Eventually Patience received letters from Robert at the front, uninjured but very tired: 'I want to sleep, if possible, a fortnight. Goodnight darling! I hope I'll dream. I kiss you!'[13] Subsequent letters convey his worries about the morale of the men who have no 'fixed ideological base'. As their tiredness increased and hopes for victory faded, their spirits had declined and they were becoming 'somewhat disinterested in things'.[14]

During April, Robert and Patience were able to see each other again in Valls. For various reasons, sometimes their meetings were not entirely enjoyable. Robert writes of the difficulties resulting from only being able to spend a short time together, 'each of us coming out of rather different surroundings, and the end of the leave comes nearer and nearer when it has only just begun'.[15] Nevertheless he adds that he'd much rather see her than not. On one occasion it seems that Patience had 'a fine flourishing fit of the blues'.[16] But their correspondence over the following months grows ever more prolific and affectionate. At the end of April, Robert is seeing little action at the front and is finding life tedious. The men of his battalion culti-

7.1 The Priorat. View of La Mola.

7.2 Mas d'en Magrinyà postcard.

7.3 Mas d'en Magrinyà interior.

7.4 Dr Jolly (left) in the sterilising lorry at Mas d'en Magrinyà.

7.5 Winifred Bates (left) with medical staff, including Lillian Urmston (right).

vate abandoned vegetable gardens for extra food, despite the occasional single shot or desultory enemy artillery fire.[17] He is now spending more time defending himself against 'thousands of fleas, light brown and – hungry'. With increased supplies of fresh food and little action, Robert starts to gain weight. Patience does not approve of the new, rounder Robert, but he seems unable to resist the temptation to eat while he can. 'I am getting fatter and fatter. I'm sorry, Dear, but I don't know what to do against it.'[18] Meanwhile, she has become as thin as a rake, and worries that he will find her unattractive. He writes, 'Pat, don't forget to eat. You, mad pancake, are sitting in front of a full plate not eating but moaning that you are getting thinner and thinner.'[19] 'It's your duty to get fatter, I'm doing my part.'[20]

From May onwards, many of the soldiers in the International Brigades were stationed in the Priorat region of Catalonia, to the north of the River Ebro. The villages of the Priorat are very small and, especially in the more mountainous parts of the region, often remote. The steeply terraced slopes of vines descend to a more open, cultivated valley where the market town of Falset serves as the commercial centre for the area. Several villages have railway stations on the line to Tarragona and Barcelona, useful for the transport of troops and for the evacuation of the wounded.[21] The International Brigades were in training in this area until orders were given to cross the Ebro to begin a new offensive on 24 July 1938. The mainly German-speaking battalions of the XI Brigade, which would have included Robert's machine-gun unit, were often not far from Falset, though they spent some of the time moving around within the area. The English-speaking battalions, together with Latin Americans and Cubans, were with the XV Brigade along the road between the villages of Marsá and La Torre de Fontaubella. Amongst the hazel bushes, they built a camp of roughly constructed shelters, 'chabolas' in Spanish, and nicknamed their new home, '*Chabola* Valley'. The Slavs of the XIII Brigade camped near Pradell. By this point in the war, the surviving foreign volunteers made up only around a third of the numbers in these three 'Mixed' or 'International' Brigades of the 35th Division.[22] The majority were Spanish and Catalans, many of whom were new young recruits.

Shortly after the retreat, Patience was sent to help set up 'a little model hospital, really, a model . . . a big farm, a dear place'.[23] Although, as usual, censorship did not allow mention of the exact location in her letters to Robert, she tells him that there is a telephone in triage and if he is not 'in line' he could ask his doctor to ring Hospital no. 2.[24] One of the few envelopes accompanying the collection of letters is addressed to Camarada Paciencia Darton, Hospital no 2, 35 División, Marsá.[25] In another letter to

Robert, she refers to the prevalence of lice when she was in Marsá, saying that she was suffering from an infestation, 'worse than you, my sweet'.[26] It would therefore seem that Patience was part of the medical unit working at Mas d'en Magrinyà, a large farm estate in '*Chabola* Valley'. There were around thirty in the team, including two other English nurses on the wards. Patience describes how, while there, they organised good lectures and discussions in the 'Red Corner', and held classes to teach reading and writing to the Spanish soldiers and staff. A letter to Robert refers to the day that André Marty, head of the International Brigades, visited the hospital. His reputation had obviously preceded him.

> I ran round like a mad woman telling the *camilleros* [stretcher bearers] for goodness sake salute the guy and then I returned to my Triage and sat translating one of his speeches in French to my two *camilleros*, which I thought would create a fine impression of CULTURE, but he never came to see us. He just cheered up everyone else though and left us expecting to be degraded to a Labour Battalion or shot.[27]

During this period of military reorganisation and training, numerous events were held to help boost morale. The troops also received visits from well-known personalities from abroad who came to show solidarity, amongst them the leader of the Indian Socialist Party, Jawaharlal Nehru, and his daughter, Indira Gandhi. There were conferences, competitions and fiestas. Soldiers, medical staff and locals took part in May Day celebrations throughout the region.[28]

> Darling Robert
> I hope you are having a nice time for May Day. We are just finishing our festivities. It was just like most fiestas except that the speeches were longer and better. We had a lively squash for the afternoon feed with everybody trying to get three helpings. D'you remember the fiesta at Christmas time when that long thin German was drunk? I got a little drunk today so much so that several people remarked on the size of my eyes . . . I'm all dressed up as a nurse today. You ought to see me looking all *guapa* [pretty].[29]

In later interviews, she gave more details about the May Day activities. It was a chance to relax, and to watch the men compete, sometimes in rather unusual sports.

> We had extra food and things sent for it, to celebrate, we decorated the place up. And we had a spitting competition. Spaniards are very good at

spitting, and some of the Americans – 'Tex' we used to call him – Tex was a marvellous spitter, he could aim. I don't know how they got so much spit ready to spit with, because I dry up if I try to spit and I can't sort of get it going. But Tex could [laughter]. He always seemed to have plenty to go and he could aim right across, so could the Spaniards – wasn't a thing I cared for – it was quite a well known thing. And we had a target up on the side of an ambulance to be spat at, and we put the people further and further away – and they got really intent on, you know, doing better than Tex. And it was as serious as can be – we had absolute hysteria watching this because they stood there, sort of churning round with their mouths getting a good gob going then – 'buong' – you see, [laughter] either booed or cheered by the surrounding crowd. It was a very good competition. Tex won.[30]

The descriptions of social and spare time activities given by Patience and other nurses on the Republican side of the lines differ markedly from those given by Priscilla Scott-Ellis, the only British nurse known to have been working in the medical services for Franco's forces. Medical staff in the Brigades usually stayed with their units when off duty, and rare periods of leave or convalescence in Britain were often spent speaking at fund-raising meetings. Priscilla Scott-Ellis, however, could leave all the 'groaning corpses' for a while and return to what she saw as 'normal life' by driving in her own car to dine at the Grand Hotel in Zaragoza with her friends in the Spanish aristocracy and the pilots of the German Condor Legion.[31]

Political education was high on the agenda while Patience was at Mas d'en Magrinyà. She wrote to tell Robert that she was trying to join the Communist Party, but still had reservations.

We are having Marxist classes now which are not bad. I asked again about joining the party but nothing came of it. They may feel I have a bad record so I am going to find out for certain. So many times the policy I read about in the official announcements is contradicted by individuals who should know what they are talking about, that I'm not sure quite what I do feel about it now.[32]

She continued to search for answers, writing the following week, 'I miss you very much particularly as we are having Marxist classes and I argue a lot in them but no one will go on arguing long enough and I thought if you were there we could fight again.'[33] It is interesting to note that by this point she is studying Catalan rather than German 'as it is more useful. Lots of the people here only speak Catalan.' Perhaps Robert had teased her about her

efforts to learn German because she adds, 'Fortunately there is no one here
who laughs at me for it, so possibly I may learn quicker.'[34]

The note written by Robert on the following day explained the absence
of some of Patience's letters in the collection that survived the war. Robert
was accustomed to living with few personal possessions. In a moment he
regretted, he had destroyed her letters.

> As stupid as I am a couple of days ago I burned all your letters. Now I
> haven't got nothing to read (remembering you). I am a fool? May be.[35]

He did not make the same mistake again and from then on, carefully
kept the letters she wrote to him.

Throughout the following weeks, Robert's letters concentrate for much
of the time on the practical aspects of his daily life; the weather, the lice,
and especially, the food. He jokingly refers to the knowledge he is gleaning
from the 'Ebro High School', for example, how to make something that
resembles coffee from unripe beans, and the amount of water you can colour
with one tin of milk.[36] Marching twenty kilometres a day is making him
thinner and hungrier. He is delighted when the men in his Brigade receive
a surprise delivery from abroad.

> From the German committee in Paris we had nice little Easter parcels with
> a bit chocolate, some cigarettes and a tin or a piece of sausage. In every
> parcel there was a piece of paper with a few lines, some typed but most of
> them written very heartily and personal.[37]

Although, as he points out, the parcels were not sent to them as named
individuals, most of the notes succeed in making the men feel that the
'comrades over there' are closely committed to the struggle going on in
Spain. Sometimes his battalion is called to hold positions on the inactive
front, which he finds tedious and frustrating. The occasional banter with
the enemy relieves the boredom. One night a fascist cried: 'Red, how many
pairs of sandals do you have?' One of the 'boys' answered, 'Two. One pair
wouldn't be enough to run after you.'[38] The men grew angry at having to
watch the enemy moving around just beyond the range of their fire.

One of the themes that emerged constantly in the correspondence
between Patience and Robert relates to communication problems while
they are apart. There are many expressions of loving and longing written
by both of them, and kisses are sent by the dozen, but at this point, Robert
still finds letter writing difficult, 'not to know what to begin with or even
what about . . . You know how I hate to write letters. I am sure, after two

or three days I'll write some more foolish lines.'[39] Patience has less trouble in this respect and she usually manages to write at great length, but she never knew whether her letters would get through to him. She was distraught when she received letters complaining that he had heard nothing from her when she was writing to him almost every day. Often, a batch of letters would arrive altogether after long delays. Each begged the other to write more often and both complained of the difficulties in reading the other's handwriting. Patience is aware that his situation is much worse than her own, but even so, is unable to suppress a little gentle mockery.

> Gosh it is cold today. It must be very cold for the soldiers who are sleeping outside. I hope you've made yourself comfortable. There are such a lot of things I want to grumble about but I feel mean if I send depressing letters in case you worry. Besides now you have formed that abominable habit of keeping my letters and expecting me to listen to you reading them when we meet, I'm being very careful what I put.[40]

As Patience attempts to improve Robert's letter writing skills, his tendency to moralise also comes in for some affectionate criticism.

> You have an aggravating way of being superior and moral when you are feeling cheerful and have plenty of work to do and you tell me off about my miserable letters, quite forgetting that you're just as bad at times. You're quite right my sweet when you do tick me off but that doesn't make it less aggravating.[41]

Despite these minor complaints, their commitment to each other and the future of their relationship becomes evident when Patience comments in a light-hearted manner,

> I wrote to my family and told them I was married darling and said that they must send out double parcels now as you were very greedy. I thought they might be more cheerful if they knew I was cheerful poor dears.[42]

The exact form taken by their marriage is not known. On some occasions the officer in charge would perform a ceremony, in others, usually when a foreign Brigader was marrying a Spanish woman, their marriage might be recorded in the Town Hall files. Few of these records survive. All such marriages were annulled when Franco came to power. What is certain is that the fact that Patience and Robert were husband and wife was recognised by those who knew them in Spain.[43] Her letter to Father Roberts written on 14 May reveals not only that she is married, but also that she is still open to opinions other than those of her husband and the 'comrades' who share his deep political commitment.

> I am more weeks apart from my husband that I am days with him so I feel rather lost when I want to refer a point to anyone whose opinion I value. I wish I had you as a cross reference. I don't want to come home till Robert can come and I don't know when that will be as it is difficult for him to get leave. Just at the moment of course we're neither trying to get it. I can have it now at any time but naturally want to wait till he gets his. You will like him very much.

Evidently, through her contact with Father Roberts, she is seeking to maintain a bond with her past beliefs, despite having explained at the beginning of her letter, 'I'm sorry, in a way, that I haven't written for so long, but I am a different person now, living in a different world and I can't connect up with my old life.'[44]

Patience was irate when, in mid-May, all her hard work and enthusiasm had unforeseen results. The American doctor, Bill Pike, assistant to the Chief of the Medical Services, Len Crome, considered Patience to be the best nurse to leave in charge while others went to begin new challenges elsewhere.

> I have been full of schemes and ideas for *camilleros* schools and organisation and what not, and got properly had. The two surgical *equips* [teams][45] that were here have moved out but left me behind in charge of the damn triage and school because there are not enough doctors so they had to leave me. Bill Pike promised to send a doctor but I feel very disgusted as the others are probably going to set up a new hospital and get more work and it is terribly dull here and now I have no one I know to talk to – that all comes of being energetic and full of ideas and not sitting still doing nothing . . .
>
> O Robert I'm so fed up at being here by myself. When I've settled down with the new *equip* I shan't mind I know but just at first I don't like it. I hope Bill keeps his promise and sends a doctor soon. I shall miss you more than ever now. By the way, I have learnt to fire a rifle. You will probably tell me I do it all wrong but I'm quite a good shot . . .
> All love
> Your Pancake[46]

A few days after being left behind in Marsá, Patience was ordered to report once again to Bill Pike at Valls, taking nineteen other members of the remaining medical staff with her on a supply truck. After a nightmare journey, she reached her destination and was greatly pleased to learn that she was to organise an eight-bed ambulance and the necessary assistants and stretcher bearers to go closer to the front. The following day, the journey began well, with everything stowed away tightly around the people travelling in the back, while Patience and Bill Pike sat in the front with the driver. After many hours at the wheel, Bill Pike took over so the driver could rest.

> And Bill started singing as he was driving, very nasty singing which I said, 'Oh God, Bill, life's hard enough without that.' And he said, 'If I don't sing I shall go to sleep.' So I said, 'All right, sing.' And I went to sleep and the next thing I knew he'd gone to sleep and we'd pitched over and I'd gone through the windscreen. And I was the only person [laughter] who could move to be hurt, all the rest were jammed tight with all the stuff they were in. He got pushed of course, in the chest with the driving wheel, but not hurt badly. I was knocked out, my face was broken up, and it looked a terrible mess. Fortunately another driver came along, English, afterwards, and we'd gone over the side of the mountain and fetched up on the only large rock sticking out, about only four foot down, so we were balancing like a comic film you see.[47]

Patience was rescued with some difficulty due to the precarious position of the ambulance, her face covered with blood. She was taken to the civilian hospital in Valls while the others continued to the front in a replacement ambulance. She was able to write a quick note to Robert, to reassure him in case news of the accident gave him cause for worry.

> Darling unfortunately I got involved in a slight accident and got in the way of a *golpe* [crash] so I am staying in Valls for a week. Bill seems to think he can get a letter to you so I am sending this by him. I'm glad you can't see me as I have two black eyes and swellings all over the place but I am quite OK but very cross at being here.[48]

The injuries were not quite as trivial as the note implies, as a later interview reveals.

> My upper lip had quite been cut right out so that you could see behind it, through to the teeth and things, and my top jaw was broken, and my nose was all over the place under one eye.[49]

However, in her letter to Robert the following day she still tries to downplay her injuries, and in the process reveals much about her feisty and determined character, with a typically English, rather self-deprecating, sense of humour. Sadly, her reference here to having Robert's baby was never to be realised and the comments made in later letters indicate that it was probably no more than wishful thinking for their future after the war was won, rather than an actual pregnancy.

Darling Robert here I am stuck in Valls going nearly mad waiting for my face to heal up and missing you terribly. Not that I want you to see me like this but I want you. My face is much better but I'm afraid my nose is a bit one sided and I have a scar over my lip. I hope you don't mind. What with you having your nose broken twice and me once, our dark haired little boy ought to be born with a broken nose to save trouble.

Please don't be worried or anything about me. I am quite OK but very bored. There is no one to talk to here except Henry and the food is awful and anyway I can't eat because my teeth were all loosened. I can't think why none were broken, you know how bad they were. Bill was very sweet to me the first night when my face really was bad and my nose was waving in the breeze and I couldn't see or talk owing to the *golpe*. You can take it for granted that I soon managed to talk. Bill asked me if I'd like him to try and get you but I said certainly not as I thought you were probably in reserve and wouldn't want or be able to come. Anyway, by the time you get this letter I shall be quite alright and back at work so you will have nothing to worry about as it will be too late to worry.

The news every day seems better. I liked the bit about capturing back the Asturian prisoners.[50] We have a radio here, out of my hearing unfortunately, but Pepe who has been very kind, comes and tells me the news. The *camilleros* [stretcher bearers] from hospital no 2 come and see me very faithfully and tell me the latest scandals. They are very surprised because I get bored with being in bed and get up and walk round. They think I ought to wait till I'm a bit more *guapa* [pretty], but I don't mind as I can't see my own face.[51]

Patience fretted and fumed. The attempts to repair the damage to her face had been poorly done and the food she was given, 'hard beans bounding around on a plate', were impossible for her to eat.[52]

[Laughing] And it drove me absolutely mad because my face was really in a terrible state, and they used to come in, open the door, burst into tears and go out. They brought the mayor of the place in, doing the right thing, who made a marvellous speech to say I'd now given my all to Spain, and I was furious because I couldn't speak properly and I was bursting with the – I mean I did tell them, I had a terrible temper – that I hadn't given my all, my face was nothing like my all, there was lots of me left, and this was a terrible way to do it and no way to treat a patient anyway.[53]

Confined to bed in a room by herself, she has time to write long letters to Robert and to make plans.

What Spain will need immediately after the war is improved communications. Don't you think it would be a good scheme if you stayed in Spain and organised a Government bus service? I could probably get a job nursing in a hospital somewhere. D'you ever look ahead darling? It seems to be the only thing left to us, but whatever we look to there is no real hope of getting it. As for the present it doesn't bear looking at . . .

You may have noticed that I feel a bit gloomy partly owing to the fact that I have half a packet of butts and matches, but no paper, so I am in a state of great indignation with life. If I could get hold of some papers, or better, some cigarettes, I should probably find a glowing future for us.[54]

Cigarettes had been vitally important to Patience since the days of her nursing training, and she was miserable without them. They become an affectionate currency between the two lovers as each tried to send or save cigarettes for the other. Robert calls her his 'dragon' and occasionally she signs herself as such, this seemingly being a reference to an addiction to smoking, rather than to her occasional fiery tempers.

Time passed slowly for Patience with little to do except raid packets of cigarettes she was trying to keep for Robert, write letters to him and, to take her mind off worrying about what could be happening at the front, read whatever she could find.

I shall know much more about Marxism-Leninism than you by the time I have finished being in bed as I have nothing to do but read and nothing to read but terribly serious books. I shall probably be wearing spectacles when we meet again.[55]

In desperation, she eventually succeeded in getting to a telephone to call the Spanish Medical Aid Committee representative, Winifred Bates, who was based in Barcelona. Winifred at first did not recognise Patience's voice as it was still so distorted by the facial injuries, but finally she grasped the words, 'Hospital', 'Valls', and 'You must come and get me'. Winifred arrived the next day and, remembered Patience, 'Of course, SHE burst into tears when she saw my face, it was most discouraging.'

They travelled back to Barcelona together and Patience spent three days in a flat that swayed alarmingly under the heavy aerial bombardment that was wreaking havoc on the city. It was decided that Patience needed more surgery but, unlike some of the other nurses, she did not have to return to England for treatment.[56] Luckily, she was able go to Dr Leo Eloesser, the American surgeon who had set up a clinic closer to the French border at Mataró. He was able to restore her features to a great extent, though her nose was never quite the same again. [57]

Patience hated being in the hospital at Mataró. She found it 'horrible'. Despite the fact that it seemed as if the place was 'full of doctors and nurses', she could never get anything she needed. Writing letters was not easy as she had a 'weird contraption' made of wire and adhesive plaster stabilising her nose after the surgery and could only see out of one eye as the bandage was in the way.[58] Worst of all, she was very jealous of two expectant mothers in the ward, both of whom wished they were not pregnant and made a great deal of fuss about nothing. By early June, she was able to walk into the shops at Mataró, where she bought a miniature chess set and board for Robert. She had heard nothing of him for nearly three weeks. There were a lot of Germans there and, despite the possibility of flirting with them a little, she found it very dull. Although feeling tired and longing for leave to spend with Robert, she fought with the doctors to be allowed to go back to work.[59] A few days later, she was back with the unit.

8

Head and Heart

All was not sweetness and light after Patience and Robert had managed to meet again sometime around 10 June. Patience's letters reveal rapidly shifting moods and a range of turbulent feelings. She was angry with him for far more than the tangible reminders of their meeting; 'Anyway, you beast, I found sixteen lice in the two days after I left you. I nearly went mental catching them . . . Darling, are you worth it?'[1] There were more serious tensions in their relationship that seemingly stemmed from Robert's reticence in expressing emotions.

The attempt to avoid sentimentality, a constantly recurring theme in their letters, was without doubt, of significant importance in the relationship. Although Patience was usually practical by nature and not inclined to be effusive, it was primarily Robert who viewed sentimentality as mawkish and a threat to positive action. His aversion to all things 'sentimental' was made clear in letters to his affectionate and somewhat forlorn parents in Palestine. His doting father was struggling to keep the family business afloat in difficult times but Robert was less than sympathetic. One epistle to his family from 1937 gives a glimpse of his personal background and conveys an impression of the philosophy that led him to Spain. The tone of the letter can be judged from a short extract; a mixture of heartfelt conviction and political diatribe, plus the impatience of youth regarding the concerns of the older generation.

I received your letters of 18 and 20 May and I do not want to hear such unrealistic sentimentality any more. My dear parents, it is absolutely not just by chance, or still less, lust for adventure or suchlike, as you seem to think, that has brought together so many people from different countries to fight in the International Brigades. It is no fun to see your best friends die, be wounded or mutilated or to 'catch one' yourself . . . You had to get out of Germany. Why? The Usankis are in South America. Why? Aunt Martha had to shut her shop. Why? Uncle Ludwig and Uncle Ede are off. Why? Did Uncle Mor leave Germany for fun? You and your like have left it all behind, but from you it is still the same old story. Are you blind or just not wanting to see – what is wrong with you? Have you got the message, one way or another? Or has your brain ceased to function? Why don't you do something? Can't you see the massive misery that Fascism has caused and will go on causing? Is suffering any different whether you are Jew or non-Jew? Only when we are all against this barbarism, which has annihilated generations, which bombs women and children from the air, has laws moreover which allow honest people to be tortured till they are crippled and imprisoned without charge for years on end, only when all unite against the fascists can we can wipe them out. Only then can conditions on earth return to normal, only then will we cease to annihilate everything that is beautiful and honourable, only then can science be put to the service of mankind.[2]

A few letters written by various members of the family to Robert in 1938 have survived and show that they continued to shower him with affection. They sent news of the violence in Palestine, the emigration of more friends and relations, and their own ongoing financial difficulties. After he told them about the wonderful girl he had met, they asked for news of 'Pat' and sent greetings to her. According to Patience, Robert's mother had joked with him that he would end up marrying 'one of those terrible Communist Party hyenas', so Robert had written straight away to tell her that he had found an English girlfriend with blue eyes and blonde hair, who was in no way a Party hyena.[3]

Robert's father was always anxious for news and begged him to write, spending hours listening to the radio to try to find out what was happening in Spain.

Son, I would be gladly with you. The whole of life seems irrelevant to me. I am 57 years old and, although still full of energy see no way out of this mess. My thoughts are almost continually with you, my son. The whole of life is indeed a struggle until your eyes are shut forever.[4]

Patience often suffered from depression too but, in contrast with Robert's father, being young and by nature somewhat feisty, she would soon rally. What exactly went wrong during her meeting with Robert in June is not clear, but, wounded and on the defensive, she retaliates. As to be expected from a young woman with an acerbic tongue, her choice of weapon is a letter to Robert containing some well-aimed barbs. In their correspondence, there had always been light-hearted references to Patience's enjoyment of flirting. Robert asks 'How are you doing with your flirts? I hope good!'[5] She told him about her flirtations with various men on the

8.1 Dr Reggie Saxton and Rosaleen Smythe (back row, right).

8.2 Drawings of mother and babies from Patience's letters.

8.3 The XI Brigade march in Falset, 1938.

8.4 The Activists Congress, Falset, 1938.

8.5 The XI Brigade on manoeuvres near Falset, 1938.

8.6 The XI Brigade fiesta near Falset, 1938.

staff, and that through flirting she was improving her German as 'it's the best way to learn a language'. However, after seeing Robert in June, a bitter note crept in to her comments on the subject.

Darling Robert

Herbert says he can take this letter to you. I was very pleased to see him again and flirted rather a lot with him which was nice for both of us. Why don't you come in by the ambulance which comes in every day from Marsa and then I could flirt with you. It comes into Falset about 6 and goes back as late as you like.

I have turned very sensible and unsentimental. After all, you're not the only person who is sensitive – d'you remember what sensitive is? It means your feelings are easily hurt. You told me yours were, but you don't seem to realise that other people's are, so I have decided I mustn't love you so much, and I mustn't take it for granted that you love me any more. The result is I am having a fine time flirting quite hard so as to get used to not being so much in love with you.

Damn this letter is not a bit what I want to say, but anyway I shouldn't be any better at explaining what I mean even if I saw you. One day when we get a leave we may find out what we are really like. You're much more self-centred than I thought, and I'm probably disappointing too. However all this doesn't stop me wanting you and loving you, but at first I was happy because I thought I could just enjoy being in love with you and not think of being proud and holding a reserve, but now I shall have to re-adjust myself. I am working very hard and don't get any time to write or do anything and I hate being here so you see I am still depressed, but don't be moral about it. Darling, if you want to keep me please write and don't be moral. I'm being very good, and working hard, and missing you terribly, and trying not to be sentimental, and trying to join the Party and being reasonable, all with my head, but my heart or whatever it is that makes me sentimental – like you, incidentally – is very sad because I can't see anything in the future. I don't care what happens to us if it happens to us together but I feel very afraid that we are not going to stay together . . .

I am just going out to lunch with Herbert. Sorry I have no envelope.

All my love and kisses, (minus a few kisses I gave to Herbert)

Patience[6]

Patience's sudden swings from assertiveness to insecurity, from annoy-ance to anxiety, while probably understandable to many women, leave Robert totally baffled. When this missive arrives, in bewilderment he hurriedly writes several letters in reply, not knowing what exactly he has done to upset her.

> I read your letter now another time. The more I read it the less I under-
> stand it except one thing. I love you and I hurt you terribly . . . You say
> I'm self-concentrated, I only guess what it means and cannot find out.[7]

He writes of the difficulties they had during their meeting; having so much to say but ending up only speaking 'nonsense'. Although unable to explain quite why he feels so bound to her, he recognises that at least in part, it is due to his admiration for her ability to overcome the challenges she meets. He therefore had been shocked when, during their recent meeting, she had spoken repeatedly about not wishing to live any more. Now he fears that it was because she was disappointed in him. Frustrated by the limitations of his English, he makes a valiant attempt to understand her worries and reassure her that even within the ideal socialist society, there will still be a place for love between individuals.

> Life is often not easy, it is better handled with two, even in the collectivity.
> Life is no life without struggle but it makes gay to hold together, much
> more than simple friendship. What is it we are living for? For the future,
> of our own, or that of youngsters, that's the same because life is an endless
> chain. Is there eternalty? Sure, you and me, we are eternal, not your skin
> or my bones, that doesn't make the very individual, but the idea of living,
> of going ahead, of working reasonable – that means collectively – of
> helping, learning and developing that is what makes a person. And that
> is not bound to an accident, or to a bullet – I wish you would get the real
> meaning out of these poor words. Darling don't worry, but enjoy our love,
> I do and am longing for continuing. Darling Patience, I want to have your
> hands in mine.[8]

Meanwhile, waiting anxiously to hear from Robert and still not having received the above conciliatory letter, Patience wrote again, now in a very different mood.

> Darling Robert – please write to me as I am afraid you are disappointed
> in me or angry or something and I don't like it. I was always afraid that
> you'd find out how silly I was really but now I'm quite worried. I am
> terribly tired and my face is giving me some trouble, also I have diarrhoea
> but we are so busy I can't do anything about it.
>   O Darling I do want you so much and I do love you so much. When I

come off in the evening about half past nine and walk home – it's about a kilometre – I always think how lovely it would be to go upstairs and find you waiting in our room or how lovely it would be to hurry home and get in first and begin scrambling the eggs for you. O I forgot, you're going to do the egg scrambling, aren't you?

I'm afraid this is getting sentimental again – it's because I'm so tired. When are we going to attack? I really am trying to join, my dear, but I haven't had time to go up to the other hospital and ask and when I come off in the evening everyone has gone. Franz [the Political Commissar] is no help. Please write.

Yours completely

Pancake[9]

After receiving Robert's letter on the following day, she writes again; eight pages full of contrition, attempting to make him understand her a little more. The letter gives details of her family background and past problems that would be unlikely to emerge in interviews or written memoirs.

Darling I am a fool and a pig both of which you probably realise very well by now, but I love you very much. And listen, darling, I told you in Valls that I've always wanted to die – I have ever since I remember thinking seriously – since I was about eleven, but I know it's wrong and I do try not to think about it. I can't stop feeling it, but I can stop thinking about it consciously and I will try a bit harder. You are quite right in saying that it is only in struggling and fighting – not only outside things but things inside ourselves, that make a person. You see, our family – my family I mean – suffers from a curse of inefficiency all through. Both pop and mother gave in to circumstances and one after the other my brothers and sister did. I saw it happening and didn't analyse it but hated it and determined to fight it in myself and for them too. The only help I had was the church I belonged to, don't be superior, I'd have been lost without it. Anyway I made a person out of myself, and became an individual with a life and work of my own and also helped my father and mother quite a lot, but I was very lonely and unhappy and always tired as I worked very hard and was not strong. You see mother and pop are defeatist and very bourgeuois (I can't spell bourgeouse) and wouldn't fight and I knew the system we were living in was the cause of it but couldn't find a solution.[10]

The letter goes on to describe how she became a nurse, despite frequent poor health which led to her being advised at one point to give up her training. She also refers to her time in Valencia and the troubles she went through due to the supplies she received from a 'British war ship'. She gives a further hint as to the cause of her transfer to the hospital at Poleñino, ostensibly as a possible 'fascist spy'. 'That was the official reason, the real one was that I was getting too much publicity and had learnt too much from an official who was in love with me.' What exactly she had learned is not specified.

Her letters reveal much about her hopes and fears. Though written so long ago, at times her outlook seems just like that of a modern young woman, determined to be independent and to enjoy sexual freedom. But, as many women will be aware, such freedom comes at a price. Patience was not immune to loneliness.

> You are quite right to think I can conquer situations and I think I can manage my own life. The only thing is that I am tired of it, terribly tired, and feel so alone. So when I met you and afterwards when I fell in love with you I thought that for once I could rely on someone else. I don't mean rely completely on some one, and not be myself or work and have my own life or be dependant, but I wanted someone I could turn to and talk to and be depressed to, and have a change from people who always expected me to look after them. But I don't mean entirely that. If two people really fit one another as I think and hope we do, it should be a fifty-fifty business, each filling in the gaps of the other.[11]

In other ways, her manner of thinking might be considered far from modern. Deprived of the consolations of religion due to diminishing faith, she was still nevertheless, searching for a moral compass. She was drawn to Robert through her belief that he was somehow on a higher moral plane than most of other men she had known. Father Roberts is mentioned in the letter, significantly, as the one other person she can trust to talk to, apart from Robert. It is unavoidable, though odd, to be aware that even their names are the same. In the same letter, she explains to Robert why she loves him.

> D'you know why I love you so much? Not because I think you're always right or because you have some brains – I love you physically as well – but because I respect your character and think you have high standards. You know I have often been in love before. You can't help if you are in love with a person or not – you can help what you do about it, and you can stop it afterwards, and you can grow out of it, but I've never been in love before with some one without despising myself, because so often people have a

much lower standard than I have. Not that I think I live up to my own
standards I know I often fail – more times than I succeed – but I have got
a high one, and so have you.[12]

Patience ends the letter on a courageous note, showing the strength of
character that was to be so important in view of what the future held in
store.

> This is a long letter, all about myself and rather sob stuff, I know. My dear
> – don't worry, I won't be a drag on you, or a dependant, but don't be
> worried if I am depressed or talk about being depressed, because I don't
> give into it in actions. My actions are much better that my feelings. I do
> want you so badly – I want your arms round me so much that I ache for
> you, and as long as you want me too I don't care. If you ever stop wanting
> me or think we ought to part, we shall have to, as you can't make human
> relationships go on unless they're fifty-fifty or at least you can't make good
> ones go on. I should mind most horribly but should get over it and go on
> fighting as I have over bad blows before. Really I am quite strong. That's
> why I just have to talk stupidly sometimes . . . But don't worry darling,
> I usually get better quickly and pick up the bits and stick them together
> and start off again.
>
> I cried over your letter when you said that about two people handling
> things better together than separately. It was just that that I felt when I
> was so depressed with you the other day but afterwards I thought that you
> didn't feel it, and my pride was hurt, in fact I was hurt altogether and
> wrote those letters. But now it is alright and please don't worry. I am only
> worried now about the international situation and Spain as now I feel that
> you and I are together whatever happens. I got a letter yesterday from you
> with photographs of a baby. Ours will be much more beautiful and will
> have a lot of dark hair. That one is quite bald.
>
> I haven't any more to say in this letter except that I love you and I miss
> you and I want you and I am working very hard and am very tired. Please
> write and don't worry. I'm not so bad as you think. I shall probably make
> quite a good comrade to you one day if you're not moral to me.
>
> Really your loving
>
> Pancake
>
> Gosh what a long letter. Couldn't you make yours a bit longer?
>
> P.S I tried flirting seriously as I thought you would be sure to want to
> break off with me and that I had better get accustomed to it but it wasn't
> any good and I hated it because I love you much too much.
>
> P.S. 2 This letter must stop.

P.S.3 Sorry, but I forgot to mention that since I found out about Communism I've nearly stopped wanting to die, and if you love me I don't want to anyway, though that is a bad reason.[13]

Feeling loved and loving in return, in combination with a strong sense of purpose, must surely be considered beneficial therapy for someone with suicidal tendencies. Later the same day, her spirits have recovered to a great extent and, sitting up in bed, she writes to him again, returning to the theme of her membership of the Communist Party.

You will be glad to hear that I think I am really managing to join the Party at last. My feelings are very mixed as I know I shall resent lots of things, particularly losing even more of my freedom. I don't know even yet if I will do it or not. You see, I agree quite entirely with as much as I can learn about Marxism and the Party, and its methods and aims and so I can't consistently stay out of it, because it deals with fundamentally important things that you can't evade and so I must join it, but I know I shall get mad later on.[14]

Her concerns about Communist Party discipline and the need to respect individual liberties, despite being at war, are made clear at the end of the letter.

I know that one day when we're living in socialised countries we shall be free, and able to live full lives, both collectively and as individuals – and even particularly as individuals – and I know we've got the devil of a fight to get that life, but even now we have the same right of liberty as individuals and don't forget it.[15]

With their relationship back on a more solid footing, a series of affectionate letters follows, commenting on daily life and the latest news on the progress of the war. Each tries hard to please the other and keep cheerful though they are apart. Robert repeatedly assures Patience of his love, and explains that just because he doesn't show visible signs of jealousy when she flirts with others, it doesn't mean that he's indifferent. Rather, it is a demonstration of his confidence in their love for each other.[16] Meanwhile, she professes her growing commitment to Communism, reads politically correct literature and writes, 'I think you would be glad if you knew how genuinely enthusiastic I am getting about the Party.'[17]

In the vicinity of Falset with the XI Brigade, daily life for Robert centred on the wide-ranging instruction programme for the new offensive being planned across the Ebro.[18] Despite the murderous heat and his tiredness after exercises and drills, he is, in the main, in good spirits, except when thinking of the losses due to the war. 'Comrades are so rare. Remembering the first days and months in Spain, one could say, all those best of the best are gone.'[19] These letters are very different from his earlier efforts, with far more emotional content, as he desperately tries to get leave to be able to see her. His tendency to be didactic diminishes and, when he reads something about Emily Pankhurst, he even asks Patience to tell him more about the history of the fight for votes for women, saying, 'You'll know much more about it, I'm sure.'[20]

Patience is pleased with the way her ward is running, and says that morale is improving with the arrival of an old friend who is organising a school to train more staff.[21] Individual patients can be a hard work – one has homicidal fits and breaks a chair to attack the nurses – but the German Brigaders she finds difficult *en masse*.

> Really my sweet they are awful. They keep grumbling about things. I am trying my best to get better but from the way they go on you'd think that everything was a direct conspiracy against them. Actually I take rather a lot of trouble to see that the internationals get fussed over, but do they appreciate it? Not on your life. . . .[22]

She passes on news about the romances between some of the other members of staff that Robert has met. Writing about other couples leads her to consider their own future.

> Anni was here yesterday. She sends a greet. Poor darling, she got two days permission to go and say good bye to Fritz before he went to France for good, and got to Barcelona 3 hours after he left so she was very unhappy. Darling I hope we're never in different countries; it is bad enough being apart in the same one.[23]

Another person who confided in Patience was Reggie Saxton, the doctor from the blood transfusion unit. He was deeply in love with Rosaleen Smythe who had been working as an administrator in the medical units since the early days of the war.

> Reggie has been here talking about Ros [Rosaleen]. He is trying to arrange for her to come and work here as he loves her very much. If he were with her all the time I think it would be all right. He wants to get married and have a baby. Queer isn't it? Can't understand it, can you?[24]

Patience certainly could understand it. There is no doubt that she was longing for a baby of her own. When she receives a photo of her brother's new baby, she remarks, 'The baby looks quite nice, but not so nice as ours will be, of course.'[25] Robert does not seem to be averse to the idea and writes in reply, 'I already wish to prove what you said about your brother's baby, don't you?'[26] Small drawings of a mother and baby have been sketched on the back of one of his letters.[27]

Their deliberations over the rights and wrongs of sentimentality continue, Robert is still having difficulty with vocabulary in this regard; 'Sensitive, sensible and sentimental – damn these 3 things, I'll never find the real distinguition [sic] out of them.'[28] With her usual practical turn of mind, Patience uses one of her long, more emotional, letters to help him learn.

> My goodness, you'll soon know exactly what 'sentimental' means when you get letters like this. To help you understand the word the sentences marked * are sentimental. I think I must be more sentimental now than I used to be, but it is your fault, so don't blame me. It all comes of loving you so much.[29]

Interestingly, the very next sentence reverts once again to the subject of politics. It seems she is determined to counteract incipient symptoms of sentimentality with a swift dose of communist theory.

> Your moral sense would be pleased if you saw me now. On my bed are 'Life and Teaching of Karl Marx', 'Lo que significa la Guerra', 'La Correspondencia Internacional' and the syllabus for a *practicante* [doctor's assistant].[30]

However, her honesty compels her to spoil the effect somewhat by adding, 'Also there is a nice frivolous, stupid novel which of course I enjoyed the most. Also a photograph of you which I look at from time to time.'[31]

Both Robert and Patience have problems with their health. Robert is suffering from severe headaches and his hands are in bandages after broken skin became infected.[32] Patience is still plagued by bouts of dysentery.

> This morning when I was washing I looked at myself in the glass and was horrified to see how thin I am. I shall have to get fatter before we meet or you will get bruises from where my bones stick out.[33]

Sometimes they write to each other several times in one day, constantly sending letters or notes with anyone who is going near Marsá or Falset. Not all get through, but the official post is equally unpredictable. For Robert and the troops, morale boosting fiestas include a sports day and a visit from a political delegation of eighty women from Barcelona. Despite having thought that the men should have been doing something more useful, Robert has to admit that it was 'rather successful'.[34] Nevertheless, tension is mounting in the Republican army. The plans for a new offensive are kept a closely guarded secret and the men are restless, not knowing what is to come. Additional activities are arranged to keep them occupied; visits from dignitaries and a delegation from *Dones de Cataluña*, 'Women of Catalonia', who supported the Republic from the home-front. There was also a day-long fiesta with the people of the village of Gratallops and a late-night trip to the cinema.[35] However, Robert has moments of despondency.

> My brain is completely dried out, there is only one moving point in it, you. I want to see you. The guys are undisciplined and bored of the heat, on one hand it is understandable, on the other side, it makes me only too often angry that I begin to shout. Anyhow, I'm nervous that sometimes I hate myself.[36]

Patience's letters grow ever more thoughtful. She returns once again to the subject of the religious influences in her life, before she came to Spain.

> In those days I was very serious minded and pure and unhappy. My religion ceased to give me any comfort or certainty but I hung on to it as it was the only explanation I could find for living. But I was young and full of life and rebellious. Mind you the Church didn't try to stop me enjoying myself, the old parson of the Church I went to was very worried and gave me lots of advice and told me to relax and enjoy myself and be young, but I was full of ideals and thought all or nothing. If I found anything was taking up my interests, except religion (which included nursing as I started because God told me to – actually very good advice on His part), I stopped it. It made life very much of a fight, but much better really than the other nurses without religion. I was much more sensible and useful to people than they were. Gosh darling I am talking a lot about myself. D'you know, when I first met you I kept being reminded about myself when I was younger, I understood so well when you made everything fit in with the Party because that was how I felt about the Church. Don't be cross darling . . .
>
>   O Robert it will be heaven to be with you again.
>   Your Pancake[37]

Her subconscious choice of words 'it will be heaven to be with you again', emphasises the link in her mind between her former religious faith and her feelings for Robert, so inextricably entwined with his identity as a Communist. The parallel she draws between the Communist Party and the Church is one which was noted by others who were in Spain during the civil war.

> It was the spiritual equivalent of changing one's religion. It was an act of Faith. The Party, like the Catholics, demanded absolute obedience. If you joined the Party, you had to renounce the freedom of thinking for yourself. You thought what you were told to think. The Party, like the Pope, was infallible. So it was an Act of Renunciation as well as an Act of Faith, and in return for what you gave up, you received Absolute Certainty.[38]

Patience makes more plans for the future, realising that 'if and when' she joins the Party, she would be most useful in England, but it would be difficult for Robert to find work there. Unlike her earlier plans for them to stay in Spain, by this time she must be considering the possibility that the war will be lost and they will have to go elsewhere. She wonders whether they could have a holiday in Russia or go to Mexico after the war. Would America be an option? But anywhere they could work together would be alright.[39] The last paragraph of her long letter to Father Roberts, in which she had told him with great candour all about her relationship with Robert, conveys the mixture of elation and trepidation she was feeling at the time.[40]

> We are more in love than ever, we just go on finding deeper and deeper meaning in life and we're both working harder than ever in our lives before and looking forward to being together after the war. I am going on working naturally. We see one another about once in six weeks. I live in perpetual fear that he is killed, but I can't ask for anything else in this world. I am waiting now for him to come. He has three days leave sometime this month and we shall be together three days running. You don't know, you can't understand the glory of looking forward to three days running, together.
>
> I hope you are pleased about it. It is the best possible thing that could happen to me. I'm a real person now:
>
> Please be happy with me.
>
> Yours
>
> Patience[41]

Robert's attempts to arrange leave to go to see Patience continue, but produce no positive results. Patience fears she will go mad when, so many times, his plans are thwarted and he is unable to visit her.

> Darling here I am waiting and waiting and imagining and longing but still you don't come. I even wake up at night if a car or an ambulance comes and wonder if you are there. How are you dearest? I hope the bombardments weren't near you, at least not too near.
>
> Today I got an application form for the Party. It makes me rather worried. I hope you will be here soon to talk to about it.
>
> Why don't you get my letters? I write so many and quite long ones; they are very silly but I want you to have them. I can't stand it when I get letters from you saying that you want me to write, because I nearly go mental waiting to hear from you and if you feel the same it makes me so mad when I think of how many I send.
>
> Never mind, we are going to meet soon. I can get permission too. What I should like to do is go out with you, with a mattress and my food – I have quite a lot, and we can lie awake at night and sleep and eat and talk all day and not do anything except be together. Unless you'd rather go to the hotel here and lead a respectable life and play chess in the P.S.U.C. [Catalan Socialist Party]? I would rather be in the country with you in the shade, with your head across my tummy and your damn lice running over us.[42]

The frequency of their expressions of love and longing for each other increase as the days go by. Patience writes:

> I don't know how it is, but I seem to love you more than ever now, and I loved you as much as I could before. Queer, isn't it? I suppose love is like every other living thing, it grows and grows. Like a baby it has all the potentialities and as it develops they come out. Being in love with you makes everything richer.[43]

As July enters its fourth week, Robert is still taking advantage of quiet times to write whenever he can.

> Only 3 hours ago I sent away the other letter but I have to tell you so much that I must write you another time, well knowing it can't be said with words, anyhow, not in letters. These are the best hours of the day: it is still daylight (9 o'clock, evening), a part of the boys are gone to see friends or to flirt with the village beauties, the heat is agreeable, somebody plays any kind of music, not nice, but loud and long.[44]

The next day, 22 July, he writes that they had received orders to move, adding, 'It is almost certain, that there are no more permissions [for leave] now.'[45]

That same day, Patience has heard news of troop movements and, still awake at 3 o'clock in the morning, she writes again.

> Darling, today I knew for certain that you wouldn't be coming – dear you know how much I wanted you and how much I was expecting of our meeting this time but I hope you have a lot of work to do. Your letters made me anxious. Are you feeling better? It is natural that you are tired. All the people who have been out here sometimes are weary and need a change. Darling I expect you are as much in a daze of disappointment as I am at not being together again. It is such a long time since we met, and last time I made such a mess of our meeting.
>
> This letter will be very incoherent I am afraid as I am terribly disappointed and unhappy because we are separated. Not unhappy, exactly, because we are only separated by kilometres and nothing else, but disappointed seems such a mild word to use for what I feel. Never mind, dearest, we will make up for it when we do meet. I have food and cigarettes saved for you, and that will go on being saved, plus rather a lot of love and kisses and rest.[46]

The letter demonstrates just how much her love for Robert was bound up with the fight against fascism. In what must be an unusual style of letter writing, given the strictures of the times and social class, her political philosophy seems to develop on the page as her words flow over the tissue-thin blue paper.

> We are very lucky to be fighting fascism directly, because it is fascism which separates us and spoils our living together so we have not only the stimulus of fighting an enemy but fighting personally as well. Do you see what I mean? We should be antifascist fighters, fighting as hard as we can, anyway, even if we weren't lovers, but supposing we were separated by other things, if we were living in socialist conditions and were separated by ordinary circumstances, we could sublimate our need for one another by working hard yes, but not in the same way we can by fighting here in Spain, when we have to make no effort to work as hard as we can. It is the thing that separates us that we can fight with all our hearts. It isn't duty or necessity or expediency which separates us. Doubtless all these things will, sometime, and then it will be hard to work so wholeheartedly and ungrudgingly but now, in a war against fascism, openly, we can acquiesce

– agree with it with all our strength and enjoy fighting – not that I'm not a pacifist – I don't enjoy killing. D'you understand what I am trying to say? The fact that I am quite willing to be separated from you, and work all the harder, maybe, doesn't mean that I am not longing for you and needing you and missing you so much that not all the work in the world could drown my sadness . . . [47]

Towards the end, she confirms his influence on her political development by writing simply, 'I wish you knew how much better an antifascist I am because of you.' Over the next two days, further ponderings have produced a clearer analysis of her anti-fascism. She has now rationalised her position and can explain more clearly why she believes that the war must be fought.

The longer I am in a country at war the more militantly antifascist I become. Like being in love with you. The longer I am in love the more I am able to be, it just gets deeper and deeper, and at first it seemed as though I couldn't love you any more than I did; it's the same with hatred. I worked as hard as I could in Spain with all my force, but now I realize more and more that fascism means war and the more I realize what war is the more I hate fascists who deliberately provoke it. All the things they do are bad, because they take away freedom but the worst thing is that fascism leads inevitably to war, and war is the greatest evil there is. [48]

However, her worries about joining the Party are still not resolved. She has the application form but remains unsure.

It is the question of freedom that bothers me. You see, I committed myself body and soul to the Church and you know I left that. The main reason I revolted against it was that I felt I must be free, and this gives me the same feeling. I know that you're never free really, you've got to submit to limitations and it is best to choose a limiting that you can agree with intellectually but anyway I will talk to Winifred and maybe wait to see you. [49]

Patience, at last able to work again on night duty after three weeks in bed suffering from dysentery, was particularly pleased to receive a visit from Len Crome. Although now a high-ranking officer, he was still as friendly as ever towards her.

It doesn't make any difference with him now he is a *Jefe de Cuerpo* [Chief of the Division Medical Services], he is just the same. He teased me a lot about you as usual but I feel so proud when anyone talks about you and me together that it isn't any good teasing me. Today I wrote to him reminding him of his promise to send me to the triage if there is work. I think he will.[50]

She also tells Robert the good news that her family are sending more parcels and that her elder brother, John, has sent a kind and affectionate letter, full of brotherly advice, but very 'bourgeois'. She has now decided that she must tell her parents the truth about her relationship with Robert, having already written earlier in the month to tell Father Roberts because, 'The truth is better than lying and saves trouble in the long run.'[51]

When Patience eventually receives Robert's letter complaining of feeling tired and being unable to control his temper, she is full of sympathetic concern. Nevertheless, being older and wiser than Robert by three years, she feels bound to offer a little emotional guidance. In such matters, their roles seem to have reversed since the early days of the relationship, though she is careful to temper her advice with humour.

> I'm afraid that your moral attitude – which I may have mentioned occasionally – is very mortified to find how weak one's will is compared with emotions. I believe you disagreed with me once when I said that you can't help what you feel, and you can't be blamed for what you feel, it's what you do about it that only you are responsible for: and gradually what we will to do, wins in the end. So don't castigate yourself for being impatient and bad tempered and fed up. It will pass off. Really dearest I am getting more moral that you are. Actually it's not so. You will see how wicked I am when we meet again.[52]

After so many weeks of training, despite the secrecy surrounding the exact plans for the new offensive, all are aware that the calm before the storm must soon come to an end; that a momentous battle is imminent. As Patience recalled years later:

> They were building roads all round, organising the thing very strongly to fight back to go across the Ebro. And we knew this, it was an open secret. We were all ready, we were longing for it. We wanted to get back, we wanted to recover the ground.[53]

At the thought of the dangers to come, senses were heightened, and passions intensified. Patience wrote to Robert, 'I think of you all the time, and dream of you when I am asleep.'[54] Her ever-present fear was that the dreams might prove prophetic.

> Last night I dreamt of you a lot, but always when I dream of you it is the same: I dream I am looking for you, but when I find you we only have time to say goodbye.[55]

At last, the day they have all been waiting for dawns. The new offensive, the Battle of the Ebro, begins; the initial aim – to recapture the town of Gandesa, just over 20 km on the other side of the river. On 23 July 1938, Robert writes to tell Patience the news.

> Most loved Darling!
> In some hours we'll march. (I'm sure this will not be destroyed by the censor as if he'll read it, we'll be, who knows it? Perhaps in Gandesa!)
>   Darling, I hope to see you soon on the other side of the Ebro (you'll go to the front as well I suppose). I'm sad that I didn't come to you, but never mind . . . Well there's not much to say now. The humour is OK. I'm sure we'll do a real good job! That's all Patience – all love, longings and kisses.
>   Your Robert[56]

9

The Ebro

Throughout the early summer of 1938, preparations had been underway for a great Republican offensive. In the early hours of 25 July, the Republican troops crossed the River Ebro in small boats and on pontoon bridges, taking the enemy by surprise. At first, they were able to advance rapidly, capturing territory and taking prisoners. Their objective was to re-take Gandesa, a key point for the success of the offensive. Patience, still on the north side of the Ebro, wrote to Robert in high spirits, 'Dearest, congratulations on crossing the river. I hear you were in charge of your company.'[1] She was to remember the days that followed with a particular clarity, her memories encompassing both hope and despair, her mind 'persistently crossing over the spilt milk of that river . . .'.[2]

> One day we suddenly were sent for, a whole lot of us, in different sections to cross to go to kilometre something on the Bisbal to Falset road, where they'd got a set-up, a huge cave . . . , very uneven, big – we could get a hundred beds up, but all higgledy piggledy and of course, rather dark in the day time, pitch dark quite early.[3]

High in the green mountains of Catalonia the wide mouth of the cave cuts a dark slash through the surrounding countryside; a portal framed by pines, the lintel a ponderous tome of rock resting heavily overhead. Situated not far from the village of La Bisbal de Falset, the cave had been chosen as a suitable site for a provisional hospital due to the protection it offered from bombardment, and because a spring of fresh water emerged within its sheltering walls.[4] But for the wounded the journey from the mountain slopes of the *Sierra de Pandols*, where the battle was being fought, to the safety of the cave, entailed a hazardous return across the River Ebro and a torturous ambulance ride along rough, winding roads.

Also working at the cave with Patience was the English nurse, Joan Purser, and the Spanish girl who had been part of their unit since the early days, Aurora Fernández. Patience described how the 'higgledy-piggledy' positions of the beds were the result of the irregular shape of the cave and the very uneven ground, which prevented the beds from being put in straight lines. 'You kept on tripping over them in the dark, hacking yourself – they were metal beds, very uncomfortable to hit on.' Further hazards included lice and scabies, ever present amongst the wounded. The ill-fitting men's trousers and shirts Patience wore at this stage of the war offered no protection at all against these parasites. She would scrub her arms and waist with Lysol, then apply methylated spirits, tolerating the stinging to keep infestation at bay for a little while. Her nursing duties were mainly carried out on the night shift. Fewer casualties were brought in during the day so she would try to sleep for a while on a mattress in a little conduit under the road. She could hear the sound of shell-fire but knew she would be safer there from the daytime bombing raids that could occur at any time.[5]

There was little chance that letters would get through to the front, but Patience wrote encouraging words that she hoped would reach Robert eventually.

> Dearest all I want is to know how you are. The boys are fighting splendidly and everyday we hear of new advances, big ones. I am very tired and we have been *bastante* [rather] busy, but I should be all right if I knew how you were. I hope you are not too tired. We will have a good rest together afterwards! I keep saying that to myself when I am extra tired.
>
> A lot of wounded prisoners have been through here. Also quite a lot of *aviacion* has been over, but we have not been bombed.
>
> Anyway we are in a good place.
>
> I can't write anymore. I've never been so tired before.
>
> Good luck, darling. Write if you can.
>
> I love you
>
> Patience[6]

Under the new system of triage developed in Spain and later to become standard practice for dealing with war-time casualties, the incoming wounded were examined and categorised when they first arrived.

> In the valley below, we had the tent which wasn't so safe and nice as our cave, but where the ambulance would get to, and then the stretcher bearers had to carry them up quite a steep place to the theatre and to the cave, once they'd been sorted out into 'serious', 'medium' and 'wait, it can go back'.[7]

Details of her nursing work and the difficulties caused by limited resources feature strongly in the accounts Patience gives of this period.

9.1 The River Ebro at Miravet.

9.3 Cave hospital exterior.

9.2 Patience's orders to go to the cave hospital.

9.4 Admissions tent in the valley below the cave.

9.5 Patience in the conduit near the cave.

9.6 Patience in the vineyards near the cave.

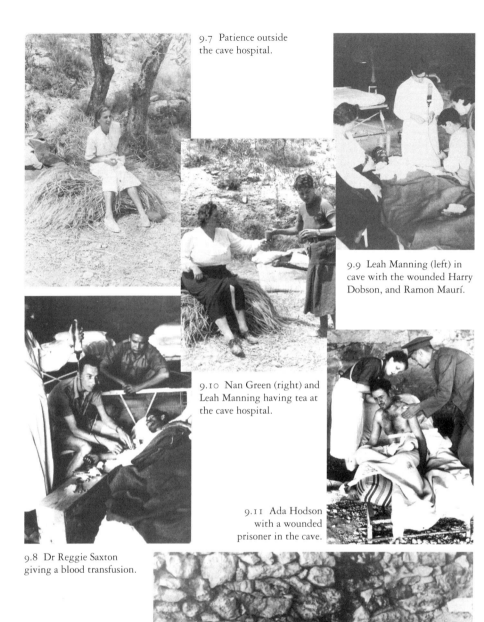

9.7 Patience outside the cave hospital.

9.9 Leah Manning (left) in cave with the wounded Harry Dobson, and Ramon Maurí.

9.10 Nan Green (right) and Leah Manning having tea at the cave hospital.

9.11 Ada Hodson with a wounded prisoner in the cave.

9.8 Dr Reggie Saxton giving a blood transfusion.

9.12 Aurora Fernández with the wounded boy, Manuel Álvarez, in the cave.

Soon, casualties from the battle began to flood back to the cave hospital, putting the medical staff under great pressure. Doctors and nurses needed all the stamina they possessed to deal with the influx of wounded.

> We had an awful lot against us. They had a lot more artillery on their side than we had and we were near to – we were obviously very near a lot of good mortars, because we had a lot of mortared wounds, and they're much bigger, they're much more smashed up things . . . And mortars take great chunks out of people if they survive at all, huge lumps have been hurled out of them, much more smashing up stuff than bullets which go through you. [Sigh]
>
> . . . We tended to get people in at night because the shelling was so enormous they couldn't move in the day. So for the first time, we got people rather long after the battle, we got them sometimes hours after they'd been wounded and some of course, we couldn't save because of that – they were already too bad.[8]

Despite such terrible losses, the number of lives saved had increased as a result of medical developments that had been made as the war progressed. In addition to new approaches to the treatment and 'débridement' of wounds to remove all damaged tissue and prevent the onset of gas gangrene, chances of survival were now also higher due to innovations in the technology for the preservation and transfusion of blood.[9] Earlier on in the war, Patience had given her own blood in an arm to arm direct transfusion, and the family had viewed her as having become part of the family 'by blood', even though the wounded man had reacted badly to the transfusion. Now, a system of collecting blood from donors in the cities was well established, serving a two-fold purpose. Not only did the successful calls for donors increase the availability of preserved blood for the wounded, but the very act of giving blood encouraged solidarity between civilians and the soldiers at the front.[10] What better way to create a sense of national identity than for the non-combatant population to become blood brothers with the soldiers who were fighting and dying for the Republic? After collection, a rudimentary classification into blood groups was carried out when possible and a citrate anticoagulant was added before the supplies were transported from the cities to hospitals near the front in lorries adapted for refrigerated storage.[11] The blood transfusion unit was stationed at the cave, run by Reggie Saxton, 'our dear Reggie', as Patience later referred to him with affection.

Photographs taken by Winifred Bates during a visit to the cave hospital show Dr Saxton giving a transfusion to a patient, the Welsh Brigader,

Harry Dobson.[12] At his side is Leah Manning, a former Labour MP and member of the Spanish Medical Aid Committee in London, who was visiting various hospitals at the front. Leah Manning was keen to be of use, as Patience recalled. Although at first it was 'awfully difficult' to think of something suitable for a visiting dignitary to do in the midst of the 'general carry-on', in the end, her presence was put to good use.[13] Harry Dobson had met Leah Manning before the war, when attending a meeting at which she had spoken about the war in Spain. Patience realised that he recognised Leah, who sat by his bedside during the night, until he died. Although Patience herself was not able to recall the wounded man's name, she remembered him saying to Leah, 'You can't kill the workers', so presumed he must have been 'a political'.[14]

Patience also referred to the subject of blood transfusions in the cave to illustrate another point she was anxious to clarify – that of the treatment of enemy wounded. The usual issues surrounding their treatment, exacerbated when supplies were short, were rendered even more complex in this case by Franco's use of Moorish troops. As historic enemies, racial tensions already existed between Spaniards and Moors, and the reputation of the Moors for extreme cruelty intensified feelings against them.[15] Patience spoke frankly about the problems that had to be overcome when a Moor needed medical attention.

> There was one Moor I remember, a Moorish prisoner we'd taken, a Franco Moor, very badly wounded in the neck. God, how he hated us, he used to give terrible looks to us, he didn't trust us at all, he expected we'd kill him the same as they killed people. But he was admitted amongst the others, and he ought to have had a blood transfusion, and the [Spanish] chaps got together and said they weren't going to give the blood of the women of Spain to the Moor.[16]

Although the Moors were hated, and Franco despised for bringing them to fight in Spain, Patience believed that there was also an awareness of other aspects of the situation amongst the Spaniards and Catalans in the unit. 'They knew quite well,' she said, 'that they shouldn't have been fighting the Moors anyway in Morocco. That was also a disgrace. They were very clear about that.'[17] The main purpose of her story becomes clear when she stresses the fact that the men, much to her admiration, overcame their prejudices. She recalled, 'When I looked round, he was getting one – this lot of sheepish faces as he got his blood transfusion.'[18]

She also praised the Spanish doctors for their surgical skills.

The Spanish surgeons were marvellous with abdominals, they'd take out miles and miles of intestine, looking for holes, because bullets or bits of shrapnel might go through twenty times you know, in the curls of intestine – one goes through a whole lot of it. And they'd pull them all out and have a look. Sometimes they'd just cut out a whole lot and join them up – they were very good at resections, excellent, marvellous.[19]

There were shortages of medical supplies and the food for the staff was poor, described by Patience as consisting of 'very mouldy bread, bits of hard meat – *burro* – donkey,' and 'tinned sweetened condensed milk' she considered 'disgusting stuff'. However, wine was plentiful, and better for the patients if clean water was in short supply.

We used to have a good deal of *vino*, which was quite a good thing – not for us, but for the patients, because it is comforting and they were so used to it, they needed it. We tried not to have spirits. The foreigners, the International Brigaders amongst them, would always want brandy, and the Spanish brandy was [laughter] *gasolina*, we used to call it, absolute gut rot – very poor quality indeed, horrible raw stuff, and that we didn't want them to have. That was always a struggle because their mates would bring it in or they'd ask somebody, you know, to slip out to get them some.[20]

The poor diet did little to help the other persistent problem that all the staff had to endure, though the Spanish brandy proved useful at times.

What was a great nuisance was if you had awful dysentery yourself and always had to be traipsing out to find somewhere to go – because that was an awful trouble. You hadn't got a loo anywhere, and that was a curse. Wasn't so bad there – plenty of bushes and rocks and things. That was awful because, I mean, you just had to get out quick half the time and sometimes you had to skip for quite a long way to find a rock – that was an absolute pest.[21]

When asked what treatment had been available for dysentery, she replied,

Nothing. Anti-typhoid, you drank brandy – horrid stuff it was, but it was comforting. And we did have a morphia mixture which was also certainly a very good thing because nothing else would stop it.[22]

She recounted the story of how she was once dosing herself in this way before going to sleep and mixed up the bottles of brandy and morphine, drinking a huge 'wallop of morphia' by mistake.

> I can still remember them walking me about, trying to wake me up and I was well away – as though I was floating above them looking down and thinking 'What are they doing with that poor girl, why can't they leave her alone?' They were smacking me and walking me up and down and trying to make me drink coffee and be sick and things. I got better, I mean, it worked, and it was a nice feeling at the time.[23]

With people of so many nationalities in the Brigades, language was inevitably at times a problem. Not only were there the practical problems associated with obeying commands correctly, or for medical staff, the ability to understand patients, but also there was the emotional anguish of being unable to communicate with the mortally wounded. The promise to convey a patient's last words to loved ones was a duty that Patience felt she owed to the dying.

> We were very good with the Brigades in the hospitals about trying to get somebody who spoke their language, because that was always a dreadful thing with very ill people, dying people – they couldn't speak – different tongues, you see. And that was where the Commissars came in. Very often there were a lot of Jewish people in the Brigades, a great many, and a lot of them spoke Yiddish and something else. And you would always try to get a Jewish person who could speak Yiddish, to another Jewish person – it didn't matter if they were Romanian or Hungarian or what they were, you could get a common language, get a message if you wanted it, that they wanted to send home or say who they were or something like that. But we had on the Ebro, in that cave, three Finns and *nobody could speak anything to them*. Nobody speaks Finnish. They were all very bad chest wounds. In those days we didn't know that you could operate on chest wounds, we used to strap them up tight and sit them up, but they were miserable. They couldn't breathe; they were strapped up tight as well as being with all these dreadful flesh wounds, very deep ones. And they were all three dying. And we couldn't get anyone who spoke Finnish and they weren't Jewish. Oh! I'll never forget them, they were such beautiful creatures, great blonde things, you know [sigh] unable to say anything.[24]

They die untranslated, their wordless deaths symbolic of so many other un-sung soldiers. Her grief at the memory of her powerlessness to help them reveals the deep feelings that lay beneath the brusque facade she usually maintained toward her patients.

Despite the fact that by this stage of the war she believed wholeheartedly in the rightness of the cause, as she heard the new young recruits singing as they marched to the front, she began to doubt that anything could be worth the suffering that she saw around her.

> And this road up to us went up to the front, past the [cave hospital] and it was lorry loads of the last call up – children, fifteen and sixteen year olds in the last call up, going up to the front. And we saw what happened when they got to the front – these terrible smashed up people, streaming in. And to hear those kids singing as they went up – it was terrible when I thought what was going to happen to them, and it got me down frightfully. We were working terribly hard, it was very uncomfortable, very dark in that cave and almost everyone who came in was pulse-less and seriously ill . . . I was on nights, well we worked most of the time, but I was always on at night, and this darkness and the discomfort and the seriousness of it – I thought it wasn't worth it, I thought no war is worth all this, this misery and this horror.[25]

Patience was one of the nurses who, having been in Spain during the civil war, became accustomed to being interviewed over the years. Nevertheless, the intensity of emotion when she talked about her experiences was often painfully obvious. Her feelings relating to this period of defeat remained particularly raw. In her narrative, she chooses to explain how she overcame her desperation by telling a 'parable', a story that has the purpose of illustrating a specific point, in this case, the moral justification for fighting the war. Although she is making a political point, her style is the antithesis of traditional political rhetoric. Her thoughts keep returning to the sound of 'children' singing as they marched past the cave on their way to the front.

> And a chap had come in, I saw him come in, long before, from outside with bundles of stuff – was let in properly. And he was sitting on the side of a bed smoking cigarettes which he'd rolled, talking to a chap – one of those deserting <u>to</u> the front who was only lightly wounded, an officer who had his arm strapped up and was going to go back. And they were talking and laughing and smoking and I was in this terrible state, running round, people dying and very wretched and these children singing in the road. So in a break – there's always a pause in these things – I went over and said, 'How can you be talking and laughing, can't you see what's going on? Can't you hear those children singing?'

And the chap was very serious, very nice man, a marvellous man, and he said he was just a Spaniard from the locality and he'd brought up fruit for us, he'd been taking it to the front but he heard about the hospital and he'd brought up – there was lots of fruit round there, apricots and such like, but of course, no use to us in the ward there, and I said, 'Well, is it worth it, all this? Can you not hear those children singing?' And he said he was an analphabetic peasant in the locality there, they hadn't even got a road only a track to their village. They were terribly poor and they didn't know much that was going on, they were used to being voted for, they were voted as so many souls belonging to the owner of the land – he just put in their votes, so many numbered. But they'd heard, a couple of years before, that there was going to be an election in which they could vote. And they went and voted, it was the first time they'd known they'd voted, they went over the tracks and voted.

They heard nothing more about it, until they heard that the village next to them was measuring out the land. So they went over to see what this measuring out the land was, and the Popular Front had got in and this was a little land reform thing, only it hadn't got to them. And they didn't know how to measure, they hadn't got anything to measure with, so they went and found out how to do these things, what was going on. The land-lord had flown, and they measured out their land. He became – he was elected the local Mayor . . . Every village had a Mayor, it would be a village council in England, but there they all had a Mayor. He was the Mayor, he learnt to read and write. They organised everything, and then he, oh, five or six weeks before this battle, the Ebro, he was sent for to Barcelona, he had a letter, it was the first letter he'd ever had – and of course, he could read it – he had a letter to go to Barcelona, and he went down to the partic-ular place on the road where he was picked up, and he went in a car – the first time he'd been in a car, with leather seats.

And he sat in this car with leather seats and he went to Barcelona where they were told that there was going to be this battle and the roads were going to be built and that the local authorities had got to be able to provide for both the refugees coming our way . . . and for the army and for anything else that was going on – he had to have these stores ready and had to be organised to do it.

And he did all those things, and they did very well at them, they managed an awful lot of food, they were ready to pass the refugees back but they didn't get any there. But he said, 'I became a man, and that's what we're fighting for.' [Pause] And he just said this all quite simply, quite straight forward, he summed up what was the matter with me, and he told me what was going on. Marvellous, the Spaniards are.[26]

For Patience, this local man expressed at a fundamental and practical level the political beliefs she had embraced. The story also gives an indication of the positive potential of encounters between foreign volunteers and villagers, however brief. Not only did he make her regret what she termed her 'defeatist' attitude at the time, but his words could be related to others in a form that clearly illustrates the issues at stake in the war. Within her personal narrative she created a successful strategy for the communication of the concept of egalitarianism, illustrating yet again the truth in the familiar aphorism, 'the personal is political'. [27]

The numerous dead were taken to a communal grave outside the village. Their removal from the cave brought additional difficulties for Patience.

> I had terrible arguments there with the stretcher bearers who wanted to take my blankets to wrap the people in to bury them, and I said no, I must have the blankets to keep people alive with – had to pull the blankets off them which was very difficult, because one didn't know if one should argue with things like that. I mean, I felt the Spaniards were probably right, but I wasn't going to have the blankets gone because I really had to have them.[28]

This was a terrible time for Patience, for reasons that did not become clear until shortly before her death. In interviews, she would sometimes pause and sigh deeply, seeming to drift into the past, especially when talking about her days at the cave hospital. One example of this occurred when she was recalling her friendship with a group of drivers that included Max Colin, Chris Thornycroft and Harry Evans.

> I was the only English nurse on nights there. I used to get up about four in the afternoon because you couldn't sleep much longer, and traipse along to my mates, the English drivers, because they weren't moving in the day either, the place had to be – the roads had to be not used except for real emergency things. And they used to brew up and have things, they were better at getting hold of food and things than we were. I mean, we had no way of getting out to get it. And there was a group of English drivers there who were great mates and help. They were marvellous, the English drivers, our lot, because they'd get anything and they knew all the proper routes. They were the people who worked out how you got your supplies, your blood transfusions and things . . . And, of course, they'd keep all the machinery going, the generator and all the lamps for the theatres. But they were very comforting, very nice to have as mates. [Pause] They were very reassuring because they were calm, and they had 'cuppas' and they

were kind when you were miserable and tired and [pause], and they were funny, I mean, they had jokes, which is also very helpful and nice. [Pause, sigh] I don't know – I was terribly tired then.[29]

The tragedy that lay behind her sadness is revealed in two letters that she kept in her collection of correspondence from Spain. The first, written in German, contained the news she must have been dreading most of all.

Front, 31 July 1938
Esteemed Comrade,

I ask you above all to accept these lines calmly. The war against Fascism is tough and takes its toll of victims. We have not been spared our share of them.

On 27 July 1938 Robert was killed, struck a mine and died immediately. A few days before, he charged me with notifying you in the event of his death. At the same time I am sending all his letters to you, yours to him as well as his parents' and ask you to notify them of his death.

We know what we have lost in him, loved by all his comrades. What distinguished him were his personal courage and his calmness in the toughest engagements. In him I too lose an old comrade, leaving Paris with him on the same day for Spain, and being with him as well with the 'Tschapjef' in the 41st Battalion.[30]

We buried him not far from the place where he fell. The Machine Gun Company has lost one of its best and so will we avenge his death.

I also ask you to extend to his parents the condolences of the whole Company at their loss.

With revolutionary greetings,
I remain
Bert Ramin
Sergeant
41st. Baon. Machine Gun Company[31]

A letter from 'Comisario Herbert', written in Spanish, followed shortly afterwards.

My dear friend Patience

I have just now received confirmation that our comrade, your husband Robert, was killed in the latest fighting. I share with you the great feelings of sorrow caused by his death.

Dear Patience, I am sure that this tremendous loss will not defeat you, because you must fight and carry on with your life and destiny. Robert died as he lived, fulfilling his duty as an anti-fascist and as a revolutionary – leading his men, he met the fascist bullet which killed him. You must be worthy of his death, fulfilling his duties without weakness.

My hope is to be able to come and see you soon, to express my feelings to you in better words than can be conveyed by this letter. I hope to receive a letter from you soon and send you affectionate greetings.

Herbert[32]

An article about Robert's bravery appeared in the German edition of the *Volunteer for Liberty*, describing how he had been wounded three times but each time had returned to the front without waiting for his medical discharge. During the battle of Belchite he had taken command of the company when the officer in charge was wounded, and his prompt action had saved many lives. He had been promoted to lead his Company across the Ebro. His death was a sad loss, not only of a good officer for the Battalion, but also of a best friend and comrade for his Company. Patience kept the article throughout her life, along with the treasured letters.[33]

A week after first hearing of his death, Patience wrote to Robert's parents to break the news to them.

My dear comrades

Please don't mind me calling you comrades. Robert talked about you so much and so often I sent messages to you that I feel I know you.

I don't know how I am going to explain why I am writing to you. However I do it, it will give you great pain so I had better say in simple words that Robert was killed on July 27. He died as bravely and tranquilly as he lived, and was killed instantaneously, near Gandesa, and was buried by his friends just near where he fell.

I know he wrote to you about me, and so you will understand why it is I that am writing to you. His friend who was there when he was killed sent me his diary and various letters, three from you. The rest were from me.

You know from Robert how much we loved one another and I know how much you loved him. For me he was perfect: I don't mean that I was blind to his faults, but that for me he was everything. What else can I say? When you first read this letter you will only be able to understand one thing, but later on you may find some comfort if I say some more about him.

I think it was hard for you to acquiesce in the necessity for Robert to be fighting fascism here but he was so happy to be here, fighting openly and with every aid against the enemy of his life. He only lived for his ideals and here in Spain he could do as he wanted and give every thought and minute of his life as a fighter so he was very happy and content. For me and for many he was a revelation of how to live and fight against the thing that is trying to ruin the world. He was content before he met me, but after we met and fell in love he was so happy that it was almost frightening. For us it was heaven. It is a great comfort to me, as much as anything can be a comfort, to remember that he didn't and couldn't ask anything more of the world. These last eight months were full of joy for him, so you must think of him as enjoying his life as much as it is possible.

He often, very often, thought and spoke about you to me, with great tenderness and love. When, in May or June, May I think, he got some photographs from you he was so pleased. You remember how careless he was about property of his own? He couldn't be bothered about anything but his work, and always lost everything, so when he had something he really wanted he used to send it to me to take care of, but when he sent these photographs he asked me not to send them with my belongings in a safe place, but to keep them with me so that he could see them when we met. In one of the last letters I got before he died he said that he had heard from you and that his younger sister had just had her 16th birthday and he would like to see her.

We are still out at the front but when I get back to the base again I will send some photographs and the book of his battalion that he was originally in.

There is nothing I can say that will make it any easier for you. Nobody can say anything that comforts me. I hear the words they say, but it doesn't help so I won't write any more. Robert said that you can understand English, but in case you can't understand all this at first I am sending a note by an Austrian girl as well.

I hate to think of your pain when you get this letter, but I have to write it. You are luckier than I am. I have known that my darling Robert is dead for eight days. You have had longer when you thought he was alive. When I go to see his Company, which he loved very much and of which the men loved him I will write again and tell you how his boys spoke about him. They loved him too. Everyone did who knew him.

Please accept my sympathy

Patience Darton

P.S. I was 'as' married to Robert but never had his name.[34]

These were bitter days for Patience. Her response to Robert's death was to immerse herself in work, though the suppression of emotions this entailed may have caused her attitude to patients to appear uncaring. Winifred Bates commented on this in the report she wrote after seeing Patience towards the end of their time in Spain. The report also explains why Patience, unlike some of the other British nurses, had never gone back on leave to England.

> She is brave at the front and never spares herself . . . She is extremely competent though rather harsh with her patients. I suspect her hardness of tongue is to cover a good deal of weariness and suffering, though I must admit it jars at times. In February, she married a fine German Communist who was killed in the Ebro offensive on July 27th. I attach a copy of a letter that she wrote to me on Sept. 3rd. At times she seemed to me very conceited and I had a fight with myself to keep my temper; I think it was worth while. She is low in health and needs rest. She has never had leave because she feared that the Committee would not send her back because of the early trouble. That seems to prove that her heart is in the work in Spain. A member of the Committee said to her, 'What will you do with a German husband who has no passport? Have you thought of that?' She replied, 'There will always be work for nurses and machine-gunners. Have you thought of that?' I shall try to persuade her to take leave for the sake of her health. If she wishes I think she should be allowed to come back.[35]

Patience declined the offer of leave and, as the Republican advance ground to a halt near Gandesa, she moved even closer to the front. Franco's escalation of his offensive, courtesy of unconditional German and Italian support, was taking a heavy toll on the Republican forces, and more medical personnel were needed across the River Ebro. Patience was transferred to a small unit with two doctors, a Hungarian and a German. It seems that Dr Jensen was instrumental in arranging this move to ensure that she was so busy she had no time to dwell on Robert's death.

> Jensen saved me. When he learned that Robert had been killed, he came and arranged for me to be transferred. I was distraught and the move to the front was like a sort of therapy.[36]

Apart from the operating theatre, there was just one tent for ten patients. She slept on a stretcher in the same tent, recalling how much she disliked both; stretchers for being too narrow to turn over, and tents because 'even a machine gun bullet is going to go very quickly through a tent'. The practicalities of treating wounds by keeping them open to allow drainage entailed a daily war against flies. They would try to improvise fly screens from mosquito netting, stretching it over frames made from bent pieces of wood. After several weeks, by this time in the month of September, she was transferred again, noting that it was to a completely Spanish, rather than a Catalan unit. 'We were moved around a lot and we got into crossfire twice and they were terribly dramatic about it you see . . . It was rather like a film.'[37] Not surprisingly, her memory of those days was hazy. Meanwhile, at higher levels, important decisions were being made that would affect Patience and all the foreigners in the International Brigades.

10

Leaving Spain

On 24 September 1938, the International Brigades received orders to withdraw from the front and to leave Spain. Based on a proposal from Dr Juan Negrín, the Prime Minister of the Republic, the League of Nations had advocated the withdrawal of foreign troops on both sides. Negrín arranged for the repatriation of the International Brigades, hoping that pressure would be brought to bear on Franco to send home the Italian and German units that were playing such a key role in the Nationalist military success. However, his hope was in vain. The order to withdraw changed the situation for the medical personnel who, like Patience, had been taken in to the Republican army. After almost a month in her Spanish medical unit, it was discovered on pay day that she had an International Brigade pay book. She was told that they were no longer able to keep her, and she had to leave. 'It was a muddle', she said, 'I was sent back to Barcelona to be sent out with the Brigade', but she ended up with a miscellaneous collection of women 'up in the hills somewhere in Catalonia'. Some were Spanish girls who had married International Brigaders, 'totally un-political, they were just beautiful creatures, dear creatures, they were very nice indeed, they were good Spanish women – they knew what the war was about and so on, but they weren't highly politically organised'.[1] However, she soon developed an intense dislike for a group of German and Hungarian women, intent on political leadership and full of their own importance. Patience grew fretful in this situation and managed to find out where the British Battalion were stationed. She then demanded a safe conduct pass to hitch a lift to join them at Ripoll, a town not very far from the French border. 'Grumpy', was how she described the mood in the British Battalion.

> Well, grumpy because we were being sent out. I mean, we were still ready to stay and fight. We didn't agree with this, and we didn't think it would work either, and it felt terrible, when the war was going badly at the end, we all knew it was going badly, and to be all sent out when we were really good and useful, it was terrible. It was bad enough losing the war without you being sent out early.[2]

Patience even describes the huge farewell parade in Barcelona, often considered one of the most moving and memorable tributes to the International Brigades, as 'terrible', seemingly because she was so burdened with feelings of guilt at having to leave the Republicans still fighting the war.

> I saw La Pasionaria through floods of tears, waving from a balcony. The Spaniards all around us were crying openly, hugging and kissing us – it was all so terrible. What could *I* do against the fact that we were being made to leave Spain? I had to accept the decision of the Spanish Republican government.[3]

Other testimonies reveal mixed emotions regarding repatriation. Feelings of relief at being away from the carnage of the battlefields were almost as evident as the remorse at leaving while former comrades were still at the front. For some, there would be the joy of going home, but even this pleasure would have been tainted with sadness at the thought of the many Brigaders who were unable to return to their own countries for political reasons, such as the Germans, Austrians and Italians, amongst a host of other central and eastern Europeans.[4]

However, Patience did not leave Spain with the majority of the British Battalion, a fact she attributes to having been on a different register of medical personnel. Instead, she was grouped together in a house in Barcelona with doctors she had known on the Ebro front, an Austrian, a German and a Hungarian. All three were in the unfortunate position of being unable to return home and were waiting for papers for entry into France. Patience's account of her journey to France with this group is perhaps the most vivid amongst the descriptions given by British volunteers on this subject. Many interviews with veterans of the civil war end with the farewell parade in Barcelona, perhaps followed by a few references to their views on the war in retrospect. Patience's account conveys the shock, both mental and physical, of crossing the border and finding herself, after almost two years, in a country not yet at war.

> And we were then told that we were going to be 'en-trained' and it was pathetic – the Spanish are such darlings – there was a whole train load of us, about five carriages, packed tight, and the railway runs along by the road. And Franco had been saying – the wireless had been chattering on – about bombing the trains of the soldiers, of us going out. I don't know whether they had done so or not, but anyway they said they were going to, or they said they had. And we were in this special train, all of us,

10.1a, 10.1b, 10.1c
Carnet Militar.

REPÚBLICA ESPAÑOLA

Brigadas
Internacionales

CARNET MILITAR

N.º

FILIACION

Estatura
Pelo
Cejas
Ojos
Nariz
SEÑAS PARTICULARES

Fecha de nacimiento _____ 8 _ 1911
Lugar de nacimiento _Dapington, Kent_
Nacionalidad _Ingles_
Profesión _Enfermera_
Estado civil _Soltera_
DOMICILIO: País _Inglaterra_
Pueblo
Calle _____ núm.
Partido Político _Anti fascistas_
Fecha de entrada en las B. I. _30-10-1937_
Fecha de entrega de la libreta _9-12-1937_

— 2 —

NOMBRAMIENTOS

Grado
Empleo
Nombrado día
visado el
Comandante

Grado
Empleo
Nombrado día
visado el
Comandante

Grado
Empleo
Nombrado día
Visado el
Comandante

— 3 —

El titular de esta Cartilla Militar nacionalidad de _____ al cabo de debidamente autorizado por la Superioridad, después de haber prestado leal colaboración al Gobierno de la República en pro de las ideas del Pueblo Español en la Segunda Campaña de su Independencia, habiendo observado siempre buena conducta.

Barcelona, a ___ de _____ de 19__

EL JEFE DE LA SECCIÓN ADMINISTRATIVA DE LAS
BRIGADAS INTERNACIONALES

— 16 —

10.2a, 10.2b, 10.2c
International Brigade
Identity Book.

Brigadas Internacionales

El *Darton*
   Patience

presta sus servicios en *35° dar 11*

El Coronel Jefe del E. M.
de la Base Orgánica.

El Jefe del Servicio
de Efectivos.

El Interesado.

HABERES PARA EL PERIODO

de	a	Pesetas	pagados por
1/I.	10/I.	100	
10/1	20/1	100	
20/1	31/1	110	R.Smyth
1/2	10/2	100	R.Smyth
10/2	20/2	80	
20/2	28/2	80	Aileen Y. Palmer
1/3.	30/3.	310	
1/4.	30/4	300	
1/5	31/5	310	Ortez

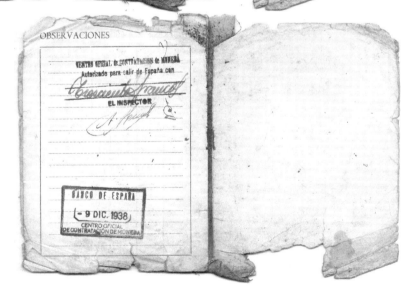

OBSERVACIONES

CENTRO OFICIAL de CONTRATACION de MONEDA
Autorizado para salir de España con

EL INSPECTOR

BANCO DE ESPAÑA
[- 9 DIC. 1938]
CENTRO OFICIAL
DE CONTRATACIÓN DE MONEDA

Internationals being sent out, and along by the road by the side of the
railway, they had two trucks with anti-aircraft guns – well, at least, the
anti-aircraft machine guns, they wouldn't have done much good but the
little aeroplanes did fly low – by the road to guard our train. And as we
went – very slow train – people from the villages came running across to
say goodbye and thank us and held up their children to be kissed – it was
TERRIBLE, we felt awful, and with all that was going on when the war
was going so badly and there they had been setting out special trucks with
people to guard us, and the people coming to thank us. And we felt it was
absolutely terrible, it was a dreadful thing. And it took a long while – it
took about four hours, a little slow train, creeping along. We went
through a tunnel which is there at Port Bou, came out the other side into
France, where they had an enormous welcoming committee, I mean, the
Spanish and the Popular Front, which is very strong in the south of France.
And they had a banquet and speeches, and of course, we couldn't – the
food they gave us, suddenly eggs and things with lots of butter, [laughter]
we were all terribly ill with it, we could hardly get through the meal. And
of course, we had to sit having speeches and whip out to the loo, and really
felt terribly sick suddenly having proper food, because Barcelona was very,
very short indeed, terribly short. I mean, there really wasn't food, you had
to go to the army depot to get your bread and lump of meat and then try
to get somebody to cook it, although actually you gave it away because I
mean, you couldn't take food when other people hadn't got it. It was very
bad indeed in Barcelona, and to suddenly have this enormous welcoming
party – you felt dreadful anyhow, about going, let alone suddenly all this
food – it felt awful, apart from being sick and having diarrhoea terribly.
Then we had to be put in a train which – a train going through to Paris
– and we were locked into a whole compartment, two compartments, all
of us, with guards on each end – horrible French Army, with a little set
up machine gun because we'd got to be seen out of the train the other end,
we were nasty dangerous creatures. This was official, not the French
Popular Front people down there.[5]

After crossing the border into France, the slow train passed through
many stations where the local people had organised Popular Front demonstrations of solidarity, singing and throwing flowers and fruit through the
windows. The carriage doors were kept locked. Patience soon became
embroiled in arguments due to her insistence to go her own way and not
follow the planned route directly to Paris. Once there, the British Consul
was supposed to escort her to board a boat for England. However, Patience
had other ideas. She had learned that by calling in at the Spanish Medical

Aid Committee in Toulouse, she would be given her train fare home. Her plan was to stay in Paris with other refugees from the Republic for as long as she could. Still having her British passport, she began demanding freedom of movement as an ordinary tourist.

Well, we got to Toulouse, where – I'd already been making statements about getting out at Toulouse, already before we started – and there was an ENORMOUS demo in Toulouse, it was in the night, about twelve o'clock, it was a huge one, being kept back by soldiers. And French soldiers keeping people back in demos in France are terribly rough, they hit you with the butt end, they bang them back – but they seemed to be taking a good part because people were swaying backwards and forwards, singing. And I had got out, the doors were locked, so I was posted out of the window, quite big windows, and I'd got a trunk I was bringing back for the Committee, a great tin trunk of stuff for the Committee, papers from the Spanish Medical Aid Committee, and this was posted out too. And then of course, the chaps cottoned on to the fact that this was happening, roars from the crowd and things, and insisted on terrific farewells. I didn't know most of them, I'd never seen them before except for the particular group of doctors that I happened to be with already from Barcelona. And tremendous roars and crowd and there was an enormous policeman, French 'gendarme', a sergeant – great huge fat thing with a huge moustache, and his belt absolutely strained round him – and two ordinary 'coppers' there to take me, to arrest me and keep me overnight and see me onto the train the next day after I'd been to the Committee, and tremendous noise and all this shouting and singing and things and roars and boos, and of course, there were these pathetic farewells from the train, people I'd never seen before, you know, I had to rush up and down the carriages being kissed and things from the platform. And you know, they're terribly high, the platforms, and I was being heaved up and down. It was all a put on thing, I mean, I didn't want to say goodbye to them, but it was quite obvious that this was a demo going on, and I was quite happy to play with it. And the train pulled out, amid more boos and things – everyone suddenly disappeared, you know, melted away, including the soldiers, and this great huge sergeant undid his belt – it was very impressive this strained leather belt round him – burst open, and he said, 'You're coming home with me, I'm the chairman of the local Popular Front. [Laughter] Everything seemed to be so queer, so dreamlike, so mad, like a film again. But my main thing was of course, this terrible business of having diarrhoea. I got my money the next day, my fares, £10 – a lot of money in those days – and the Mayor took me round Toulouse, gave me crystallised violets, the last thing I wanted. All I wanted was to be left in quiet peace to get to a loo, you know, a decent one. But however, I lasted the day till I was put on a train.[6]

On arrival in Paris, she was met by the British Consul who tried to persuade her to return home immediately. But Patience had already arranged to meet the three doctors she knew in order to help them arrange papers for entry into Britain – Fritz Jensen, Caspar Kisch and his brother, Egon Erwin Kisch.[7] The Consul was given a firm refusal – Patience was not giving up so easily.

Paris was swarming with impoverished refugees and after buying a third class ticket home, she had enough money to stay in Paris for two weeks, living in a cheap hotel. The days were busy, filled with efforts to help others who had recently left Spain.

And we'd already started organising in Barcelona for some of the doctors to go to China – Germans and Austrians, because where could they go and what could they do anyway? They wanted to go on fighting – they wanted to go on doing something, and China of course, we all knew about, we had read *Red Star over China* which was one of the books being passed round in Spain. We knew all about Mao and the rest of them. And there was this group of seven doctors who wanted to go to China, because at least it was somewhere to be – they didn't particularly want to leave Europe but they wanted to go on being somebody in something. So we were starting to organise a committee and they wanted me to get people to get them to England. In those days it was fairly easy if you had somebody who'd say they'd look after them and they were only going through anyway, you could get papers for England, to let them land anyway. So we were organising that and I was about a fortnight in Paris, and it was just after the *Anschluss* in Austria and the place was full of Jewish refugees. Paris was perfectly beastly, and in the south of France we'd had all this glorious being given violets and things, but in Paris they hated all of us – all the foreigners, all the refugees – all broke, nobody wanted us. The hotels didn't like us. I must say, it was a bit hard on the hotel because I was staying in a hotel with three of these doctors, and all their friends, particularly the Austrians, came in to have baths in the hotel. Well, it was a bit hard on the hotel. [Laughter][8]

Just before Christmas, Patience's money ran out and she was forced to use her ticket back to England, still having had no success in arranging papers for her friends.

The train was frightfully cold and I had bare legs and I had only borrowed shoes because we only had, of course, cotton *alpargatas* [sandals] in Spain, I didn't ever have shoes. And I borrowed shoes from somebody else which didn't fit me, they were terribly uncomfortable – my bare legs – I got frightfully chapped with the cold. And I had a woollen skirt, a nasty woollen scratchy skirt that I'd got in Barcelona, and I'd still got my army 'mac'. And the porters wouldn't help me because I couldn't tip them so I had to cart this trunk on and off by myself and get it onto the boat. It was very difficult; it was a nasty tin trunk, too big to pick up to carry it by its handles.[9]

She arrived back in England without a penny to her name, just a third-class ticket to Victoria. Exhausted, she sat on the trunk which had 'Spanish Medical Aid' written all over it.

However, the porter saw this, said 'What's all this then?' So I said, 'It's Spain, I've just come from Spain.' 'Oh!' he said, 'Well you can't carry that can you?' He put me in a first class carriage and told the people there that I'd come from Spain and I was to be given tea and things. Very surprised they were. Oh, dear, how I cried, because it was so nice after the French being so horrid – this darling porter. And anyway, they made polite enquiries. I had tea, it was very nice having tea on the train, I've always liked it. But I was a bit amazed, so were they, and nobody seemed to mind my ticket was a little third class ticket. But when I got to Victoria, I really was rather stuck because I didn't know how to get out of the station. I knew my brother was in London and I could look it up in a telephone book. So when a porter came again with my trunk, I said would he lend me tuppence for the phone – I'd give it him back when my brother came, and I was from Spain – tra la! So he said, 'Yes, yes, yes.' He gave me the tuppence, took me to a phone box and waited outside. And I got my brother, and the porter was still there when I came out, so I said, 'It's all right, he's coming', and he said, 'That's all right, I wanted to see if you got through, dear', and he tramped off again. So again, I mean, this was terribly upsetting because France had been horrid, perfectly awful, and all these terrible things from the refugees, and leaving Spain was so terrible. Then coming back, suddenly people were so kind and so marvellous about Spain.[10]

She was not to see Spain again for almost sixty years.

▌▌
A Different Life

On her return to England in December 1938, Patience was aware that nothing would ever be the same for her again. Years later, she reiterated the words she had used in her letter to Father Roberts, 'And of course, then, I was quite a different person, going to have quite a different life.'[1]

She went first to visit her parents. While she had been away, they had moved to the quiet Buckinghamshire village of Dinton, near Aylesbury. Any letters she had written to them from Spain have not been found, but her comments indicate that perhaps they were few and far between. She told an interviewer that during the civil war the local paper had carried reports on 'Aylesbury nurse in Spain', adding, 'which was lovely you see, you didn't have to bother writing'.[2] Though her relationship with her parents was never very close, she was perhaps not quite as unsympathetic towards them as this remark implies. In April 1938, she had written to Robert, 'I had a terribly pathetic letter from my father yesterday begging me to come home. He should have got my last letter by now, so I hope he feels better.'[3] Perhaps it is not surprising that while caught up in all the drama and tragedy of war, she had given very little thought to the worries her parents might have had about her.

However, on her arrival, the welcome she received from her mother was warmer than she had expected. She was surprised and rather pleased to hear that for some time, Phillis had woken every time she heard a car at night, thinking it might be her daughter coming back. Patience had laughed and pointed out that she certainly would not have arrived in a taxi. But the new life that Patience foresaw for herself did not meet with the approval of family. Her younger sister Hilary, a trained social worker and a stalwart church-goer, was more inclined to conventional philanthropy than socialist revolution. Her brothers, the elder a conservative 'good citizen', the younger 'positively reactionary', were appalled by the changes Spain had wrought in their sister.[4] They had managed to refrain from criticising her marriage to a German Communist and, after hearing the news, had written to her in Spain. One had merely asked what her name was now, and the other had said he was glad she had found someone to 'look after her'.[5] Now they were faced with the reality of her presence once again, the ardently left-wing Patience was viewed by them all as somewhat of an embarrassment; the 'black sheep' of the family.

During her short stay at her parents' home, Spain was never far from Patience's mind. She gave a talk at the local Women's Institute and organised a collection for Spanish relief in the village shop. But soon she was on her way to London, hoping to find work. Two glowing references from people she had known in Spain recommended her highly for any nursing post. The former Labour MP, Leah Manning, remembering her visit to the cave hospital, praised Patience's calm efficiency and stamina.

> I have had the opportunity personally of seeing Miss Darton at work in the most difficult circumstances. I spent the night on duty with her in a temporary hospital in a cave during the Ebro offensive. There were about forty grave cases, mostly abdominals and chests, a large percentage of whom were dying. Miss Darton's only help consisted of two untrained boys (sanitarios), During the whole night she never ceased work once, for injections were constantly needed, help with blood transfusions and attention to haemorrhages. Miss Darton had been on constant duty for weeks before the offensive yet never once did I see her serenity disturbed or any suggestion that she was tired.[6]

Dr Reggie Saxton's reference was no less favourable, highlighting her resourcefulness and ability to work under challenging conditions.

> I worked with Nurse Darton as my Ward Sister on many occasions in Spain, and never had a more efficient or justifiably self-confident nurse. In particular I recall a severe typhoid epidemic in October and November 1937, when, with a severe shortage of food, clothing, heating and lighting, utterly inadequate sanitary accommodation, completely untrained assistant nurses and overcrowded and uncomfortable staff quarters with a minimum of furniture and privacy, Miss Darton ran a typhoid ward with great efficiency. I could only give the patients a minimum of attention as I was Superintendent of the hospital as well as Medical Officer for that ward, but I had complete confidence, justified by results, in leaving the major part of the treatment in her hands. The ward contained usually 30 to 40 severe cases. Her capacity for dealing with severe surgical cases appeared to be no less, as I had occasion to observe in the wards of the Casualty Clearing Stations where I was for many months Medical Officer in charge of Blood Transfusions. Miss Darton's ability for developing a friendly atmosphere with people of other nationalities was

11.1 Nan Green on the boat coming back from Mexico, 1939.

11.2 Isabel Brown.

11.3 Fritz Jensen.

11.4 The Mayor of Southport and Mr D. N. Pritt MP with an ambulance which had served the IB in Spain and was being used to collect funds prior to being sent to China in May 1939.

11.5a and 11.5b Street demonstrations for Czechoslovakia.

11.6 Patience working at the Czech Refugee Trust Fund.

11.7a and 11.7b Patience in the audience at a concert and presentation for the Czech Refugee Trust Fund. PD notes: 'Front row – senior staff (including me, 6th from right) of CRT. This was farewell to Dr Betty Morgan, (a Liberal ex-MP). Dr Elizabeth Allen, later head of Civil Liberties is on my left.'

notable. Her assistant nurses, who were Spanish, were devoted to her, and the patients of many different nationalities contrived to make her understand and appreciate their needs without difficulty. You may be confident that whatever conditions were to face Miss Darton, she would deal with them with efficiency and courage.[7]

On 4 January 1939, the minutes of the Spanish Medical Aid Committee note that a letter had been received from 'Nurse Darton, returned from Spain, asking whether we could assist her to obtain a non-resident post under the London County Council.'[8] She was interviewed by the LCC and offered work lecturing nurses on the organisation of hospital services under war conditions and surgical nursing in wartime. She spent three months teaching the hundreds of LCC nurses the new techniques and practices she had learned in Spain.[9] To give these talks, Patience had to travel by bus several times a week to one of the large nursing homes at the top of Highgate Hill. Paid a pittance, she only had enough bus fare to get to the bottom of the hill. She remembered feeling very riled to see the nurses she was to teach speeding by in their comfortable, specially laid-on coaches, while she toiled upwards in her ill-fitting shoes. In her lectures, she spoke about the effectiveness of the triage system in front-line hospitals, and about the use of bottled blood for transfusions. She was particularly proud of the new methods that were developed in Republican Spain for the treatment of wounds to avoid the onset of gas gangrene, 'that ghastly plague of WWI which killed in great torment, almost as many as died of wounds'.[10]

Throughout this time, Patience began to meet other people who had recently returned from Spain. Some were to become close friends during the following years. One of these was Nan Green, who had worked as an organiser in the medical units. Her husband, George, had been killed during the Battle of the Ebro, just before the International Brigades were withdrawn.[11] Nan had a flat in Coram Street with another nurse from Spain, Ena Vassie. 'They took me in', said Patience, 'because when I came back I had no idea what to do.'[12] The Spanish Medical Aid Committee had given her £8 but she did not know how to set about finding somewhere to live, having always lived in Nurses' Homes when she had worked in London hospitals. The three women soon became part of a social circle, drawn together by their shared experience of the civil war.

There was a huge group of Brigaders nearby . . . and lots of Spaniards, we brought quite a lot of Spaniards over in one way and another.[13]

Around this time Patience also became friendly with Isabel Brown, the

Communist Party campaigner and speaker, well known for her success at raising money for the Spanish Republic.[14] She had visited Spain herself in the early days of the war as part of a delegation from the British Anti-fascist Committee and was also involved with the campaigns to help the Spanish refugees held in terrible conditions in the camps in France.[15] When Isabel's husband, Ernie, went to Spain on a special mission almost at the end of the civil war, Isabel was worried about him and asked Patience to stay and keep her company for a few days.[16] It was Isabel who sponsored Patience for membership of the Communist Party of Great Britain, for which she had to complete the customary probationary period.

After all her hesitations and doubts about the Communist Party, Patience at last decided in favour of membership. Years later, she said that joining the Party had made her feel she belonged 'to something that I'd already got used to and was part of me, and was part of what I wanted to be, and what I wanted things to be'.[17] If Robert had lived, Patience may well have eventually joined the Party, but with his death, the balance tipped decisively towards membership. It was a way of keeping close to the ideals they had shared. Although never referring directly to the possibility that he might be killed, in her letters to him she had said that should he ever leave her, she would mind 'most horribly' but would get over it; that after experiencing 'bad blows' she always went on fighting. She assured him that she would be strong enough to 'pick up the bits and stick them together and start off again'.[18] She was right in the assessment of her own strength, but after a blow so devastating, the fight she faced to come to terms with the loss was to last a lifetime.

By working for the Party, Patience was not only assuaging her own grief through action, she was also carrying the torch of Robert's political dreams onwards, attempting to mitigate the loss to the cause brought about by his death. Nan Green would have understood this. Both had experienced a similar bitter bereavement and were equally determined to overcome their sorrow through activism. In this they were not alone. Other women were also metaphorically picking up the rifles of the men who had fallen in Spain. One wrote to the *Daily Worker* on hearing the news of her husband's death at the front, 'I am proud to know he died for a cause he held so dear. I will do all in my power to continue his good work, and I have decided to join the Communist Party, of which my husband was an honoured member.'[19]

Through her contact with Isabel Brown, Patience met Angela Haden Guest, also recently returned from Spain, and the two women formed a close friendship. Although not a qualified nurse, Angela had been responsible for the running of the convalescent hospital at Benicasim, working mainly with a German team led by Dr. Fritz Jensen, the Viennese doctor Patience had known in Spain. Angela, whose brother, David, had been killed in Spain during the Battle of the Ebro, was the daughter of the Labour MP, Dr. Leslie Haden Guest, and Carmel Haden Guest, the writer and former suffragette, both of whom were very actively involved with the Spanish war.[20] Angela had returned to England together with a German doctor from the International Brigades, a relationship that provoked some amusement and frank comments from Patience.

> Angela came out with one of the German Brigaders. She was very stiff and proud about not having any sex, about not being tied up with anyone and being a virgin, which she was and remained for ever such a long time . . . She kept it up longer than the rest of us, much to the grief of this extremely nice chap, this German doctor – beautiful creature he was. Lots of the others would have, you know, fallen down for him but she wouldn't.[21]

Always popular and prepared to work hard, Angela joined the Communist Party at the same time as Patience. Being 'a nice fiery person with a well known name', Patience recalled that Angela had been in great demand as a speaker. The two women were to remain friends for many years until Angela's death in a car accident in South Africa, after which her son became Patience's ward.[22]

With Franco's final victory drawing ever closer, Patience and the other doctors and nurses formed a group known as the 'The British Medical Unit from Spain'. Their aim was to raise funds for Spanish relief and to add their voices to the campaign to change the British government policy of Non-intervention, well-known to have worked largely in Franco's favour throughout the war.[23] Patience described these days in interviews, seeming to find great pleasure in remembering the excitement of their activities at a time when there was still a slim hope for the Republic, if only another world war had broken out in time to generate new allies.[24] She recalled being part of 'a little gang running round doing lots and lots of things'.

> I mean we were busy all the time – lots of demos in those days – lovely demos – 'We demand arms for Spain', and we could often do things – women you see, particularly Nan Green and me because we spoke so nicely that the police didn't stop you in the same way that they did the others. We used to do a lot of popping round in and out of the undergrounds, in Trafalgar Square and Piccadilly Circus on the big demos – great big – really hundreds and thousands of people – up and down these undergrounds and the police pushing you around a great deal. And if I got pushed around I used to tick the police off and they used to take it you

see, because I'd got a nice voice – the same with Angela [Guest]. We'd get up again and start another little 'We demand arms for Spain' somewhere round the top of the underground, particularly in Piccadilly Circus and Leicester Square – you can get quite a long way up and down – Ah me! It was quite different in those days.[25]

Nan Green spoke of two particular protests they organised.

Some of the nurses got up a little group, five or six of them I suppose and went to see Mrs Chamberlain to ask in a humanitarian way for help to Spain. When they got to Downing Street they were told that the family were at Chequers so they immediately took two taxis and went off there, but by the time they got to Chequers, [laughter] there were barricades up at the gates and they'd taken the precaution of taking the press with them, so we got a story but we didn't get anything out of Mrs Chamberlain. Many actions like this were taken. Angela Guest, who was always a person who liked taking explosive actions, got a bottle of red ink and splashed it on the doorstep of Downing Street, saying it was the blood of the Spanish people. But she was a great girl, she was always doing things like that.[26]

By now working full time as a Deputy Sister on a hospital ward for the elderly, Patience was asked to report on the conditions there to the Matron she had known before going to Spain, now in charge of hospitals for the LCC. Patience was horrified by what she found. The ward was in an establishment that had formerly been run as a 'Poor Law' hospital in conjunction with the workhouses. Some of the key issues for concern that she raised with the Matron continue unresolved today. These included leaving elderly patients in soiled beds, 'very bad for people, and demoralising', poor food and an unbalanced diet, resulting in 'avitaminosis' for long term patients, and cost cutting on basic supplies to save money. 'I failed to do anything about it,' she wrote regretfully afterwards.[27] This was due to a combination of factors. It was discovered that she was 'narking', and she was 'boycotted like anything'.[28] Ostracised for telling tales, she left the post after three gruelling months, feeling the strain of working full time while taking part in campaigns for Spain and speaking at numerous meetings. She would fall asleep as soon as she sat down. She was still suffering from bouts of dysentery, a problem that returned to plague her for years. Her manner of dealing with this problem was as practical as usual, and her observations as customarily frank.

At the time I knew of all the women's available loos – including some secret ones. The best ones were in big hotels – Cafe Royal etc., but timing was important for those.[29]

As she rushed around London, struggling against the demons of personal loss, physical illness and exhaustion, and fully aware of the dire situation that the Spanish Republicans still faced, she had difficulty in tempering her feelings of anger and hatred when she saw the British Fascists campaigning out on the streets.

It was terrible seeing them. One of the places I had to change, at Highgate somewhere, on some steps, I can't remember where quite, there were always some real Fascists, some British Union of Fascist people, and I felt very strongly I ought to kill them. I mean, it was instinctive with me, I ought to push them down the steps, I felt, under the tram.[30]

Then came the misery of witnessing from afar, powerless and sorrowful, the death throes of the Republic. Newspapers on 22 February 1939 carried reports of Franco's triumphal entry into Barcelona and described the spectacular parade that lasted over three hours. The procession along the *Diagonal* was led by the Italian Legionary Army. General Franco rode in an open car, preceded by his 'picturesque Moorish bodyguard, their trappings jingling and glittering in the sun'.[31] On 29 March 1939, the headline read, 'MADRID GIVES ITSELF UP TO FRANCO. Mussolini and Hitler Rejoice.'[32] Movietone, Universal and Gaumont newsreels carried footage of the tragic exodus of refugees and the arrival of the victors.[33] By 31 March 1939, all Spain was in Nationalist hands. On 1 April 1939, a bulletin was issued from Franco's headquarters, 'Today, with the Red Army captive and disarmed, our victorious troops have achieved their objectives. The war is over.' The Pope sent a telegram to congratulate Franco on his 'Catholic victory'.[34] It is hard to imagine the grief and bitterness that Patience and so many of the people she knew must have felt when they heard the news. Decades later, she said with a sigh, 'But we lost, we lost everything.'[35]

Those who had been together through so much while supporting the Republic were trying their hardest to keep in contact and help each other in a spirit of solidarity. Patience received a sad letter from Ramón Mauri, a young Catalan who had been part of the medical team in Valls and at the cave hospital during the Battle of the Ebro. He had assisted Dr Reggie Saxton with the blood transfusions. Now, in February 1939, he was with Dr Olsina, also from the unit, together with other International Brigaders and thousands of Republicans in the concentration camp on the beach at Argelès in France. Conditions were appalling. Lack of food, medical treatment and even shelter, meant that the refugees were dying like flies. 'Life here is very distressing', wrote Ramón. He requested her most politely to find out if it would be at all possible to arrange for them both to come to England. Perhaps she might be able to send them a little money by post-office 'Giro' to make life in the camp a little more bearable? He gave the name and address of a French visitor to the camp, who had kindly paid for the stamp and posted the letter on their behalf.[36] It seems likely that Patience then contacted Reggie Saxton, probably because she herself had no money to send. Unfortunately, Reggie was also short of cash, so he appealed to Dr Len Crome, who had been Chief of Divisional Medical Services in Spain.[37]

> Dear Crome
> You may remember Ramon Mauri. He assisted in the lab at Valls and became Henri's transfusion assistant. He was in his last year at school (aged 17) – a very good lad. Is it possible to get such a case to England? I am absolutely broke (total assets between 10/- and 15/-), but have prospects of acquiring a few hundred quid in the near future. Will you please send Ramon £5 immediately and I will undertake to repay you. I have never failed to pay a debt yet. If you will find out about the possibility of getting him to England, I can probably find him hospitality amongst my friends.
> Yours fraternally, Reggie[38]

A 'Giro' payment did get through to Ramón in the camp. According to Ramón's son, his father would always speak with great emotion about the help he had received from his former colleagues. Arrangements were in place for him to go to England but, at the last moment, he decided to risk boarding a ship bound for home. [39]

The group formed by the medical personnel from Spain joined forces with other veterans from the Brigades who founded the International Brigade Association [IBA] in March 1939.[40] Patience was voted on to both the London and the National committees. The London office in High Holborn was always bustling with activity. At first, much of the work centred on helping Brigaders who were unable to return to their own countries, in addition to the thousands of Republican refugees, many of whom were still being held in camps in France. Funds were raised to help pay for a boat to take some of the refugees to Mexico and Nan Green was sent out to travel with them.[41] Reggie Saxton, now working as a doctor in Reading, was the driving force behind the opening of a 'Casa Española' for twelve Spanish refugees.[42] Other campaigns were organised on behalf of the political prisoners being held by Franco in Spain, amongst them a group of ten

British Brigaders who were still in San Sebastian jail. In April 1939, all but two were released. Brigaders of other nationalities were to remain in Spanish prisons for years.[43]

Patience was soon preoccupied with the group of Austrian, Czechoslovakian and German refugee doctors from Spain who were planning to go to China, where they intended to support the Chinese Communists in their fight against the Japanese. As their own countries were now under Nazi domination, China offered a new front to continue the battle against fascism. The doctors had all needed sponsors to come to England from France, and Patience had persuaded her parents to sponsor the Austrian doctor, Fritz Jensen.[44] A special committee was formed, known as the China Medical Aid Committee, and arrangements made in collaboration with the Chinese Red Cross for their journey.[45] Along with Dr Kisch, who had been the chief of the Czechoslovak Surgical Unit in Spain, and Dr Becket, a German, Jensen left England in May.[46] The fact that he managed to get to China at all was probably quite an achievement, in view of the contents of a letter to Harry Pollitt, leader of the British CP, from André Marty, the French Communist who had been the Commander in Chief of the International Brigades in Spain. Marty wrote from Paris in May 1939 naming Jensen amongst several other doctors he considered 'bad elements, Trotskyites, a divisive influence'. The Aid Committee for Spanish refugees in France had therefore refused to accept them, or to recommend them for service in China, 'whatever their professional competence'.[47] Widely known for his extreme views on the dangers of subversives, in this case it seems that Marty's opinion must have been disregarded.

At one point, Patience had thought she could go to China along with Jensen and the other doctors.

> I wanted to go, and was interviewed by the Chinese ambassador, a very polished customer, who seized on the idea.[48]

But it seemed that the Committee did not approve of sending out nurses, so this time Patience's plans were thwarted. Eventually however, years later, she was to get her way and go to China.

Further aid for China included the supply of an ambulance. The vehicle had already been at the front with the International Brigades in Spain. Originally used in Southall, the ambulance was certainly not in the first flush of youth but it was well built and serviceable. After a refit and a tour through towns to collect donations, it was sent off to China by the mayor of Southport from the town hall steps. Charlotte Haldane, who had been a staunch supporter of the Republican cause, thanked the Mayor on behalf of the China Campaign Committee.[49]

At this time there was growing concern amongst members of the International Brigade Association about the direction being taken by the International Communist organisation, the Comintern, and the increasing numbers of denunciations of those who had deviated in any way from the Party line. 'In those days the Comintern was denouncing around', said Patience. Their policies resulted in discord with the British CP leader, Harry Pollitt. Patience described how the IBA representative, Peter Kerrigan, would report back to their committee after attending Comintern meetings in France, 'still white with rage, hardly able to speak for pent up fury'.[50] The news of the Nazi–Soviet Pact in August 1939 posed further problems for those whose support for the Spanish Republic had been bound up with dreams of a new social order. It seemed unbelievable to many on the Left that the Soviet Union could have signed an agreement with Germany to maintain neutrality should either side enter a war.[51] Attempts by some Communists to put forward arguments in support of the actions of the Soviet Union at this time were firmly dismissed by Patience.

> I didn't – I still don't agree with that fancy thing about it being a Capitalist war, and Imperialist war, it wasn't. No, no, I was all for fighting Hitler, in fact I was quite determined to fight Hitler. I remember arguing with Isabel [Brown] about it. Isabel wanted to know what I thought and I said quite clearly that I didn't agree, nor did Harry Pollitt, you see. Harry resigned as Secretary, dear Harry, he was very good to me. When you have one of these terribly elaborate things that you have to work out the theoretical things of it, they're nearly always wrong, I find – these highly worked out political things. Straight forward things are usually better.[52]

The situation in Europe deteriorated. Demonstrations on the streets of Britain urged the government to 'Stand by Czechoslovakia', but the calls went unheeded and the policy of appeasement prevailed. When the Home Office seemed about to hand several million pounds of Czech money held in British banks to Nazi Germany, Patience was amongst the many people in Britain who were outraged.[53] After a public outcry, some of the money was released to be used for the Czech refugees who had come to live in Britain. A new organisation, the Czech Refugee Trust Fund (CRTF) was formed to administer the money, and Patience became largely responsible for the Medical Aid Department.[54]

When Patience first started working for the CRTF in June 1939, her

post entailed dealing primarily with individual cases, but it soon developed
into a more organisational role. The work consisted of running an office in
London, eventually with a staff of seven, arranging for British doctors and
hospitals throughout the country to treat the refugees in hostels, and a
'panel doctor' for isolated cases outside London. This was in the days before
the National Health Service, so throughout England, refugees were
accepted onto a local General Practitioner panel for twelve shillings and
sixpence each. Hospitals were also paid to treat them.[55] Czech refugee
doctors were not allowed to prescribe, so this was often done by Dr Crome,
one of the doctors always regarded very highly by Patience in Spain. Born
in Latvia, Len Crome had studied medicine in Edinburgh, and in 1934 had
become a naturalized British citizen. After the Spanish civil war he returned
to England and, believing that a world war was imminent, he applied for a
commission in the British army. Despite his qualifications and his experience in front-line hospitals, his application was turned down on the grounds
that 'every candidate for a commission must be a British subject and son of
British subjects'.[56] He therefore continued working in his medical practice
while continuing to help the Spanish refugees in the French camps and the
Czech refugees in Britain.

Patience's work was not easy. Although the refugees she was working
with had come to Britain from Czechoslovakia, many of them had been born
elsewhere and had been living there in exile. There were endless confronta-
tions between different groups – Hungarians, Polish, Jewish, Germans of a
variety of left-wing persuasions, journalists and writers. Patience wanted to
help them all but found their quarrels tiresome.

> When I was young I was sure that all the differences between different
> nationalities would disappear and that eventually there would only be one
> nation. In the Communist Party we believed in the ideal of a great inter-
> national community – an ideal that we were very fond of and defended to
> the hilt. Later on, I saw very clearly that this idea that national character-
> istics would disappear wasn't right. It's in our blood to have our own
> national identities and our national characteristics and temperaments will
> always be a part of us.[57]

Meanwhile, Dr Jensen was beginning to regret being so far away in
China. In September 1939, eager to be in the thick of the fight if war should
break out in Europe, he wrote to Len Crome, just before setting off for a
two-month tour of the front in an advisory capacity to the Chinese Red
Cross. He pleaded with Len to discuss the matter with Patience and other
former comrades from Spain, and to try to persuade the Chinese Medical

Aid Committee to pay for his return trip or, if that failed, to raise funds he
could borrow and would repay as soon as he could.

> I am very anxious to get back to Europe and to take my place anywhere
> in the fighting line near Germany. I feel that nothing is actually as impor-
> tant as that the right people should be at the right time on the right spot.
> The efficiency rate of my work here is not at all *so* satisfying that I could
> take the risk not to be there when we are going to smash Hitler and to
> provide him with a good successor . . .
>   I ask you therefore as my friend and comrade to do all in your power to
> provide a place for me anywhere where men are fighting for our common
> sake; be it that there are existing units of volunteers of Spaniards, Czeks
> [sic] or Austrians or Germans or be it that the English or French Army
> would take a man like me with the Spanish Nationality and valid Spanish
> papers born in Prag (Czechoslowakia). [sic][58]

Many former International Brigaders, like Jensen, were hoping that the
outbreak of war would give them another chance to defeat fascism.

12

Bombs on Britain

The outbreak of the Second World War on 3 September 1939 gave former International Brigaders the chance to volunteer for the services, though some encountered difficulties due to their involvement with the war in Spain.[1] Others were able to contribute to the war effort in different ways, for example, in the Air Raid Precautions service or the Home Guard. Doctors who had been in Spain, such as Len Crome and Reggie Saxton, were eventually called up to serve in the Royal Army Medical Corps. Patience's war work was varied. Fears of a gas attack were initially high and her first call-up papers sent her to run a 'gas station' in Stepney.[2]

Through working at the Trust Fund and her friendship with Len Crome, Patience at some point in 1939 met Felix Horowitz, a Czech doctor, known to his friends as Horo, who was living as a refugee in London.[3] It was there that he got to know Patience who, after the death of Robert, had begun the process she had described as picking up the pieces and sticking herself together again. She did not plump for a life of celibacy. Horo and Patience began what her family would have referred to as an 'affair'. In a photograph taken of them in 1940 at the Trust Fund, Patience has written the caption, 'Boyfriend – "Horo" – smoking'. Another photograph shows him once again puffing away on a cigarette; seemingly as addicted to tobacco as Patience. Horo, with his broad, high brow, strongly reminiscent of Robert's, would doubtless have also been attractive to Patience because of his left-wing commitment and dedication as a doctor. Letters he wrote to Len Crome indicate that he was a thoughtful man, inclined to despondency.[4]

London as a city at war has been described by writers, poets and in reports from the general population recorded in the Mass Observation project. When campaigning for aid to be sent to the Spanish Republic, Isabel Brown had said, 'It's Guernica today, it'll be Paris and London tomorrow,' and she had been right.[5] However, as the German bombs fell in their thousands and London burned, the prophecies of Bertrand Russell, that London 'would become one vast bedlam, the hospitals will be stormed, traffic will cease, the homeless will shriek for peace', did not become reality.[6] Instead, a 'business as usual' attitude prevailed. Even at the height of the Blitz there was a sense that London's spirit of continuity was indomitable, that it had survived disasters before and that regeneration would take place. Patience had met Stephen Spender in Valencia, where he had questioned his pacifist beliefs. Now, having experienced a raid over London, he mused, 'I had the comforting sense of the sure dark immensity of London.'[7] He seemed to believe that the suffering normally endured by the poorest members of the population throughout the ages had somehow inoculated them against this new devastation. 'The grittiness, stench and obscurity of Kilburn suddenly seemed a spiritual force – the immense force of poverty which had produced the narrow, yet intense, visions of Cockneys living in other times.' It would have been interesting to hear Patience's views on his musings. She was to spend the war busily dealing with the practical business of sorting out the problems people faced as a result of the war.

One of Patience's personal anecdotes illustrates that life went on despite the craters and mountains of rubble in the streets. Patience became friends with another intrepid woman moving within left-wing circles at this time who was living near her in London. Frida Stewart had driven an ambulance to Spain on behalf of the National Joint Committee for Spanish Relief and had worked in Murcia at a children's hospital and then later, in the Press Office in Madrid. On her return to England, she had been a key fundraiser for the Basque Children's Committee before going to France to help the tens of thousands of refugees in the camps.[8] When the Germans entered Paris, she was interned but managed to escape, returning home with a message hidden in cigarette paper from the French Resistance for General de Gaulle in London. She and Patience had never met in Spain but had much in common: their upper-middle class background, their work with refugees, and their membership of the Communist Party. When Frida was expecting her first child, Patience called in to see her one day on her way home from work. As usual, Frida was busily involved in the preparations for a forth-coming campaign, while grumpily complaining of indigestion. Patience, as a trained midwife, recognised the imminent arrival of the baby. This had resulted in a dash across London in the blackout. Fortunately they arrived at the hospital in time.[9]

In 1941, Patience's work with the CRTF ended and she was given a testi-monial by Sir Henry Bunbury, formerly the Director of the Trust and now the Chief Establishment Officer at the Ministry of Health.

> I have known Miss Patience Darton for about two years. During that time she has been in charge of the medical and allied services for refugees in the care of the Czech Refugee Trust, of which I was Director till November last.

12.1 Len Crome in uniform during the Second World War.

12.2 Dr Felix Horowitz and Patience.

12.3 Dr Felix Horowitz (left) with Patience and friends.

12.4 Frida Stewart and friends with field kitchen in France.

Back From German Internment Camp

YOUNG CAMBRIDGE WOMAN'S ESCAPE

" French Counting on Britain "

THE story of how a young Cambridge woman escaped from a German internment camp in France by crawling through a hole in barbed wire, was told to a " Cambridge Daily News " representative a few hours after she had arrived back at her home on Saturday evening.

Miss Frida Stewart, daughter of Dr and Mrs H. F. Stewart, of Girton Gate, Huntingdon Road is the young woman concerned.

With Miss Rosemary Say, of Hampstead, she succeeded in making her way through France and Spain, eventually returning to England by plane from Lisbon.

When France was over-run by the Nazis, Miss Stewart was working for a refugee committee in Paris. "I tried to get out," she said, "but it was difficult to get a conveyance, and with about 4,000 other women I was seized by the Germans. I was interned, and for five months we were kept in a military barracks used as an internment camp. The conditions there were very bad, both in hygiene and in food. When I was moved to another camp the hygiene was a bit better, but food was still scanty. And you can imagine that we were greatly cheered by the Red Cross parcels which arrived from time to time.

FRENCH PEOPLE HELPED.

In the camp Miss Stewart met Miss Say, and they decided on their bid for liberty. We escaped by crawling through a hole in the barbed wire found the camp, she went on," and made our way through occupied and unoccupied France to Marseilles. All the time the French people helped us, and everywhere we found they are

Miss Stewart

just counting on Britain to relieve them. Some of them even said they wished they were coming to England with us."

At Marseilles the two girls had to wait some time for their papers to get into Spain, but eventually they arrived and the girls reached Lisbon, from where they flew back to this country. In London they had, to use Miss Stewart's own words, "a nasty shock" when they saw the effects of the bombing. As for the future, she hopes very soon to take up some form of work to help the war effort.

Miss Stewart was educated at the Perse School, and afterwards did various form of social work. She spent two years at the Manchester University Settlement, lectured with the W.E.A. in Yorkshire, and organised entertainment for Basque refugees.

WORK FOR WAR REFUGEES.

When war broke out she worked on the entertainments side of the Y.W.C.A. and went abroad to work for war refugees. In December 1940, she lived with an English friend who had married a Frenchman, and also attended lectures at the Sorbonne. She was left alone by the Germans until all the English were rounded up because of a disclosure that someone was using the wireless to give away information.

12.5 Newspaper article: 'Young Cambridge woman's escape.'

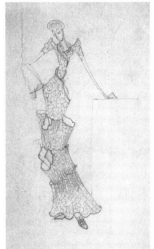

12.6a, 12.6b, 12.6c Cartoon drawings of Patience by Diana Gurney.

12.7 Patience, Jack Shafran (USA) and Paddy O'Daire at an International Brigade reunion in 1943.

This Records
the Loyal and Valued Services of

PATIENCE MARY EDWARDS DARTON.

to the United Nations Relief and Rehabilitation Administration in its Great Work of Relieving the Suffering and Saving the Lives of the Victims of War in the Liberated Countries

Director General

Washington, D.C.
31 December 1946

12.8 UNRRA Certificate.

In handling a by no means easy or straightforward task of organisation, her initiative, resourcefulness and sound judgement have been outstanding. She showed a happy combination of a fundamentally sympathetic attitude with realistic common sense. She thinks clearly. She has great energy, always wants to see things for herself and can get people to do what she wants. Of her courage, her two years in Spain during the civil war are sufficient evidence.[10]

At the same time, she was given a wonderful accolade by Lady Mary Murray, whose son, Basil, she had nursed during her first year in Spain.

I am asked to give a note of personal recommendation to my friend Nurse Patience Darton. The tie of gratitude which binds me to Nurse Patience is so personal – i.e. the rendering of service to a dying son in Spain – that I am biased. But I believe that anyone to whom she gives of her skill and devotion would find himself biased in that sense. She is a nurse of long and large experience and a most gallant and devoted woman, full of courage, energy, thoughtfulness, sympathetic and eager – I only hope that she may find scope for the qualities of head, hand and heart with which I believe her to be endowed.[11]

These glowing references led to a post as Organising Secretary of the Stepney Reconstruction Group where Patience was responsible for researching and compiling evidence for Ministry of Health Inquiries.[12] She was pleased with the results.

We gave rather effective evidence, some of which was used verbatim in the County of London Plan. I still have the Evidence. It reads quite well, though in those days it was considered very revolutionary to suggest garage space for council housing. I wish I had kept the essays from local schools which we were able to organise. I can still remember some. 'If I could choose my house I would like to have curtains on all the windows.' 'I should like a tap and a lavatory indoors.'[13]

This work occupied her from 1942 to 1943, during which time she was based at Toynbee Hall. Whilst in this post, she met Diana Gurney, who was working there in the Citizens' Advice Department. Diana was an artist who had studied at Westminster School of Art as a pupil of the British painter, Mark Gertler.[14] When they first met, Patience was living with a group of refugees in a hostel in Putney which was due for closure and demolition. Diana offered Patience a room in her Chelsea flat and was able to use her lodger as a model. Amused by the length of Patience's legs and the dilapidated state of her housecoat, she produced several humorous cartoon drawings of her. Meandering smoke from a cigarette forms part of the composition and accentuates the languid atmosphere conveyed by the pose. They also show that Patience had adopted the hairstyle that was to serve her for the rest of her life; a long plait coiled around her head. Two more serious portraits were never finished as Patience wouldn't sit still for long, but they capture the striking beauty of her features. Living with Patience was not easy as the flat was soon 'invaded by Brigaders and Czechs', one of whom Diana found in the bath. A certain Captain Horowitz 'was some sort of fixture, much taken with Patience'. Eventually, Diana's mother wanted to move in with her and she had to ask Patience to find somewhere else to live.[15] She shared a house with her sister, Hilary, often putting up American and Canadian old friends from the Brigades when they were on leave in London. These visitors usually brought a welcome relief from rationing in the form of large food parcels, though on several occasions hungry soldiers arrived out of the blue and ate the lion's share of their meagre supplies.

In March 1943, Horo was at last accepted by the Royal Army Medical Corps, serving first as a lieutenant, then as a captain. He worked for a time in Britain before being posted abroad, but kept in touch with his friend Len Crome, a prolific and accomplished letter writer. In July 1943 Horo wrote to Len saying that he had received a letter from Patience who was 'full of beans, working on an IB celebration which takes place soon'.[16] This IB reunion in London was a great success. Bill Pike, the American doctor who had worked as Len Crome's assistant in Spain, was in England and had been able to attend. He wrote to thank Len for his 'heart-warming' letters and to tell him about the reunion.

> In this cold damp England of yours, blast this rain and the fog, letters like yours are better than any fuel, because they last, and the glow lasts and the feeling that you are not alone stays with one and it's a good feeling.
>
> About three weeks ago I was down in London again where I saw many of our old friends at a reunion. Nan, Patience Darton (remember when I fell asleep at the wheel, smashed the car and Patience's nose and got 10 days arrest from you – but was permitted to go on with my work and you forgot to have the money deducted from my salary and I forgot to remind you? I still have the paper signed by you amongst my precious souvenirs), Margaret Powell (notice I mention the women first), Hans, Harry Evans, Chris Thornycroft and American lads. It was swell.[17]

Patience's next contribution to the war effort was as a factory nurse at Cossor's, a firm involved with research and development of radar. She spent almost eighteen months there, from 1943 to 1944, until beginning work for the United Nations Relief and Rehabilitation Administration [UNRRA].[18] In a letter written later to accompany a CV she explained her work as Assistant Medical Procurement Chief, as usual, with a touch of dry humour.

> This was not as dull as it sounds as although we had official 'Bases' worked out by the United States, these had to be translated into real needs with the representatives of all the allies. Theoretically making Yellow Fever Vaccine – I still don't know why that was UNRRA but it was very stimulating, and then suddenly found ourselves supplying Europe long before the plan envisaged.

There were many disagreements between the allies over the best way to administer supplies, especially with the American Army. Patience was outraged over one such instance that took place after the liberation of Antwerp in 1944. The fleet of supply ships was stretched beyond limits, trying to deliver essential goods for a starving population. The Americans insisted that one of the ships should carry supplies of cleaning materials for their soldiers who, according to Patience, had three uniforms each, rather than the single one allocated to the British soldiers. Worse, it was well known that some of the 'luxury' foods destined for the American soldiers would in fact be designated, as rules decreed, to the prisoners of war. The workers at the port of Antwerp, reduced to eating tulip bulbs, had to off load mountains of food from the ships without being allowed to taste any of it, whilst at risk of losing their lives under enemy fire. Eventually, they went on strike, and said Patience indignantly, 'The Americans took up arms to fire on the workers.' Fortunately the European allies were in the majority and the situation was resolved without loss of life.[19] With the liberation of the concentration camps, her work increased, in part due to the constant difficulties posed by bureaucratic regulations. At one point, she was unable to send supplies of sanitary towels for women released from the camps because they were not included on the official list of medical supplies. Finally, she sent quantities of first aid bandages to be converted for the purpose instead.

> Belsen – theoretically we did not go in till 6 months after AMGOT,[20] but Belsen and other camps changed that. Likewise Czechoslovakia and Yugoslavia didn't want AMGOT but did want supplies. My chief was out

of the country as much as he could be, and I first held the fort, fighting
for shipping and transport at the highest levels. There was one other
doughty feminine fighter from the Ministry of Food on the Cabinet
subcommittee meetings, but I thought many times then that if some
disease struck down women between 25 and 35, all the secretaries and
Assistants, WAAFs, Wrens and the ATs who were really running the war,
knew where everything was, kept all the minutes and saw to all the follow
throughs, total and complete chaos would ensue at once. The immediate
needs having been met, and our carefully structured supplies flowing, I
went down to the West Country with two little secretaries to take over,
sort and pack all the US medical supplies in this country.[21]

Before beginning work for UNRRA, Patience had handed in her
Communist Party card, but continued to work on the Executive Committee
of the IBA. When she had to undergo two interviews with MI5 during this
period, Patience wrote, 'great defence put up by chief, who said "so
what?"'[22]

Despite the ongoing difficulties of life in a country at war, Patience and
her friends in the IBA continued to hold events. Nan Green wrote to Len
in March 1944 to tell him about their recent annual weekend, held around
the time of the anniversary of the Battle of Jarama. She sends him a copy of
the conference report and writes excitedly of the presence of fifteen
nationalities at the reunion and twelve at the conference, making it the 'best
we've ever had'.

> About 200 were at the Reunion, and it was a good sight to see how many
> people met there who had not seen each other since Spain. We sang songs
> and Miles[Tomlin] tootled on his whistle. The conference next day was
> serious and businesslike and I am sure you will approve of the document
> and decisions taken.[23]

Meanwhile, Patience's relationship with Horo was seemingly no longer
so close, though it is clear from later letters that they remained friends.[24]
When he wrote to Len Crome to congratulate him on being awarded the
Military Cross in September 1944, Horo was in poor health and spirits, and
the sadness in the tone of his letter implies that he and Patience had
parted.[25] The following year, now with the rank of captain, he wrote again
to Len before being posted to the Middle East, hinting at unresolved
emotional matters in England. 'I wish I could see you and speak about a lot
of things which go through my mind, but it is difficult to write about all
that,' adding without giving details, 'I would like to see our friends and

settle personal affairs, as you can imagine.'[26] He attempts to end on a positive note:

> After the nightmare of the last ten years in Europe, the people hope for a new world. The fight will go on to materialise these hopes.[27]

When the Second World War drew to a close in 1945, Patience celebrated along with thousands of others in London.

> On 8 May we heard the news that Germany had surrendered we knew that the war was over. I went to Piccadilly Circus where I met two friends, then arm in arm together we walked on to Buckingham Palace with a great crowd of people. We all held hands and danced. Everyone was dancing in the streets. It was unforgettable! The street lights were switched on. The fact that the lights were on again was an important part of the end of the war because all through the war London had been in darkness. I remember it so well. Marvellous![28]

Despite the Allied victory, there was indeed still a great deal to be done to build the hoped-for 'new world'. One way in which Patience tried to contribute to this aim began in 1948, when she became National Welfare Organiser to the Infantile Paralysis Fellowship.[29] In addition to case work, her responsibilities included the organisation of local voluntary workers in different parts of the country, grant applications, and the preparation of evidence for Ministry of Health Inquiries.[30]

In 1949 a brief but intense campaign brought Patience's organisational talents into play. Gerhart Eisler, a prominent German Communist living as a refugee in the United States, had been arrested in 1947 and brought before the House Un-American Activities Committee. He refused to testify and was given a gaol sentence. On his release he was re-arrested pending a deportation order, but granted bail. Rather than waiting for the conclusion of the legal process, he jumped bail and, in May 1948, stowed away on a Polish ship, the *SS Batory*, bound for Gdynia via Southampton. Whilst in the British port, police forcibly removed him from the ship and placed him under arrest to await extradition to America. Patience became the Honorary Secretary of the Eisler Release Committee, drawing on the support of British Communists, Trade Unionists, MPs and groups such as the National Campaign for Civil Liberties [NCCL], and mounting vigorous public demonstrations against his arrest. When the subsequent court hearings established convincingly that he had not committed any crime in Britain and could not be extradited to America, he was released and allowed to proceed on his way. Patience wrote an article about the case for *Civil Liberty*, the journal of the NCCL, thanking all those who had helped in the campaign for his release, and the press for their support.[31]

Celebrating the defeat of fascism on so many fronts at the end of the Second World War had brought hopes that Franco's dictatorship would also be brought to an end. But it was not to be. Within Spain, those who had supported the Republic continued to be subjected to various forms of repression. Elsewhere, many former International Brigaders continued to suffer for having fought in Spain.

> And we used to say, during the war, when Europe was free we'd be able to go everywhere, you know, and always have friends.[32]

Sadly, this hope was not to be realised. Not just in Europe, but in the United States and the Soviet Union too, there were dark days ahead for the veterans from Spain.

> A lot of very stupid and horrid things happened to Brigaders in the different countries – terrible things, undeserved things, because they'd been [in Spain] they were not trusted.[33]

A war had been won but there were still dreams to be dreamed and battles to be fought.

13

Opening the Chinese Puzzle Box

When Patience had gone to Spain in the 1930s, it was still considered by most British people to be a wild and largely uncivilised country – its people dangerously volatile, even when flamboyant gypsy flamencos had been the dominant image rather than the deadly dance of bloody civil war. In 1950s Britain, China was the 'Mysterious East', known by the majority for little more than willow pattern tea sets and the oriental arch-villain of popular fiction, Dr Fu Manchu, 'the yellow peril incarnate in one man', whose exotic robes and long, menacing fingernails were only surpassed by his even longer and more sinister moustache.[1] Patience's friends in the IBA would have understood her reasons for wanting to go to work there, but what ever would her family have thought of her decision to live in such a very *out*landish land?

This was merely one of inumerable questions I should have asked Patience about the time she spent in China from 1954 to 1958. Why, oh why, I repeatedly asked myself, hadn't I asked her more about her later life? Surrounded by Chinese memorabilia in her cluttered, cosy room, we had talked about her parents, her childhood, nursing training, and most of all, Spain. I found out how she had felt when back home in England, and how she viewed her involvement with the civil war in retrospect. I still try to make excuses. Like other people who had interviewed her, the focus of my research was Spain and the civil war. I attempt to justify my omission by telling myself that she was always tired and emotionally drained after talking of her work as a nurse at the front. I hadn't wanted to exhaust her completely by further questions. But – the nagging voice of my conscience continues to chastise me – I could have gone back to talk about China another day.

So, when beginning to write this chapter of Patience's biography, I somewhat reluctantly began to review what I knew about this period of her life. Very little indeed! Having cooked lunch for me one day, our conversation at table had turned to our children, and I learned that her son had been born in China – she was highly critical of the medical attention she had received.[2] That was the sum total of all she had told me about this period of her life at first hand. Could I find out more? Perhaps one particular Englishwoman's experiences in the vast territory of China's past would remain veiled forever in the mists of historical obscurity. The trail to follow Patience to the Orient began, leading me eventually to the opening of a new panorama in the landscape of her life.

Patience had only ever written a few introductory pages to her autobiography, but when I re-read the copy she had given me, amongst the recollections of her early life I found a short passage comparing the harvests she had seen in England as a child with those she saw later in other countries. With such an eye for detail, I lamented that she had never finished the script.

> The big flails that were used in my mother's day were still hanging in the barns, but when I was a child in Orpington a great threshing machine, (steam powered, the wonders of science, what you'd call high tech) used to go from farm to farm . . . I have three times seen threshing done since then. In Spain, on a threshing floor, and then winnowing it by throwing it up into the air so as to blow the chaff away, and the rhythmic group would be in a haze of chaff, like a cloud of glory; and in Poland in 1952 and in China. The nearest harvest that I saw (the country was close up to the walls of Peking then) was just the same – except on the Western Hills which for the great part are made of low grade soft coal (often open cast, and carried into Peking on panniers on camels. They use to go past our dining-cum-bedroom window). There on the Western Hills, the threshing and winnowing floor was beaten coal. It was queer to see a black threshing floor, but the chaff didn't seem to come off black.[3]

What more could be gleaned about this period of her life from the literature on the subject of China in the nineteen fifties? Thousands of books had been written about the Spanish Civil War, so surely I would be able to find more about those who had gone from Spain to China? Several doctors Patience had known in Spain had already gone there at the end of the civil war to help in the fight against the Japanese.[4] Following the establishment of the People's Republic in 1949, other veterans of the International Brigades were to follow the same path. What had motivated them to take such a step? From the perspective of the Left, there were striking similarities between the two cases as the historian, Tom Buchanan, points out.

> Both China and the Spanish Republic had been victims of fascist aggression in the 1930s, suffering high levels of civilian casualties, and the image

13.1 Threshing in Spain.

13.2a, 13.2b Peace Conference card, 1952.

13.3a Peace Conference crowd scene.

13.3b
Peace
Conference
entrance.

13.3c Peace Conference welcome message.

13.3d Peace Conference speakers on the stage.

13.3e Peace Conference speakers with bouquets.

13.3f Delegates at the Peace Conference.

13.4 Patience (left) at the Peace Conference.

13.5 Nan Green & Ted Brake in China.

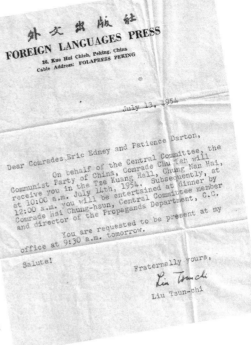

13.6 Foreign Languages
Press Invitation.

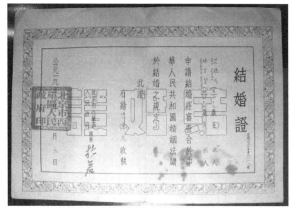

13.7 Marriage Certificate: (from right to left): Marriage Certificate (in three large characters), followed by the name, age and sex of the contracting parties, then: "Have applied to marry and upon verification it is found that this is in keeping with the Marriage Law of the Peoples Republic of China". It is issued by the Xicheng (west city) District of Beijing, signed by the district head and dated 5th March 1955.

13.9 Horo's gravestone in Bushey Cemetery.

13.8 Patience and Eric Edney's wedding phototograph.

13.10 FLP English section, (Patience back row, centre).

of a 'new' China struggling to shake off the shackles of the old was almost identical to the left's interpretation of Spain in the 1930s.[5]

I knew of others who, like Patience, had been first in Spain and then in China: David Crook and Nan Green. Both had lived in Peking [Beijing] at the same time as Patience, and fortunately, they had written their memoirs. Both had also attended the Peace Congress of the Asian and Pacific Regions held in Peking in 1952, an event to which Patience was also invited. David, Nan and Patience formed part of the team of interpreters and translators at the Congress as a result of their knowledge of Spanish. David, who had gone to China in 1947, was working in Peking as a teacher.[6] He noted that International Brigaders with a knowledge of Spanish were welcomed at the Congress because the majority of Spanish speakers in China at that time were either Catholic priests or professional athletes – not the ideal candidates to present China's aspirations and political policies to foreigners.[7]

Like Patience, in 1952 Nan Green was making her first visit to China, and she devotes several pages of her memoirs to descriptions of her impressions. Patience must have experienced a similar feeling of 'cultural shock' as Nan, who on finding herself in such a different civilization was struck by the light, the colours, the scents, sounds, and the people. Nan wrote of the post-revolutionary euphoria that still abounded and the copious tears of joy that were shed during the welcome ceremonies. Amongst the interpretors was Aurora Fernández, the young Spanish woman who had trained with the British nurses and had returned with them to England. According to Nan, they all lodged together in a Chinese-style home, with rooms built around a central courtyard and a 'devil screen' facing the main entrance to prevent the entry of hostile spirits, believed only able to travel in straight lines. She and Aurora were probably the most skilled of the group, and Nan remembered that her final task was was to interpret at a meeting of the then foreign minister, Chou En-lai, and a Latin American delegate who wanted to establish diplomatic relations with the new China.[8] According to David Crook, Patience's responsibilities were not quite so grandiose.

> At the conference, Patience was prepared to take on any humble tasks which would serve the group of translators as a whole and did so tirelessly. This work attitude was no doubt responsible for her being invited to work in China later.[9]

Nan went back to China the following year and in 1954 began work for the journal, *China Reconstructs*, one of the earliest magazines aimed at a foreign readership.[10] Her husband, Ted Brake, joined her there, to work as an editor on the journal of the All-China Federation of Trade Unions. In that same year, Patience was also given the opportunity to return to China to work for the Foreign Languages Press. In a CV written much later in her life she stated briefly that her work consisted of the sub-editing of reports, magazine features and books. She then added an explanatory note:

> These were translated in Chinese English and I endeavoured to put them into readable English. Sometimes my efforts were rewarded; but in more highly political material the original jargon was restored.[11]

The Foreign Languages Press had been newly created specifically to translate selected Chinese books into other languages, but was occasionally also responsible for translating politically acceptable foreign books into Chinese. Research has been carried out which gives background information on how those from abroad, like Patience, were employed.

> A few other trusted foreigners living outside China who had worked with the Chinese Communist Party [CCP] in the past were invited to return, mostly to work as language polishers for CCP foreign propaganda organs . . . These chosen few foreigners were known initially as international friends, to distinguish them from the foreign detritus of assorted imperialists, missionaries, and the like who were being cleaned out of new China.[12]

But the Chinese system of *waishi* – the management of foreign and diplomatic affairs – included the full spectrum of relations, not only state-to-state but also people-to-people. As such, any dealings with foreign residents in China were subject to stringent controls, some of them readily apparent, others more subtle.[13]

> Despite occasional objections, even in the hardest times in China CCP functionaries treated the international friends with particular privilege. 'Privilege' in the worst of times meant that they got more to eat and better food than all but the highest of Chinese leaders, in better times it meant that they were given high salaries and comfortable accommodation far superior to ordinary Chinese. As the international friends were acutely aware, privilege was one of the means with which foreigners were reminded of their outsider status. . . . The underlying message was that

foreigners were only allowed to live in China at the will of the government. China was to be run by the Chinese and they would only use foreigners as and when it suited them.[14]

Nevertheless, despite this attitude and various practical restrictions, such as the requirement to carry registration booklets and permits to travel outside their areas of residence, research has shown that in 1950s China, amongst 'foreign friends' and Chinese alike, there was generally a great deal of idealism and enthusiasm for the new government.[15]

> There was a strong sense that things were getting better and better, and that life had improved dramatically since 1949. In contrast, the Western world seemed fascist and aggressive. Foreign supporters of the People's Republic of China were disturbed by the spread of McCarthyite attitudes in the Western world and United States support for former war criminals in Germany and Japan.[16]

This was the political atmosphere in which Patience was to live for the next few years. However, I knew that at this time additional factors were also having a great impact on her life. She had not gone to China alone. Also invited was Eric Edney, a former International Brigader and Communist Party official, the man who was to become Patience's husband. Fluent in Russian and with a good grasp of Chinese, he would have been considered a useful asset at the Foreign Languages Press.

Born in 1908 in Wooton Rivers, Wiltshire, the son of a farm worker, Eric Edney had won a scholarship to Marlborough School, where his wide reading led him to communism. After leaving school at sixteen with excellent exam results, he began to work for the Post Office.[17] In January 1937, he arrived in Spain but was wounded in February during the Battle of Jarama. Afterwards, he worked at the British Battalion's post office and was appointed as a political commissar.[18] The entry about him in the Moscow archives described him as 'petty bourgeois' and his conduct as 'good'.[19] He was repatriated in April 1938 and for several years was the editor of the magazine *Spain Today* and at some point also took on an official role in the Communist Party.[20] His own writings included poems in which, like other former International Brigaders, he drew on his experiences in Spain to express the commitment he felt to the 'cause'.[21]

I was aware that Patience and Eric had known each other before going to China, though their paths had not crossed in Spain. They first met at one of the International Brigade reunions after the Second World War.[22] Patience had explained in an interview that through Eric's work for the East

German news agency in Britain in the post-war period, she had learned
more about the situation there.

> Eric was the East German news agent [in Britain] when they sent the
> Germans out for being spies. Eric was the whole office. And when we went
> to Germany, we used to hear their problems they had with the Soviet
> Union, which wanted to set up factories and things, use the German
> know-how but to use the stuff that was pre-war and the Germans wanted
> to have things that were ahead. They had terrible quarrels about it,
> terrible. And it was very difficult to work with the Russians because in
> lots of ways they were curiously old-fashioned.[23]

However, this was the only reference she made to her husband during
several lengthy interviews, despite all their years of marriage and the fact
that he was the father of her only child. The bare bones of Eric Edney's life
were accessible, but as a personality, he still seemed strangely insubstantial.
I searched for further information about Eric elsewhere but, despite his years
of commitment to Communism, his footprints in the political jungle were
barely detectable.

The few studies and memoirs I had found relating to the subject of
foreign workers in China did not mention the Edneys by name and there
were very few people still alive who had known her well at that time. The
trail was becoming ever fainter, petering out into a dry desert – the 'sands
of time'. Disappointed, I envisaged a somewhat perfunctory and unsatis-
factory chapter covering Patience's life from the end of the Second World
War until I first met her in 1994. Only one hope remained. After Patience's
death, her son had kept a portion of the many papers she had accumulated.
He had already kindly allowed me to see the letters he had found, dating
from her time in Spain. Perhaps, when emptying her house, he might have
also salvaged vestiges of her Chinese memorabilia. I ventured to enquire if
this was the case, but in the twelve intervening years, the boxes he had taken
home with him from her house in London had become buried in the usual
accumulation of discarded family belongings; perhaps in the loft, or in the
deepest recesses of rarely opened cupboards. Was there anything from
China? It was possible.

The weeks and months went by without news. Who wants to spend a
precious weekend digging through dark nooks and crannies to find dusty,
and perhaps somewhat distressing, reminders of a mother who had died
more than a decade ago? I dared to pester him. Could I come and talk to
him about his mother again? Might he have remembered where the boxes
could be? We arranged an evening to meet at his house. When I rang to

confirm the appointment, he mentioned having unearthed a few things from her China days. I suppressed a small flutter of hope – no point in anticipating more than a couple of faded postcards and some Chinese trinkets.

For historians, there is great joy to be found in the sight of a table piled high with unplumbed riches on the subject of their research. The excitement felt by an intrepid explorer, 'to boldly go where no man has gone before', can also be found when delving into a collection of private papers, in delightful disorder, with all its secrets still awaiting. Patience's boxes from China included ornate documents in Chinese mixed with typed letters in English, drafts of articles and reports – and the photograph albums; a pictorial record of Patience in China – a veritable treasure trove of imagery. It was a wonderful moment for me.

A bright red card, stamped with Chinese lettering in gold, contained a carefully folded letter on tissue-thin paper. It was an invitation for Eric Edney and Patience Darton to attend a reception and dinner on 14 July 1954, just after their arrival in China.[24] A large document with handwritten Chinese ideograms, decorative border and an official stamp was, in fact, her marriage certificate.[25] I opened the photograph albums to find several studio portraits of the couple with a caption indicating they were wedding photographs. Patience is sitting stiffly on a stool, the formal style of her hat and suit – square-shouldered and with a sharply pleated skirt – in keeping with the frozen immobility of her smile. And here is Eric, standing behind her, almost as painfully thin as Patience. The intellectual's stereotypical depth of brow is a notable feature, one he had in common with Patience's former lovers. But, I thought as I saw Eric's picture for the first time, his rather abstracted air and heavy tortoise-shell spectacles certainly did not give the impression of a man of action. It was hard to imagine him, even when twenty years younger, fighting as a soldier at the front in Spain.

A small brown cardboard box held a cache of over thirty letters from Patience: the majority being correspondence with her sister, Hilary. At this time Hilary was living in London's Camden Town, in the large, somewhat run-down house in Oval Road that the two sisters had bought together after the war, renting out some of the rooms to supplement their income. Many of the letters to Hilary were undated, but as the process of reading and sorting them began, I saw that this problem could be overcome. The letter announcing the forthcoming wedding had been preceded by another, breaking the news that she was expecting a baby. The letters therefore could be put in order by following her progress during the months of pregnancy, her first days as a mother, and by watching through her eyes as the baby changed into a little boy. Perhaps because she knew her sister's views differed so radically from her own, Patience wrote little to her sister of a political nature, but the letters revealed much about the cultural experience of living in nineteen-fifties China. Hilary's replies were also in the collection.[26] Her letters kept Patience in touch with life at home in England; the family and financial matters, the garden and the antics of the much loved cats. Sisterly confidences are few and far between in Hilary's letters. In contrast, at times with all the intimacy of a diary, Patience had typed away to Hilary in her usual forthright manner; her words giving personal glimpses of a stranger in the strange lands of China, marriage and motherhood.

There were no letters in the collection describing Patience's arrival in China. The first I found was dated 31 January 1955, and began with sad references to an old flame. Hilary must have written to tell Patience that Horo had died early in the New Year. After serving with the British Army in the RAMC until 1945, Horo had returned to London, becoming a British citizen in 1947 and working as a doctor in the Regent's Park area. Patience had feared all was not well with her former 'boyfriend', but had already heard the sad news of his death through Nan Green.

> I had terrible feelings about him from Christmas onwards and although I was upset I was not surprised. Of course I still have a feeling that he wouldn't have had pneumonia if I had been looking after him, but nobody could have done anything about the leukaemia. I can't imagine how he got it so suddenly, but it is like a cancer of the blood stream. It is irreversible. Poor Horo, I hope he was not too conscious, because it was so sad everything falling to pieces at once, and suddenly nothing left for him at all, no life or anything all of a sudden. I hope he was too ill to realise it. I'm afraid my letter was too late for him.[27]

It is clear from her additional comments that Patience's relationship with Horo had continued on a friendly footing. Apart from the letter she had written to him, 'nothing in it except gossip and trying to write cheerfully', she referred to Horo's financial affairs in detail; his mortgage, car repayments, life insurance and his will. Her attitude towards his family was seemingly less than sympathetic.

> I know he made more than enough, but he kept on spending too much on his family. Each time he went to Israel or Norway it took all his savings, about £100 each time. But there was a lot of property in the house, so there should be something for his family. Goodness knows why they seem to expect it.[28]

Horo had died on 9 January 1955 and was buried two days later in Bushey Cemetery. He was only 51 years old. Patience was still in China when his memorial stone was consecrated the following year, the inscription below the Star of David reading 'Deeply mourned and sadly missed by his brothers, sisters, relatives and friends.'[29] Patience would certainly have included herself amongst the latter.

Shortly after the death of Horo, Patience must have heard about the death of another old friend, Dr Fritz Jensen. He had worked in China until 1947 before returning to Austria. He died when the aircraft in which he was travelling crashed on the way to the Bandung Conference. Chou En-lai should also have been a passenger on the same plane, and an assassination attempt has been considered the likely cause for the crash.[30]

This first letter from Patience to her sister, like many others that follow, contains additional notes and comments from Eric, in which he often gives Hilary instructions regarding what to do with his stamp collection, his *Record Collector* magazines or his gramophone. It seems his editing work continued even when reading his wife's correspondence as he adds the remark, 'I've read Patience's bit and told her it needs editing and cutting, and that it's dreadfully preachy and didactic: but you know she wouldn't admit she's wrong.' Patience has written by hand in the margin 'pooh'. On the last page, it is through Eric that we hear the first news of Patience's pregnancy. Now aged forty-four, she may have been thinking that it was unlikely she would ever become a mother. Eric writes,

> Patience thinks a little facsimile is on the way, so we are touching wood. She has already got round to eating bags of cucumber, which all expectant mothers do here – God knows why – and discussing names for him/her.[31]

Alongside this news, Patience has added, 'seven weeks!' Elsewhere, the letters indicate that the pregnancy was not accidental, and that both had been involved in the decision to try to have a child.[32] Patience was at an age when she could no longer postpone plans for having a baby and she had already been told twice that she ought to have a hysterectomy.[33] But her decision cannot have been taken lightly. Eric was already married with a daughter in England and, at that time, was still waiting for his divorce to be finalised. She must have been fairly certain that he would indeed marry her when he was free to do so. Though Patience was a courageous and independent-minded woman, she would have known that life as an un-married mother in the 1950s was a daunting prospect, and that the social stigma would still be a handicap for the child.

Several weeks later, with Eric's divorce finalised, Patience wrote to

Hilary with news of their forthcoming marriage. She certainly chose to marry Eric with her eyes open to some of his failings. When writing to her sister about Katie, Eric's daughter, Patience remarked, 'She has her dad's brains, I hope she hasn't got his character. This is for Eric to read by the way, but I mean it too.'[34] On another occasion she commented on Eric's lack of potential as a breadwinner and the fact she would need to go on working, 'I knew beforehand that Eric wouldn't be able to keep himself, much less his responsibility to Katie, and I am quite willing to lump it, but I must be able to make preparations to lump it.'[35] However, when criticising Eric in the letters, her general tone is humorous rather than bitter. Despite the degree of understanding they seem to have had at the start of their relationship, the marriage was not to end well for Patience.

Margaret Powell, the nurse Patience had known since Spain, was asked if she would put an announcement in the *Daily Worker* about the marriage. The wedding itself, on 6 March 1955, was a low-key affair.

> Eric and I had a very sweet wedding. We expected it to be in the afternoon after the office on Saturday, and both were going to smarten up in a mild way in the lunch hour. Imagine our surprise therefore when our best man came in the morning at ten-thirty and said come along. We had to go over and fetch Eric, he works in another building across quite big grounds, and he came down saying he was being rushed into it, much to the concern of the best man, who is a poppet but without a sense of humour in English.[36]

So the ceremony took place making use of a wedding ring given to Patience by one of her colleagues who had been married twice and had one to spare, with the bride wearing 'padded dirty blacks and torn pullover' and a groom who hadn't shaved.[37] The best man was anxious that the official business of the marriage he had arranged in the Registry Office should make a good impression on them, 'very proud indeed of his dear Republic as well he might be', said Patience. However, as they waited, the Registrar had to deal with other cases, and the golden image the best man had wished to present of the 'new China' was somewhat tarnished.

> In came a bashful young couple. 'Ah my dears,' beaming social worker smile [from Registrar], 'have you come to get married?' Both at once, to get in first, 'Not on your life, we want a divorce.' Smile fades, stern lecture, must do more than want it, bring back your work mates and arbitrators, serious step, very retrograde with young people, can't do it today. Unfortunately, the next couple also wanted a divorce! But the only

contretemps was a nasty old feudal daddy who was trying to get married
without producing the bride. He got a very friendly lecture, but told
absolutely nothing doing, the woman is as important as the man, and she
has to be completely willing and in love with you. I fear he was trying to
get a free *baomu* [servant], but it didn't come off . . . We had a lecture,
questions on the marriage law, what provisions for Katie, what arrangements for ex-wife, close scanning of decree (Dated January 31 by the way,
but we only got it in the middle of February.) Are you both making a free
choice, do you both want to help one another in work and home, how long
have you known one another, (a bit taken back when we said since 1939),
do we know that in China money, property, land, everything is completely
equal property of man and wife? This to Eric. But our dear best man filled
it all in for us and I really feel that he performed the ceremony. We have
a large certificate each, in colour, one made out with my name first and
one with Eric's, and a seal and a stamp on the back of the decree into the
bargain.[38]

News from England marred this happy mood. Before the couple had
their wedding photographs taken a week later, Patience heard that her
father had suddenly died. She was relieved that it had happened so quickly,
believing that her mother would have been unable to cope with him
through a serious illness. She sympathised with the problems this now
posed for Hilary; an unmarried daughter expected to shoulder the responsibility of caring for an elderly parent. Horo, who would have been a
dependable friend in such circumstances, was sadly no longer there to offer
her sister support.

I expect you miss Horo very much as he would have been kind and helpful
and been able to talk about it. Which ever one did die first would have
made an awful problem for you and the remaining one.[39]

The austere atmosphere of the wedding photographs is explained by this
unexpected loss. Both Eric and Patience had 'dressed up like mad' for the
portraits, but other plans for the studio shots were changed.

We were going to have large bouquets and Eric a great red rosette and
have best man and seven bridesmaids in the photo, but cancelled because
of pop.[40]

A small, private dinner for the foreign contingent was held shortly after
their marriage. The couple were given numerous wedding presents,

including some for the coming baby. One of the gifts – a book – amused Patience greatly, especially in view of earlier comments that Eric, 'the mean toad', had made, comparing her blossoming bust measurements unfavourably with those of her sister.

> Last night we had a small, private dinner of the foreigners. One of them had racked his brains to think of a present, had hunted in vain, and then suddenly ran into a book in the second hand market, 'What every young husband ought to know'. It is absolutely killing, and we had readings from it. I seem to be ticking over merrily, getting bigger already, and as for my bosoms, as good as yours. Eric wants me to have my photo taken in a tight pullover to send to you. I never realised he was jealous of your figure for me, I'm not. It just shows how even the most unexciting men have these ideas, the little book is quite right that all men are nasty sex-ridden creatures who have to control themselves. The little book also says that the reason women have a higher moral and spiritual sense is because they tend by life to be unable to get to church on Sundays, what with cooking and children being ill and other responsibilities, so they have this higher nature so that they can still be moral. Later on, when the children get bigger or the husband is earning more, they can go to church again and don't lose the habit. It doesn't say what happens to the servants' morals, who are doing the cooking instead, but I suppose they are women too and can also last out. It is a convenient theory, but innocently takes it for granted that the late Victorian Age in America was what all life was leading up to, hence I suppose women were endowed with suitable feeling in the Garden of Eden ready for 1880 New York life. It doesn't make any comparisons with nasty savage women in other climes. On the whole though, the little book is on the side of the angels but plays down any pleasure in sex for either, men shouldn't and women don't. It is the lower part of us which the author is glad to see can be got under control at the age of 45 if you take cold baths and plenty of exercise and don't share even a room with your wife, much less a bed. Best to start off with two rooms and two beds well apart. Also once a month is quite enough.[41]

A key person now entering Patience's life was Gwang Ying, the Chinese *baomu* whose services as a housemaid, and later, as nanny, Patience relied on so heavily over the next three years. The trials and tribulations of learning about each other's cultural differences was a protracted process that was explained to Hilary in great detail. Apart from Gwang Ying's habit of putting too much garlic in the food, there were plenty of other minor tensions.

Must write to ma sometime this week, perhaps tonight at home. I get unnerved typing at home though because Gwang Ying lurks so, breathing heavily, so as to watch the marvel. She did the same thing when I did a bit of darning on my thick nylons. They don't darn at all. They patch with anything that comes handy in the way of cotton.[42]

But when Gwang Ying's mother moved in too, Patience began to appreciate her *baomu* rather more than before.

I realise more and more how extremely sophisticated Gwang is to accept as much as she does, and with such grace and enthusiasm. Her old mother, who never thought to read, heaven help us, hasn't got as far as telling the time, so her household here is having a rather difficult time. The old duck has also a strong feeling that only her local village dialect is understandable and refuses to understand the local accent or Mandarin. I think we shall have to get a couple of sheep and some chickens, and make a little paddy field for her. I'm sure she won't be able to do anything but peasant work. She's been wished on to the Spanish comrades now, and another friend of Gwang is trying to control her. The Spaniards are mad to pinch my Gwang but there's nothing doing, I tell them it takes two to make a Gwang, and one of them's me, so they must also learn to work the miracle, and do some of the work themselves to show her.[43]

Elsewhere in the letters Patience makes references to friends made in China, such as David Crook and his wife, Isabel, an anthropologist. Gladys Yang and Ruth Weiss were also mentioned.[44]

It is interesting to consider the extent to which Patience might have been aware of the way in which, as a foreigner, her activities were being monitored. One historian of the period has stated, 'In the 1950s most resident foreigners were assigned minders who would spy on them and find out their views on various issues.'[45] Informers would be asked by the Ministry of State Security to 'keep an eye' on someone, and translators or guides were frequently asked to report on foreign guests and experts in their charge. This supervision was pervasive.

Sometimes Chinese people who were previously unknown to a foreign resident would be assigned to meet them accidentally and become their 'friend'. In addition, Chinese colleagues were encouraged to report on the views of their foreign workmates to senior staff. Some foreigners also became notorious for informing on other foreign residents. Foreign residents knew that their overseas mail was being read both by the Chinese authorities and officials outside China so they tended to be very guarded about what they said in letters. Those designated as 'foreign friends' were discouraged from mixing with 'bourgeois' foreigners from the diplomatic community or non-communist journalists, and they were expected to live a relatively Spartan lifestyle. The few who indulged in decadent pleasures such as listening to rock and roll music and drinking excessive amounts of alcohol were criticized.[46]

Eric and Patience would have been unlikely to fall into this latter category and if someone was informing on Patience's activities, there would probably have been little to say. Working and sleeping were all she could manage to do for the next few months, other than making plans for the birth of her baby. 'Painless' birth, drug-free, was the norm in China. As a midwife, Patience had trained in 'co-operative' childbirth, but that had all been a long time ago. She asked Hilary to contact Margaret Powell who was also a qualified midwife, to see if she might be able to send her up-to-date information on the management of childbirth.

> Could you ask Margaret Powell to send me Dick Read's book,[47] and any more and better ones, because it is all 'painless' so called here and I had better mug it up. I should be alright as far as subconscious feelings go, and conscious ones too for that matter, but I am old and tired and a bit narrow, so I had better do my own co-operating I think.[48]

She hoped that a friend from work would be present to help her when she was in labour. Whether or not this friend was required to report on her to the Chinese authorities would probably have been of little concern to Patience. She was immersed in the preoccupations of pregnancy.

> Classes here are not as good as at home, and it will be tiresome having to have a baby in Chinese. I hope to have my best friend here with me, my desk mate, as she speaks English perfectly, doesn't lose her head and has had one painful in the US and one painless here – a model mother.[49]

Patience gave Hilary strict instructions not to tell their mother at this stage about the pregnancy, presumably to avoid confronting her with the reality of pre-marital sex. 'I am four months and a week now, must soon tell Ma that I've started, but it's only a month since I got married.'[50] However, Patience was not accustomed to such masquerades and found the deception difficult, writing later, 'Oh what a tangled web we weave, I am so bored with writing lies to Ma, but suppose I had better keep it up now.'[51] Such obfuscation seems remarkably out of character for someone as normally outspoken as Patience, even given that her mother's sensibilities might have been of an extraordinarily delicate nature. The fact that religion had played an important part in Patience's upbringing probably helps to explain her unwillingness to tell the truth in this instance. But, whether from reluctance to face maternal wrath, or from a wish to avoid distressing her mother, the make-believe was maintained.

It seems that Patience herself still found religious ceremonies appealing, even though no longer a believer. She was certainly fascinated by the different cultural traditions in China.

By the way, I meant to tell you. There was a lot of Easter here, it dragged on because all the Russian Orthodoxes had it a week later, so there was rather a lot of bell ringing and midnight masses of one sort or another. Good Friday too had a lot of tolling twice, which seemed rather queer, but there was an actual performance of Stainer's Crucifixion, the last thing I expected to find in Peking. I didn't go because I only knew about it afterwards from the daily news release. All the papers carried the various do's [sic] religiously, same as they do the Moslem ones. The chaps are killing about it in the office, very disapproving narrow minded blighters, it's part of their constitution. But fancy old Stainer! No Matthew Passion though. Pity. We shall be able to get a long playing of it now that we have a long playing gram. Wireless out of order now though. Deep gloom reigns, poor Eric can't play his records . . . The shops which cater for western food had chocolate Easter eggs and rabbits, Russians have rabbits it seems, no sillier than eggs when you come to think of it, [Margin note from Eric 'They had eggs too.'] and Pasque cake, a long shape like a blunt sugar loaf with sparse currents and cinnamon, tasting like an unfruity Christmas cake. I have a feeling that we have Easter cake in some part of the country, saffron, is it? Easter being a moon festival it coincided with Ching Ming, Bright and Clear, when you go into the country to enjoy the beauty of spring now. It is really the day when you go to your ancestral graves and bow to the ancestors and sweep the graves. But they always made a picnic of this, having swept the graves they sat down and ate on them and now it is a general spring outing. The peasants keep it better, because they haven't budged from their ancestral village, but most workers and townspeople are too far away from their original homes now, what with one thing and another. All the places of work, schools and offices have an outing. We were very puritanical and had it on a Sunday but quite a lot have it in working hours, a much better idea.[52]

Unfortunately for Patience, due to an important ceremonial occasion on the same day as the outing, she was only able to imagine walking amongst the trees in blossom; a brief escape that might have reminded her of happy days in Spain.

> Our Office went to the nearby (30 miles) hot springs and climbed a mountain, but we were incommunicado waiting for one of our big do's, blast it. I was longing to get out of these walls and climb gently up a mountain through the apricot trees all in flower. Pooh to protocol, though as a matter of fact it was THE VERY GRAND DO, even though we only figured as others present. Eric was taken aback at being presented arms to, having always been at the other end, but the presenters were sweet and grinned as well, seeing how excited we were. They have got lovely manners, even the guards behave like welcoming hosts. I must say, one feels a mug bowing one's way through, I felt like the dear Queen, but you can't just sweep by nose in air, and the guards are as thrilled as we looking at the bods, I don't know who inspected who more closely.[53]

The parade reminded her of an anecdote she had heard about 'Harry's boy', in all probability, the son of the CP leader, Harry Pollitt.

> We heard a nice story about Harry's boy who is doing his call up now. Of course he has a lot to put up with and the army is very alarmed, quite superstitious, but a lot is just plain teasing. On Christmas day parade they had all gone to bed late after a booze up and had Church parade in the morning with a general inspecting. Harry's boy was standing like a ramrod in line with the others, and when the gang went down behind him they stopped for what seemed hours with the most ghastly silence. Then the general asked the major or what not, and the major asked the sergeant, 'Who is this?', was told, said 'Hm' and passed on. Everyone but Harry's boy was dying [of laughter] it seemed. The others had stuck on a huge hammer and sickle on his back. I think the general was very sensible to take it like that. As a matter of fact I expect he was amused.[54]

Patience anticipated that attending the lengthy May Day ceremonies might be more than she could physically endure in her condition.

> You really need to be in training for these things, besides I can't get into any of my best clothes. I am feebly asking to go and watch the parade from a hotel near the square, because I don't feel like four hours solid watching, but I expect we shall get into the grand stand where one can slip out of

the back and have tea. The parks are all wired up with loud speakers and floodlights for country dancing and I badly want to look around and see the party in the square and the families and tribes in the parks. The minorities beat every one else hollow for dresses, but our uniform blue coat and trousers look very nice too. The evening do is lovely for October 1st but, judging by the preparations, May Day is even better folklorically. It will be sad only being an onlooker. Some of the others here are arranging a barbecue at five but it's over the other side of the city and I don't know that I want to go so far, except that it is nice to have a gossip with the out of towners who we don't see often.[55]

This same letter, many pages long as usual, reveals Patience's skill as a letter writer in full flow. One paragraph in particular, eloquently encapsulates her sense of humour.

We bought a companion book to 'What every young man should know', 'What every man of 45 should know', but it is not helpful, no need to bother after 40, you've had it by then, the 'SEXUAL HUSH' closes down, they say. Also they have a lot about excesses, with which is included TEA, smoking of course, drink and sex. I was outraged about TEA. DO YOU WANT YOUR CHILD TO REMEMBER YOU DRINKING TEA AND SMOKING? I ask you. My child has already got a strong pre-natal feeling about tea I should think by now, if that's an excess, I give up. Also you mustn't ride bikes, or sit on soft cushions – it excites the parts. Some people are easily excited I should say.[56]

However, reading the little book also made Patience reflect on the relationship with her father as she grew up. The repressive nature of the advice it gave dated from the days of his youth.

Pop would have loved it, I fear, I don't mean exciting the parts, poor thing, but the emphasis on excess, tea and sex lumped together. The trouble was we read the book too late, it really is what pop was brought up on and would have helped us to understand him when we were 15 or so, instead of just being bored by his carry on. You didn't get so much of his interior life as I did, he used to go on for hours about it to me. Oedipus the wrong way round, I used to think resignedly. Too late for us to have countered it I suppose by the time we were old enough to cope. My goodness, what a background, this book is a real eye opener.[57]

Patience was discovering many new things in China, both about a different culture and about herself. As I read through her letters, I too was finding new facets to her character. It was like opening an intricate Chinese puzzle box, and finding the secrets hidden within.[58]

14

Falling in Love Again

As the weeks went by, Patience was becoming anxious, waiting for good books on pre-natal exercises and relaxation techniques to arrive from England. She seemed sure that Eric would be prepared to join in, although it's difficult to know how much of his involvement was at Patience's insistence. She writes, 'I must begin soon or it won't be all that painless, besides, Eric must practise too.'[1]

However, being a qualified midwife and observing numerous expectant mothers was not the same as experiencing pregnancy oneself. Patience was intrigued, and sometimes horrified, at the changes taking place to her body as the pregnancy advanced.

> The little creature is now wriggling, it feels like a small fish leaping for mosquitoes. I never felt faint the first time or anything, it's a swizzle. I'm still not sure when it's just wind or when I feel life beneath my heart. These people who describe these feelings are too poetic. What is left of my poor stomach is high up under my beautiful bosoms, you never saw anything so horrid, and my umbilicus points upwards, all flattened out. I can easily look into it to wash it now, but it's so flat it can't go on getting full of Peking dust as it used to when it was a neat little hole, quite difficult to get into. Bosoms completely wasted. They can't stick out as far as my stomach, let alone my great abdomen. It is a shame, they'll never be like it again, much better than yours and not at all pendulous, just right. So far no untoward symptoms, other than cravings for good plain cut off the joint, baked potatoes and veg, followed by stewed fruit and custard. None available.[2]

Normally thin, Patience became almost emaciated after an attack of bronchitis that lasted for a month. Nevertheless, her 'little incubus' continued to do well. An American-trained woman doctor was supervising her pregnancy at this point, which was helpful as far as communication was concerned. Patience, now increasingly aware of Chinese cultural niceties, explained 'she can speak the language and I argue with her myself, not

173

through an interpreter so no face is lost'. Patience must have been less than humbly respectful, finding her doctor to be 'full of trite psychological phrases which turn me up'.[3]

As Patience continued her work at the Foreign Languages Press, eight hours a day, six days a week, she found the gruelling schedule increasingly arduous. Plans for a holiday were an attractive possibility, but still not definite. She would have liked something simple, but the officially proposed destination was distant and exclusive. She complained to Hilary, 'We are wrapped up in cotton wool at the wrong time, and worked like slaves otherwise, what a life.'[4] Nevertheless, she was finding much of her work interesting, but was disparaging about the use of so much jargon. Eric, Patience, Gladys Yang, Ruth Weiss and Sid Shapiro all worked on a variety of publications. Patience hoped that Hilary would read some of their output and offer a stern critique of form and content, adding, 'we relish criticism and have lovely meetings about it'. Her dislike of political rhetoric and theoretical discourse is clear.

> I have developed a bloody good critical sense of all the nonsense I would never read before, for my sins. Get hold of a recent copy of *Chinese Literature* and guess which are my handiwork. Those ghastly philosophical-political bits at the end have been touched by me for the most part as have the short stories. Not all of them and anyway Eric has firmly mauled them around afterwards, he is the last word. See if you can recognise mine. We can all tell one another's, but Eric always points out the Dartonisms, and says what would Hilary say about that . . . [5]

Summer came, and with it, an adventure that Patience was to write about at length; a trip to Lushan, the prestigious mountain resort, retreat of the elite. The holiday, Patience told Hilary afterwards, had been trying in many ways, not only as her pregnancy was too far advanced for comfort during much of the long, hot journey, but also because the trip had been organised with 'masses of precautions of various foolish kinds and no common sense'.[6] These frank comments to Hilary were included in milder form in a detailed article entitled, 'Holiday Journey in China', possibly written for publication in one of the propaganda magazines. The long journey by train, two nights and a day, gave Patience the chance to observe the changes that were taking place. The porters, train staff, sleeping arrangements, and even lavatory facilities – all were scrutinised carefully. During the course of her work, she had read a great deal about the agricultural reforms being introduced in China, and now she saw the practical results of these policies. From her window, as the countryside passed by, she could see peasants labouring in the fields. She tried to decide whether the inhabitants of each village were working together as a co-operative or a mutual aid team, or still as an old-style family group. In her article she writes of Hankow, the Yellow River and the Yangste, but does not describe the remainder of her holiday in Lushan. Her letter to Hilary gives a little more information, particularly about some of the problems that arose. It seemed that not everyone in China found it easy to fulfil the expectations of the new regime.

> Boat down the Yangtse at 7 next a.m. Lovely new boat, everyone bursting with pride. Sprung beds, bedside lights, fans in room, chairs and tables, big lounge. Here the ultimate shame came to our courier. She is the well brought-up daughter, Western educated, of a very high up general, who saw the light in time (just). She had of course been to Lushan in the old days, I am sorry to say along with Chiang and Co. Her mother had a house there with a swimming pool. She is very pretty, dresses well, perfect lady, dumb as dumb, but with an innocent sweet nature. Her manners are beautiful, exactly the same to everyone, but unfortunately she has no brain, a Pooh.[7] She works in my office and I know her very well . . . On the boat, the security man came at once, having been notified about us by efficient Hankow, and took strong exception to Dora not being armed. Dora giggled, but was upset. Dora armed would be about the most insecure thing I could imagine, by the way. I wouldn't trust her with a toy pistol with caps, not that she would want to have such a nasty thing. But she is terribly willing and earnest, and cries like anything when she's criticised for not being an earnest female. Then she is criticised for crying. However, we laughed about her being armed.[8]

The steep ascent to Lushan was a nerve-wracking experience; negotiating hairpin bends in dense low cloud, 'rain and wind howling, cataracts foaming off cliff on one side, precipice with un-seeable bottom on other'. They arrived in the late evening, exhausted, but there was still the formal welcome for senior comrades to endure.

> Eric speechless, ears blocked feeling the height, me green as grass from the drive, and longing for bed, and Dora on her best behaviour having to do all the translation of speeches of welcome, and effusive thanks from us.[9]

On her return to Peking from Lushan, life became even more onerous for Patience. Temperatures reached 110 degrees in the shade and humidity was high. She continued to drag herself into the office everyday as it was cooler there. The new doctor assigned to her case met with her approval, 'English

14.1 Patience in the mountains. The Chinese writing says: Souvenir of visit to the Fairy Cave at Lushan, 4 July 1955.

14.2 Patience, Eric and the group, showing in the background the Lushan floods of 1955.

14.3 Patience with Dora (Chang Su-su) and Eric.

14.4 Patience, Eric and Bobbin.

14.5 Gwang Ying with Bobby as a baby.

14.6 Bobby with Gwang Ying.

14.7 Where the Great Wall of China runs to the sea, Summer 1956.

14.8 Ming Tombs trip 1956, (left to right) Denise, Luis La Casa & Jorge, Patience and Eric.

14.10 Patience and Isabel concoct a feast.

14.9 Patience on a stone camel – Avenue of Beasts, Autumn 1956.

14.11 Meal with friends: Yang Hsian-yi, Patience, David Crook, Gladys Yang, Isabel Crook at the Crooks' house in Zhonghaitan, (Central beach), Beidaihe seaside resort.

14.12 Patience working at the FLP.

14.13 Patience, Bobby and Gwang Ying, Peking, West City.

14.14 Eric, Patience, Avis Hutt, Nan and Ted.

14.15 International Women's Day 1956 (Patience wearing a hat, back row).

14.16 Gladys Yang, Ruth Weiss and Patience, International Women's Day 1956.

14.17 Janet Springhall, Jean Gallacher and sister, 1956.

14.18 Nan Green, Ted Brake and Harry Pollitt, Peking 1956.

trained, not American', though being pregnant had its problems. 'I can no longer see the ground under my feet, it's like always carrying a tray.' Eric managed to keep his sense of humour, writing in a note to Hilary, 'The Chinese call this part of the year – late July, "fu" which the diccker [sic] defines as "dog days" – but it is obvious that it is really onomatopoeic, like the English "phew!"'[10]

Patience's world changed completely with the birth of her son in September. Her letters show that she surrenders gladly, without the slightest protest, to the overpowering strength of her maternal feelings. By now almost twenty years had passed since she had been writing to Robert in Spain, planning one day to have his baby. But, despite the passage of so much time, he had never been forgotten. She named her son 'Robert'. She loved her baby as passionately as she had loved his namesake. In the letters to Hilary, Patience's wonder at this diminutive being who has captured her heart is expressed throughout the reams of pages filled with the minutiae of his daily routine, his every new accomplishment, and all the torments and delights of motherhood. At first, she refers to him always as 'the bobbin'. Gradually, as his independence increases, he becomes 'Bobbin' with a capital B, then 'Bobby', but never it seems, 'Robert'.

Seven pages of the first letter she writes to Hilary after his birth are missing. The sheet, bearing the number eight, gives the explanation, begin-ning as it does with 'Don't give ma this page.' It becomes clear that the lost pages were all about the actual birth, to be saved and shown first to their mother, then to other friends who were keen to know what it was like to have a baby in China. Like most new mothers, despite the ongoing medical problems that were to plague her for some time, Patience was so absorbed in her baby that the pain of childbirth retreated rapidly into the past.

> I have already forgotten how tedious everything was, when I look mawk-ishly at my little bobbin, who is really an unusually beautiful and talented child, of course.[11]

Patience was now to find out more about Chinese attitudes to children and methods of child rearing. Chinese colleagues gave Eric and Patience a scroll to mark the birth, using ancient script and replete with traditional symbolism. Congratulations were given on the birth of 'a jade playing crea-ture', indicating a boy, considered 'very valuable and counts as a grade one birth'. The girls in Patience's office objected strongly to the use of this Chinese symbolism, saying it was reactionary and feudal. At first Patience rather liked the notion, then changed her mind.

'Jade playing' suits him very well as his Chinese name is Bah-bee, which I say is short for Robert. Popular name, though a little old fashioned nowadays. It means treasure . . . Stop Press. I have now heard that little girls only get a broken bit of pottery to play with, and the congratulations, if any, merely say, 'We hear you have a small shard-playing object born to you.' Pah, I don't wonder the girls in the office took a poor view of using this feudal nomenclature.[12]

Celebrations were held, as was the custom, when the baby was one month old.

The mother is then technically visible. Up till then in the old style she has not been out, read a word, got up, eaten anything cold (including fruit) etc. I had to do some of the things, like drinking milk with brown sugar and chicken soup, but I didn't keep in bed a day.[13]

By this time her baby was getting 'nice and plump', 'not so like a skinned rabbit as he was', though she did admit that when awake, he was 'rather an anxious little fellow, looking like an old couples' child'. The pages she writes about him would fill a small book that could be entitled, *What Every Mother Should Know About Falling In Love With Her Baby.* A letter to Hilary, written just before Christmas 1955, contains a passage that conveys the happiness she was feeling to have her longed-for child at last.

The little wretch is so sweet now that he laughs and chuckles so that I am completely disarmed anyway. He shouts and denounces me when I put him down, and then when I go over after letting him do it for about 10 minutes, and find him black in the face, all the clothes kicked off with fury, his little clenched fists froggy cold, and tears squeezed out of his eyes, and speak to him, he stops, gives a touching catching little sob with large pathetic blue eyes and then turns his face into the pillow, looks up to make quite sure that muggins is still looking, and breaks into chuckles, with his wicked eyes sparkling with fun. He also loves me to sing to him, though he seems to take it as a rather low music hall joke. He laughs so much, with such coos and dimples that it is really too much, very rude. I agree that I can't sing, but he need not make it quite so obvious.[14]

Patience was to go back to full-time work very soon after the birth, but spending more time at home for several weeks had allowed a little time to meet other mothers living within their compound. Breast feeding was a hot topic of conversation.

Did I tell you that one of the other mothers in the compound says I'm just like her? Everyone always asks how the milk is, and I told them that I am a bit one sided, an awful lot in one, not so much in the other and baby fancied one side more than the other and had to be bullied every time to take from the small side. She said she was like that and whipped out her bosoms. I hesitate to call them by the name. One was completely atrophied, like mother's little money purse, a flat brown flap, about two inches. The other was like a brown sock with a small tangerine in the toe, hanging down below her waist. She is still breastfeeding her 7 month old, who practically stands and swings on it. Lots of mothers feed toddlers. They just sit down and let the toddler stand up and pull it out, like strap hanging. They don't mind at all about looks, nor do the men. Apparently the breast here is what it should be, not an adult erotic symbol at all, purely a mammary gland for use. The men don't get excited about it, and don't admire or want women to have a bosom in our sense of the word. But I still can't stand it when my compound friend joins our little mother's circles and says her bosom is just like mine . . . [15]

Eric was fulfilling Patience's expectations as a new father, and was seemingly entering into the experience wholeheartedly. In the New Year of 1956, Patience wrote that Eric and his son still looked very much alike, adding, 'it looks absolutely killing to see Eric lying down on the floor kicking with him'.[16] After work, Patience relished the hours she could spend with the baby. 'Eric is just as bad, we sit there cooing back at our bobbin.'[17] There were certainly tensions at times between Patience and Gwang Ying over child-rearing customs. Patience believed Gwang Ying would give in to his every whim, whereas she herself was inclined to take a firmer stance. Gwang never left him to cry for even a minute, and insisted that all Chinese babies slept with the light on. 'There's some superstitious pap about it', Patience complained, 'Gwang won't dare leave him in the dusk when she's looking after him.' However, it appears that some of the discord was due to Patience's jealousy because the baby was spending so much more time with Gwang Ying than with her; 'He sees so little of me all day, except Sunday.'[18] She regretted not being able to show him off to her family at home in England, writing with unadulterated pride, 'How I wish they could see my bobbin and see how ineffably superior he is to anyone else's baby on earth.'[19]

Meanwhile, as Gwang Ying was 'conquering illiteracy' by going to classes three nights a week, Patience was learning Chinese with a personal tutor.[20] Her teacher, however, did not seem to grasp what was required of him. As far as Patience was concerned, she had no need to learn how to issue orders to her child in Chinese as she always spoke to him in English. What she wanted was to learn how to give clear instructions to the *baomus*. One of the lessons was on Chinese terminology within family relationships. She was surprised to find that there was no word just for 'brother'; one had to specify either 'older' or 'younger' brother. The customs relating to the naming of women were even more deplorable.

> Did I tell you I lose my name too? Except to the baomus and others who knew me before as an important government foreign friend and still call me Pay-Shen-Dze I have now degenerated to being Bao-bee-de Mumma. Bobby's mother, which is all the name married Chinese women ever used to have. Many women had no given name at all in the old days. They used their fathers' surname till they were married and then their husbands', but had no given name at all. If they had no children or only girls they weren't even so-and-so's mother.[21]

In March 1956, when the offices of the Foreign Languages Press were relocated to the outskirts of Peking, the Edney household also had to move. Patience and Eric had different opinions about their new home. Eric seemed pleased, describing a 'brand new building about a mile outside the city – outside the old city walls, that is – the city is growing enormously. It's much more commodious and bright than the old place which we'd grown out of badly.'[22] Patience was less enthusiastic.

> We live at the office now, worse luck, in new Peking outside the city, beastly, in a modern block of jerry-built flats. The kitchen has a better stove and the hot and cold runs beautifully quickly otherwise everything is worse than our nice little Chinese tumbledown compound.[23]

Around this time, Patience had to return as an in-patient to hospital for treatment for her 'guts'. In the tradition of countless stand-up comedians, she manages to make an uncomfortable problem the butt of her humour.

> The doctor is absolutely killing. He lives for his work and sees life entirely in terms of piles, and expects one to do the same. He told me before that I should just lie down for a few hours ALWAYS when I went to the lav and blandly waved away any idea that it might not always be convenient or possible. He is scared stiff about having me as a patient, just on general principles because I am foreign. There aren't any runes or fancy things about air and water and humours about piles, or I would have to have a lot of rigmarole explanations. They are more poetic and fancy about the actual piles themselves, which they don't reckon are just nasty varicose

veins but sweet little entities, falling into several categories, named after flowers and animals, depending on whether they are on the N., S., E., or W. of the bottom! They are all very bland and frank about it, and had an illustrated article for *People's China*, the heavy-weight periodical Eric works on, and were surprised it was turned down for the English edition. Our pictorial magazine did it however, with illustrations of the eight categories, and a picture of the bottom, and a photo of the operation being performed, enlarged! Again the English edition did NOT have the photo of the operation, which gave the name of the patient! I suppose you would recognise him from that angle anyway.[24]

Work and the baby took most of Patience's energy during the following months. Sight-seeing trips included a visit to the Great Wall of China, and the Ming Tombs, 50 km north of Peking. Opportunities to get together with other British people for some sort of social life seem to have been limited, though there were occasions when they would have drawn together for mutual support.

Resident friends of China were bound not only by their ideological commitment to Chinese communism but also by displacement from their own societies. However, research on the subject has shown that it was through politics that much of their social interaction took place.

For many pro-CCP foreigners living in Beijing from 1952–1959 the focal point of social life was political study groups. Foreigners in the capital were not permitted to attend the study groups for Chinese personnel held at their work units. Their study groups were divided along language and national lines. Unlike Chinese citizens, attendance at a political study group was not compulsory for foreigners, but there was a certain amount of peer pressure and most attended. The groups read translations of Marxist-Leninist thought, selected articles of Mao Zedong thought and discussed contemporary political issues.[25]

David Crook recalled Patience at one particular study group meeting, shortly after the Soviet Union entry into Hungary on 4 November 1956.

Patience was an active member of the British study group in Beijing and I remember how indignant she was on learning of the Soviet incursions into Hungary, expressing herself with characteristic candour.[26]

Although letters to Hilary rarely contained references to politics, the Suez crisis, also in November 1956, did raise the subject. Patience had heard the news of a huge demonstration in London. The crowd had chanted, 'One, two, three, four, we won't fight in Eden's war,' in protest against the invasion of Egypt.[27]

> I had many congratulatory remarks about the almost unanimous reaction
> of over half the population of England, which had full treatment in the
> press here including photos in the biggest paper of the demo in Trafalgar
> Square which made me very homesick. I had enough in Spain of having
> to be ashamed of my country's rulers and trust, dear sister, that you are
> registering your disgust of Eden etc.[28]

Ironically, whilst living in one of the few Communist controlled countries in the world, owning a property with her sister in London was presenting Patience with problems that provoked a wishful backward glance to her more conservative roots. Tenants in the rooms they rented out at Oval Road and income tax liabilities were constantly recurring subjects in the letters to her sister. 'In a way I am sorry we have such nice labour MPs in both S. and N. St Pancras as I feel like writing to a good Tory one and saying where is this property owning democracy, if you can't have a little property and let it without losing money heavily on the deal?'[29] In the coming year, Patience's sympathetic opinion towards Chinese officialdom was to be put to the test.

15

Clouds over the Peking Picnic

The Hundred Flowers Movement, despite the pleasant image it conjures in the mind, brought distinctly unpleasant experiences for Patience in 1957. Possibly motivated by the relaxation of strict communist controls in the Soviet Union, Chairman Mao Zedong invited criticisms of the Chinese Communist Party's policies, based around the poetic slogan, "Let a hundred flowers bloom, and a hundred schools of thought contend," aiming to 'promote progress in the arts and sciences and a flourishing socialist culture in our land'. Eric and Patience were caught up in the backlash.

> Mao said to the peasants, 'tell me frankly what you think of the Party. Tell me your complaints. My goodness! They had millions of complaints. The Party was in a panic and was so angry that they started to frighten people, trying to put an end to the Hundred Flowers. Eric was not used to biting his tongue – very English – and said, 'We English are accustomed to speaking out and discussing our problems in public. If the Chinese don't want us to do so, they shouldn't ask any English person to come here.' After saying this, Eric was arrested and I was interrogated too. The Chinese wanted me to denounce my husband, but I said 'No, no.' I didn't want to say anything bad to discredit him – although I often thought he was wrong, I wasn't about to criticise him over this. Then, the Chinese said, 'Very well, we'll put you in prison and take away your son.' Bob was still under two years old, and the Chinese were fully prepared to do it. In a situation like that, it's difficult to decide what to do. One isn't a heroine, just a normal person. I thought perhaps the Chinese wouldn't dare keep us in prison very long, and Nan Green came to visit me and said that if they shut me away as well as Eric, she would look after Bob, and she stood outside the prison with a placard in protest. Anyway they didn't lock me up, but the situation was horrible, horrible.[1]

Not surprisingly, in 1957, Patience's thoughts were turning increasingly towards going home. However, the business of leaving was not as simple as might have been expected. Sometime in the summer, a letter to

Hilary mentioned that there were problems relating to their departure.

> Our time has now been settled. They seem to have ambivalent ideas here!
> We were always firm about having a time, i.e. not here for ever, but when
> we found they were so surprised and grieved that we had our own ideas
> about it we had long arguments. I don't know why, except as a sort of
> compliment to our indispensability, as all the others here have perfectly
> ordinary contracts. However, it is now settled that we come back after four
> years, that is, next June.[2]

But instead of being settled, matters actually became much worse.
Correspondence and transcriptions of meetings with Chinese officials were
carefully kept by Patience, recording details of two serious misunderstand-
ings, the first relating to the general principle of assistance for foreign staff
returning home, and the second, to accusations that the Edneys had misap-
propriated £800, given to them before they left England. Due to the
complexities of currency exchange between China and the rest of the world,
this money had been sent from the Chinese via Czech comrades and then,
the British Communist Party. When finally the sum had been handed over
to Eric and Patience, it was on the understanding that the money was to
cover their financial commitments in England while they were away, such
as their mortgage repayments and Eric's alimony payments to his first wife,
plus money for their journey. Despite the fact that they had asked for confirmation of this arrangement several times after arriving in China, they had
heard nothing further about the matter. Now the Chinese were insisting
that the money had only been loaned to them and should have been
deducted from their salaries. This had never been done, so repayment was
being demanded as a lump sum, a very large amount to find in those days.
Patience and Eric did not have the funds available to meet this demand.
Believing that they were staying till the following June, they had spent
their savings on tickets for Eric's daughter Katie to visit them during the
summer holidays. Then suddenly, they had then been told by the Foreign
Languages Press that they should leave almost immediately, six months
earlier than previously stated.

On 30 November 1957, Patience and Eric met with Feng Hsi-liang and
Lo Liang. Feng's manner was hostile and dismissive as he reiterated the official view that 'The £800 should have been repaid, and we think it should
still be repaid out of your salary.' Lo was rather more conciliatory, but both
seemed resentful of the fact that as foreigners, the Edneys had been paid
more than their Chinese colleagues. The acrimonious tone of the meeting
caused Patience great distress, as a short extract from the transcript reveals,

not only because of confusion about the date of their departure, but also due to the insinuation that they had been involved in some sort of financial chicanery.

> *Patience:* Once this spring and once last year, Comrade Yang Chen-fang was very much surprised at my raising the question of our going home at all. He said it was not a matter for me to decide. When I said that we had always understood that we were only here for four years, he was very surprised at that too. . . . I was very surprised that Comrade Yang seemed to think that any time limit was none of our business – that we were simply sent under orders. . . .
>
> *Eric:* I find it very strange that all this financial matter has been allowed to drift until this date – three and a half years after we arrived in China. We took the very first opportunity of raising it – the very day we arrived, and on many occasions later. And we took the first opportunity of reporting back to the Party in Britain that we had done so, and the fact that we had got no results. My own conscience on this matter is absolutely clear.
>
> *Feng:* Well, if you have any other questions, you can raise them with the leadership.
>
> *Comrade Feng left.*
>
> *Lo: {to Patience}* If you are not satisfied with anything, you can take it up with the leadership.
>
> *Patience:* Comrade Lo Liang: be human. Of course I am not satisfied. How would you feel if you had virtually been accused of embezzling sums of Party money? No, of course I am not satisfied.

Nan Green demonstrated her sterling qualities of reliability and dogged determination by taking up their case and arguing for clarification of the matters of principle involved that would also affect other foreign employees. She sent several letters and spoke at length with the comrades of the Liaison Bureau pointing out that had the Edneys known they were going to be sent home so soon, they would have saved more and not spent money on Katie's visit. The Bureau attempted to offload the problem on to the Foreign Languages Press (FLP) or the CPGB, but Nan was not so easily put off and fought valiantly again on their behalf.

> *Nan:* We don't think this is a matter for the FLP. It is a question of principle. And there is not much time. The principle is, are comrades returning to get 'notice' here or in their own countries. 'Notice' is no use here for finding jobs. They have no jobs in England. They have no 'refer-

15.1 Patience and Bobby out shopping, January 1957.

15.2 Patience and Bobby at Pentacho.

15.3 Group excursion with donkeys at Pei Hai To.

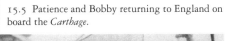

15.5 Patience and Bobby returning to England on board the *Carthage*.

15.4 Patience and a view from the temple, 1957.

ences'. Eric is not young. The CPGB will not have funds to support them
(it asks us for funds) and it may not be able to find them jobs either. If the
comrades had been told that this matter would be dependent on their
savings, they could have saved. We can all do that as long as we know.
Bureau: If they have financial difficulties they can ask the Party for help.
Nan: I have explained that they have difficulties. They don't want help.
They want to know what is the principle of the thing. Is it a principle that
comrades returning home should not receive any help to settle them in
their own country?[3]

Patience wrote a long and anguished letter to Betty Reid of the National
Organisation Department in the CPGB, explaining the whole sorry saga to
her at length. She admitted that the problem had been exacerbated to some
extent by Eric's difficult relationship with his employers and Chinese
Communist Party officials.

> An added complication is that Eric baffles them, originally with his
> accent, and subsequently with his British working-class reaction to
> things, so that everything is done through me, and I often have to carry
> messages to Eric which he doesn't agree with.[4]

The support of Nan and her husband had been crucial when they had
been faced with unjust accusations.

> I was very heartened to find how kind and sensible Nan Green and her
> husband were. We went straight round the night after, not knowing quite
> what had hit us, and Ted's sterling commonsense made me want to cry.[5]

After raising the practical issues to be resolved, Patience made her attitude to their difficulties clear.

> Now nothing I've said has to be taken to mean that we are not heartbroken
> at all the mess, I rather less than Eric because I'm only an accessory in that
> old-fashioned, feudal way they have here. Eric has nothing like the crimes
> on him that he is accused of, but both of us take full responsibility and
> are very sorry. We tried and tried not to do the wrong thing, but in the
> end just being was wrong. I don't have to tell you that none of all this has
> been said or even hinted at to anyone who has been here, nor will it be
> said to anyone after our return. It's a very nasty little molehill, but we
> don't propose to make a mountain out of it.[6]

After Nan Green's intervention on their behalf, the matter was referred to Wu Wen-tao. At a subsequent meeting in early December, the atmosphere had changed completely. Wu Wen-tao had succeeded in discovering the source of the misunderstanding and was full of apologies for the 'inconvenience it has caused you comrades'. Embarrassed, he admitted there had been 'shortcomings' over the matter and promised that regulations would be worked out for future cases. 'We hope that you comrades will also help us with criticisms and suggestions so that we can improve.' Patience, still unhappy about the accusations that had been made against them, offered to continue 'polishing' translations after returning to England to help to pay any outstanding debt, but it was made clear that it was not necessary to repay the £800 as had been previously stated, and that they would be given help to arrange their journey home.[7]

Eric's comments to Wu Wen-tao on this occasion reflect his unease at the disparity in the salaries earned by the foreigners and the Chinese, so pointedly remarked upon by Feng Hsi-liang and Lo Liang at the earlier meeting. As already noted, 'privilege' was used as a manner of re-enforcing the divisions between the Chinese and other nationalities. Eric had been concerned for some time about the salaries for foreign employees, thinking them too large, saying that they 'put a barrier between us and the Chinese comrades'. He had discussed this with some of the other British employees, and had wanted to raise the matter officially, but had been told not to do so, because the 'Chinese Party took everything into consideration when fixing salaries'. However 'comradely and helpful' their meeting had been that day, it was a pity, said Eric, that they had not had such talks in the past as it would have saved a lot of trouble, and also saved the Chinese Party expense. Being so overpaid, many of them had given large sums to the British Party and *Daily Worker*. This was all very nice, explained Eric, but should not have been done at the expense of the Chinese Party. He believed most comrades from Britain would welcome frank discussion on salaries and possible readjustment downward in many cases. 'In any case', he added according to the transcript, 'if today's meeting had done anything to improve relationships, it would have been well worth while.'[8]

At the end of December, another document records assurances from representatives of the Bureau of Experts' Affairs about arrangements that had been made for financing the Edneys' journey home. A small resettlement sum would be paid into their bank account in England. Once again, it was stressed that the accusations against them had been made in error.

When the Edneys came to China, £800 was sent to the CPGB for their family commitments and part travelling expenses. THIS MONEY WAS

PROPERLY USED. Due to a misunderstanding we did not get this clear. We regret this misunderstanding. I repeat: we know that the money was properly used, and the misunderstanding has been cleared up.[9]

During Katie's visit, this unpleasant and stressful business had been kept firmly under wraps. 'Of course,' Patience told Betty Reid, 'we gave her the impression that all was sweetness and light.'[10] Poor Katie, now aged thirteen, was naturally 'madly jealous' of the new rival for her father's affections. Bobby, however, was accustomed to the idea of large Chinese families and was thrilled to have a sister. When she had first arrived, in typical teenage fashion, Katie, as her new step-mother commented, was 'determined not to be impressed by anything, or else is not impressed or indeed open to impressions'.[11] During the last week, however, she had apparently decided to make the best of the situation and matters improved.

Patience had been considering for some time the possibility of having another baby, but now discovered medical reasons that made a further pregnancy inadvisable. During a check up, she managed to see her delivery notes, and found that half had been written in English. Her records stated that she had suffered from the dangerous and potentially fatal complication of childbirth known as pre-eclampsia, and that her blood pressure had gone up alarmingly after the delivery. 'I knew I was poorly but I have been frightened retrospectively now!'[12] Worried about how they would manage to remain afloat financially on their return to England, Patience decided that she had more than enough to cope with already, without further additions to the family.

As the date for departure grew nearer, Patience began to feel really homesick. Nevertheless, rather than travel back as quickly as possible, she hoped that a few days in Canton and Hong Kong, followed by a slow boat home, would give her the opportunity to see a bit more of the country. She had told Betty Reid how restricted their opportunities for travel had been.

> None of the wretched foreigners here have seen so much as a measly factory for the past eighteen months or even had a duty trip to a farm. It will be nice to have something in China to talk about favourably and forget the nasty block we live in, to say that it's fun working for a people's democracy.[13]

Even more importantly, the slow voyage would give her the chance to rest and recover from the worries that had left her almost numb with exhaustion. However, one short trip towards the end of her stay had been possible, and Patience remembered this particular October day she had spent with her son with great pleasure. Like thousands of other people, Hilary and Patience had read books by Ann Bridge, internationally famous for her novels that combined romantic fiction with a well-researched perspective on foreign cultures and an inside view of certain key historical events. Ann Bridge in reality was Lady Mary Dolling Sanders O'Mally, the wife of a British diplomat who had lived in Peking in the 1930s. One of her books, *Peking Picnic*, would have been of particular interest to Patience.[14]

We had the most heavenly outing to a temple in the hills, one of the temples that comes into Ann Bridge. There is now a magnificent mountain road to it, right inside the mountains. The trees were changing colour and the sun was hot as hot and the persimmon trees looked like Christmas trees, bare crooked branches covered with golden shiny fruits, and winnowing and harvest all over the place, heaps of corn cobs thrashed and un-thrashed and whole cobs drying under the eaves like Spain. Bobby loved it, and Sao Pang, a four-year old, who has a passion for persimmons, had never seen them growing before and felt that it ought to be kept a secret that such glorious things existed, otherwise everyone would go and take them. They were terribly cheap there – practically nothing for the eight months' work it is to grow them. They're cheap enough here in town but most of the cost is for carriage and selling. Bobby was a great hit with the local peasants who came up in a business like way to sell persimmons, walnuts and eggs. I was also offered two live chickens but felt I couldn't cope with them on the long ride back with Bobby. It is a most lovely temple, all cleaned up now, but still lonely and sleepy, with exhibition 'Crysanths' in big pots and gingko trees and huge statues and room after room of Buddhas and door gods and dead abbots. It has a magic spring which comes out of a dragon's mouth, runs round a little courtyard in an open mazy drain and is then piped with prehistoric pipes through every courtyard and then across the moat, like a Roman or a Moorish aqueduct, down to the village below. The little courtyard with the water maze was where the emperor used to sit and float his wine cup to cool the wine. One of the emperors who enlarged and rebuilt it about 1500 retired from the world there, but it was rather a worldly retirement from the world, he took his wives etc. An emperor's daughter before him was a very holy nun there who spent her whole life praying in front of one of the Buddhas, never moving, there are two holes in the floor (marble) where she knelt.[15]

Then came the frantic business of packing up their lives for the journey home. The final farewells were not easy, as Patience explained in a long letter to Hilary when once on board ship.

> I only stopped crying in Hong Kong as we kept on having send offs and everyone was so lamblike. A huge send off at the station, and poor Aunty Gwang out of control, it was dreadful. I hope she is now basking in three months' pay etc, plus perks and masses of photographs in her village.

The month-long voyage home on the Carthage P&O gave Patience time to reflect on the changes in her perspective after four years in China.

> Hong Kong is really beautiful but man is very vile. Goodness how horrid capitalism is, also American cultural oppression, also beggars, poor things.

In comparison with travelling in China where such efforts had been made to offer a good level of service, P&O standards were a dismal failure.

> Goodness, did I feel the draught on this boat straight away. No smoking in dining room, stewards didn't help with children, children not allowed in tea room, you can't sit here, no meals kept if your child won't go to sleep, you'll get good service if you tip . . .

Two-year old Bobby was excited by everything and was soon adapting to the change of language. 'He is talking only English already' wrote Patience, 'and we know he _is_ forward as he talks like a four year old and picks up new long words all the time, in context.'

Patience also had plenty of time to observe her fellow passengers, describing them to Hilary as distinctly 'second class'.

> There is a comic silence here when we say we came from Peking, but now about half the people come up to be friendly, and the other half with avid curiosity. Of course they can't make me out with my obvious upper class accent, but I'm used to that.

Being once again back in a British social environment after living in China, Patience was struck by the racist attitude of the woman in charge of the nursery.

> She said 'Isn't it fortunate he turned out fair', as though Chinese colouring is catching _and_ unfortunate. Also, 'Was there anyone there for the poor

little thing to talk to?' And when I said yes, 600 million, she said, 'No, I meant nice people . . .'

Always strongly anti-racist and keen to defend the rights of the workers, Patience nevertheless manages to combine these sentiments with a remarkable degree of snobbery when faced with the reality of the great mass of ordinary British citizens.

> I thought I would enjoy relaxing in a less rarefied atmosphere than I have been in, but what with these lower middle class types and the P&O undiluted exploitation of passengers and crew I don't.[16]

Patience had told me how she and her sister always pigeonholed people by class moments after they had opened their mouths. They had learnt this skill as young girls and the habit was so ingrained it had become second nature. Without doubt, many of those from a similar background to Patience would have considered her a traitor to her own class. She had become a member of the Communist Party and had worked for years to put an end to class-based society. This did not mean, however, that she rejected *all* the values of her class. A biographer has the power of selection and must tread carefully the path between hagiography and hatchet job. How easy to omit character traits of someone you admire that could be considered unattractive or no longer politically correct. I decided to include Patience's comments on her fellow passengers. The richness of her individual personality is to be found through an awareness of her inconsistencies and foibles as well as her strengths.

Patience arrived home on 18 February 1958, her experiences in China having opened up a wider world for her, not just because of the sights she had seen, or through living and working in a communist country, but also because she had felt the range of emotions from adoration to anguish that are part of motherhood. She wrote later 'I wouldn't have missed those four years for anything.'[17]

16

Reprise

Thirty years after the Spanish civil war, the writer, Josephine Herbst, went to a showing of *Morir en Madrid* – To Die in Madrid – the film by Frédéric Rossif. As she watched the stark black and white documentary footage of death and destruction, the memories of her time in Spain came flooding back and she felt as if she too were dying, or indeed, that she had died.

> . . . it came to me that in the most real sense my most vital life did indeed end with Spain. Nothing so vital, either in my personal life or in the life of the world, has ever come again. And in a deep sense, it has all been a shadow picture for years and years . . . most of the time since then has been lived on buried treasure of earlier years, on a kind of bounty I could still take nourishment from.[1]

Patience would almost certainly have seen the film when it was released in the 1960s. Might she have felt the same? Friends who knew her well in later years remarked that Spain always seemed to have a hold, like a clenched fist, over her heart.[2] Towards the end of her life, the ties that bound her to other old comrades in the International Brigade Association grew stronger, rather than weaker, as public awareness of the Brigaders' role in the war increased, first in Britain, then finally, at long last, in Spain.

The years between her homecoming from China and the only return visit she ever made to Spain, although less dramatic than her earlier years had been, were certainly not without incident. After she returned from China, Patience's life settled for a while into the more hum-drum routine of being a housewife, nursing her bed-bound mother, and bringing up her child. Eric found work, firstly for the German news agency, ADN, then from 1966 till his retirement, on the editorial staff of the *Soviet Weekly*.[3] But when her marriage eventually came to an end after almost eighteen years, Patience had to face both emotional and financial upheavals. Eric and Patience had always seemed an unlikely couple; even their son thought it 'weird beyond belief' that they ever got together.[4] Nowadays, Eric might well have been diagnosed as suffering from one of the syndromes within the autistic spectrum. Enormously intelligent but socially inept, intensely absorbed in his special interests but lacking imagination and frequently depressed, he seems to have shown many of the typical behavioural patterns associated with such disorders.

Patience told her neighbour, Pauline Paucker, that Eric was becoming 'odder and odder', and 'wouldn't come out of his room'. The cause of this behavioural change may well have stemmed from the fact that Eric was bisexual. Coming to terms with this must have been extremely difficult both for Eric and for Patience. Not surprisingly, she never said much about it during interviews. Pauline was sympathetic when Patience told her the news of Eric's departure in 1973, 'Now he's asked for his Russian library and he's off, and I have to get some money somehow.'[5]

> Patience was selling inherited pieces of very fine furniture and her own collection of books, and wanted my opinion as to their value. All her father's publications were to go, children's books illustrated with colour-printed woodblocks of the Evans kind, really nice; it was very sad, I thought, that she had to lose these.[6]

Eric went to live with a man much younger than himself, Francis Youling, who had been partially disabled in the Korean war where he had earned distinction for his bravery. Eric effectively took on the role of his carer for many years. Bob continued to see his father occasionally and found him to be happier than he'd ever known him to be before.[7] With her customary skill in practicalities, when Eric died in 1989 it was Patience who managed to organise residential care for Francis in a hostel for distinguished members of the armed forces.[8]

Following her separation from Eric, Patience managed to pick up the pieces of her life yet again, but the numerous CVs and copies of letters for applying for jobs indicate that it was far from easy. Bob was still at school and she was now almost sixty years old with no recent employment experience. At first, she managed to find work as a part-time dietician and cook in an old people's home in Hampstead. Then came several years of employment by the Schools Council, first as an assistant in the library, then as cataloguer of their small specialist library.[9] In 1974, when Bob went to Cambridge University to read Natural Sciences, Patience continued to work, cataloguing an exhibition for the Schools Council, until in 1976 she was made redundant.[10]

Meanwhile, after almost forty years of dictatorship, the death of Franco in 1975 was having a huge impact on the lives of people in Spain. His much longed-for demise created waves that reached out to affect former

International Brigaders too. As Spain took the first steps towards creating a new democracy, the IBA took on a new aim. The focus moved to remembrance, to keep the memory of the International Brigades alive as a symbol in the on-going international fight against fascism. Whilst in Spain people were living through twenty-five years of the *pacto de olvido* – the tacit decision to forget the past, or rather, to turn a blind eye to it – in Britain, the process of preserving the memory of the war was beginning in earnest. The fortieth anniversary of the start of the civil war in the year following Franco's death took place at a time when oral history was growing in popularity. Projects to record interviews with those who had been involved with the war in Spain were begun by various institutions.[11] Media interest gradually increased as each anniversary went by, resulting in articles based on the personal recollections of individual Brigaders. Some of the veterans had already written their memoirs with a retrospective perspective, and now, through talking to historians, students and journalists, many others found that the time was ripe for reflection.[12] Patience was amongst them, saying in an interview in 1984:

> You know, when you go out when you're young to a thing like that, everything, one thing after the other, just happens, and in lots of things you feel, 'That's the way it is', and you don't draw conclusions until afterwards.[13]

There was certainly a great deal to reflect upon, not least, the commitment to communism that Patience and the majority of the Brigaders had made in the 1930s. The horrendous truths that had emerged of mass repression and annihilation under Stalin, Soviet expansionist policies, and the violence of the Cultural Revolution in China, were amongst the many issues of concern for British Communists. Nan Green wrote of the 'painful process of real thinking' that was required to 'unlearn blind faith' in the Communist Party and the Soviet Union. For her it was a slow change, beginning with the Nazi–Soviet pact, and ending with the final realisation that there were many Soviet acts that could not be defended.[14] Patience endured the same dreary rain of disappointment and disillusion, regretting that the CPGB had depended to such an extent on the Soviet Union, inevitably being damaged by the failures of socialism there.[15] She was still struggling on as a Party member in 1994, but it was far cry from her youthful ideals.

> I belong to two things – the Democratic Left, which I despise like I don't know what, and I belong to what's called the Communist Party of Camden. But you see, it's a contradiction in terms and we can't really be

16.1 Patience and members of the International Brigade Association committee at the Marx Memorial Library, 1996. (Seated from left to right, John Dunlop, Len Crome, Dave Marshall and Patience; standing from left to right, Dave Goodman, Bill Alexander, Simon Hirschman, John Longstaff.)

16.2 Patience and Bill Alexander at the IBA Memorial, Jubilee Gardens, London.

16.3 Patience at the unveiling of the IBA Memorial with Margaret Powell and Lillian Urmston, Jubilee Gardens, London, 5 October 1985.

16.4 Arganda Bridge crowds, 1996.

16.5 Patience with Angela Jackson, Arganda Bridge, 1996.

16.6 Photo of Patience from the obituary in *El Periódico*, 'Morir en Madrid'.

anything. We still call ourselves Communists and we're split into dozens
of splinter groups. And quite a lot of them are the rather fierce ones who
think that the Soviet Union was right all the time – that all the wrong
things about the Soviet Union were right – we had terrible arguments
with them.[16]

Whilst satisfaction in the implementation of communist theories dimin-
ished, for Patience and Nan and many others who had served in the
International Brigades, pride in the role they had played in the Spanish civil
war continued to be sustained. 'What a fortunate group we were, those who
went to Spain,' wrote Nan in her memoirs, 'with a clear, uncomplicated
cause that has remained untarnished to this day.'[17] Patience too, looked
back at those days and remembered the triumphs rather than the tensions;
a shift in perception that differs notably from the views expressed in her
letters from the 1930s. When asked how the different nationalities within
the medical unit got along, she replied,

I remember it only as a great enormous group of marvellous friends – all
of you working together and all of you respecting and honouring one
another.[18]

Patience remained closely involved with the work of the International
Brigade Association, working on the committee for many years and
eventually, despite her dislike of mathematics, became the treasurer.

For those who actually experienced the events of the war, commemorative meetings are not only about the past, they are also about continuing to
live with the memories. Their importance as an occasion for public decla-
rations is matched by their value as a space for private interactions.
However, Patience rejected the idea of joining the other veterans when they
were invited to return to Spain in the 1980s. Her words illustrate not only
her concern for the feelings of her comrades, but also the relatively low value
she places on her own part in the war, with its not inconsiderable adversi-
ties, such as the facial injuries she received when thrown through the
windscreen of a lorry.

I wouldn't go when Franco was there, and when the Brigaders went back
you see, people make an awful lot of fuss about nurses and the chaps were
looking forward to it so terribly, you know, this was going to be their
welcome back, their recognition, and I had a terrible feeling – in the first
place, there are a lot of ghosts for me in Spain and I hadn't got anyone in
particular to go with who would know that [pause] and some places I

wouldn't like to go back to, it had too many memories [pause]. I knew
the Spaniards would be marvellous to them – to us, but that if there was
a nurse, they make a terrible fuss of us and this wouldn't be fair, the chaps
were so looking forward to this enormous 'do' . . . Mind you, I'm very
proud of having been an International Brigader and having a pay book and
so on, but one does get much more attention, and it was they who did all
the fighting – the chaps – much worse for them.[19]

But much more can be understood on closer examination of this passage
from the interview. During the pauses, with hindsight, it becomes clear that
she is slipping away from the present into a past she had shared with Robert.
Although in the many interviews she had given over the years Patience did
not mentioned him by name, privately, with close friends, she occasionally
alluded to her lost love.[20] Once, during a power cut at Oval Road, Patience's
neighbour, Arno Paucker, had been singing civil war songs to her down the
telephone to keep her spirits up in the dark. His wife recalled that when he
began to sing the 'Peat Bog Soldiers', one of the most popular marching
songs amongst the German Brigaders, Patience had asked him to stop.

> He'd reached the *Moorsoldaten* – but here she said, "No, not that, it makes
> me weep. My lover was German and he was killed on the Ebro. He was a
> German Jew."[21]

Although Patience had said that Spain held too many 'ghosts' for her to
ever want to return, by 1996 she had changed her mind and decided to
accept an invitation to attend the international 'Homage to the Brigaders'
in commemoration of the sixtieth anniversary of the war in Spain. In a newspaper interview shortly before leaving, she spoke publicly, for the first and
last time, of why she had been so reluctant to return.

> The memories upset me terribly . . . A chap I was deeply in love with, a
> German, was killed on the Ebro. I'm going to make efforts not to go back
> to all those places where I was with him.[22]

The journey that Patience made to Spain in November 1996 therefore
represented not only the reprise of an early formative experience, but also a
courageous decision to face the pain of re-living the past.

Despite poor health and frustration with the limitations of age, or
perhaps because of those very reasons, she rejected medical advice to stay at
home, determined to take part in the 'Homage'.[23] She felt that this time,
the Brigaders were returning at the request of the Spanish people. At long

last, the Spanish government was going to fulfil the promise made to the Brigaders by the Republican prime minister in 1938 and award them Spanish citizenship. The ceremony in the Madrid parliament buildings was to be part of a packed programme of commemorative events lasting several days. A large group of British veterans were making the trip, many of them accompanied by their families. Patience's son Bob agreed to go with her, unsure of whether or not he was doing the right thing by helping her to go when she so frail. I, too, was a member of the group, by now having made good friends amongst the Brigaders as a result of my research on the involvement of British women with the war. The organisers had invited me stay in the same hotel as all the veterans as a translator and general dogsbody. I was delighted to be able to take part in the historic occasion and help in any way I could.

In truth, the logistics of the event were daunting. Coachloads of veterans from all over the world, many in wheelchairs, had to be transported from one tribute to another. The organisation may have been shambolic, but the atmosphere was exhilarating. It was like living in a slightly surreal theatrical production. The overture took place at the airport where the veterans were greeted with banners and embraces. The opening act took place a few miles southeast of Madrid, by the old Arganda Bridge. During the civil war, the narrow iron span crossing the waters of the Jarama River had linked the capital city with Valencia and the rest of Republican Spain, but the price paid to defend it had been high. The International Brigades, including the British Battalion, fought alongside the Republican troops at Jarama in February 1937. Of the 500 British volunteers that had gone into battle on the first day, as many as 136 were killed, a similar number wounded, leaving less than half the battalion on their feet.

By 1996, the bridge was no longer a vital artery for the city. It still stood, but severed from the main road; a monument to the past, bypassed by a new superhighway. But on this bright November day, the obsolete bridge was subject to another assault, this time a peaceful one. I didn't count the coaches that brought the veterans, but someone did – there were apparently eighteen of them, plus two ambulances. Convoys of cars jammed the road with all the people who wanted to pay tribute to the veterans. While new arrivals were decanted, crowds thronged across the bridge, even though there was nowhere to go except to the other side and back again. Patience sat in her wheelchair in the sunshine, seeming a little bemused at all the commotion. We chatted from time to time, between the interminable speeches that were made to inaugurate a new memorial to International Brigades, a large iron three-pointed star – the symbol of the Brigades.

Later that day, at the concert held in honour of the veterans at the Palace of Sports in Madrid, the arrival of the Brigaders was greeted with thunderous applause. Shouts of *No pasarán* reverberated from the rafters till throats were raw. Well-known singers sang flamenco and folksongs from the heart. Poets and actors declaimed with oratorical gusto. But perhaps it was when the original recordings of the songs from the civil war were played that Brigaders and audience alike were moved most of all. At the end of the concert, while the old tunes were still playing, the Brigaders were asked to go up on the stage where the crowd would be able to see them and show their appreciation. As the old soldiers made their way shakily to the stage, a Spanish friend pointed out that there were no women amongst them, all were men. We asked Patience if she would like to go up too. Clearly, there should be at least one woman to represent all the nurses who had worked in Spain. She agreed. As we made our way through the crowd, I could see that Patience had been right – people did love to make a fuss of the nurses. So many people wanted to kiss her as she passed by that it took us several minutes to reach the platform. I helped her on to the stage so she could stand with the other Brigaders as the crowd cheered and chanted. A television camera swung overhead, sweeping around and above the veterans to record their faces, filled with emotion, and transmit them to the viewers all over Spain. Someone sent me a copy of the programme later. There she is, in the last few frames, in the midst of old comrades, smiling happily but somehow remote from them all.

The next morning, she was admitted into hospital, impossible to rouse from sleep and slipping deeper into unconsciousness. I was at the hospital with Patience and her son throughout the following night. She never fully regained consciousness but held tightly onto my hand. Perhaps there was some comfort in it. If not for her, then for me. I wondered how many times she had held the hand of someone as they lay dying during the long nights in Spain. The next day, 6 November 1996, aged eighty-five, she died.

The symbolism of her death was recognised in the newspaper report, *Morir en Madrid*, 'To Die in Madrid', published two days later. The title of one of the most famous documentaries made on the Spanish war was now a headline for her obituary.[24] If there were ghosts waiting for Patience in Spain, she had gone to join them.

I thought of Patience dying in Madrid when I read a letter she had written to Robert only a few days before he died. One particular passage stood out – one in which she was regretting that they had spent so much time apart.

When we are together again we will make up for it. We will rest and eat, and eat and rest; occasionally, we will talk. But most of the time you will

be in my arms and we will just make love, and argue. We may go so far
as to kill a few lice now and again. My arms are aching to hold you, dearest.
I do want you so much. I am going nearly mad waiting here.
Your Patience[25]

17

'Patience on a Monument, Smiling at Grief'?

But Patience's death does not take us quite to the end of her story. One last act of the drama remained, to bring down the curtain on a poignant finale.

Patience's body was flown back to England for a funeral some days later. In the tradition of the International Brigade veterans from Spain, the flag of the British Battalion was draped over her coffin. The packed room listened as Bill Alexander, former Commander of the Battalion and head of the IBA spoke of the work she had done in Spain. David Crook had sent a letter to be read out by his son about her time in China, and Councillor Gloria Lazenby spoke about Patience's recent work to place a plaque to the Brigaders in Camden Town Hall. Bob spoke about her role as mother and grandmother, mentioning that he had known almost nothing about the man he had been named after, only recently discovering that Patience had been married to his namesake in Spain. He had intended to ask her more about it on the way back to England. As she had requested, *Freiheit!* the song of the Thaelmann Battalion, was played during the ceremony.

But while the farewell was being played out in public, a duty had been fulfilled in private behind the scenes. Years afterwards, I read the final moving postscript to Patience's remarkable life in the short memoir that her neighbour, Pauline Paucker, had written after the funeral.

> Later, I heard from another, disapproving, neighbour who is a friend of Patience's sister, that detailed instructions in Patience's will for the conduct of her funeral stated that her husband's blood-stained uniform greatcoat, which she had brought back from Spain, was to be wrapped round her body and cremated with her. 'A horrible task!' my informant said. 'Her poor sister, having to find it and drag it to the undertaker's – and it was heavy!' I thought it was a beautiful gesture.[1]

Though in some ways macabre, the story demonstrates that Patience had a clear sense of the importance of symbolic acts, whether private or public.

She would probably have approved of the small private ceremony of closure that took place when Bob and his family took her ashes to Spain and scattered them in the cave where she had worked as a nurse during the Battle of the Ebro. Patience certainly was well aware of the value of public remembrance as an instrument for transmitting a message, taking part in the process of memorialisation herself, both as icon and activist.

When the sixtieth anniversary was approaching, a book was prepared to commemorate the occasion entitled, *Memorials of the Spanish Civil War*, dedicated to the subject of remembrance. The richly illustrated book gave the stories leading up to the unveiling of nearly forty memorials throughout Britain, honouring the volunteers who served in Spain.[2] One of the photographs shows Patience nursing in Spain, an image that seems to epitomise the notion of the nurse as a 'healing angel'. Gently bending over the wounded man to instruct a Spanish girl in the skills of nursing, she is bathed in a radiant light from a nearby window. Also included in the book is a photograph taken at the inauguration of the plaque for the International Brigaders in Camden Town Hall in 1995. Patience, no longer young, is shown gazing at the plaque she has unveiled, reading the words that have resounded through her life, now etched boldly in brass before her, ¡NO PASARÁN![3] In effect, she too is included on all the plaques and memorials to the International Brigades in Britain and Spain. In the cave near la Bisbal de Falset, a plaque in memory of the British medical personnel includes the photograph of her at work as a nurse in Spain: 'Patience on a monument' in one, very literal, sense.

There is no doubt that Patience in some ways wished to live a life that would compensate for Robert's death. In the final interview before her return to Spain, when she spoke of Robert publicly at last, she had added, 'His death altered my life, but I've tried to make up for it.'[4] Sentiment, sorrow, survivor guilt, all were implicit in her statement. How had she lived her life? 'Like Patience on a monument, smiling at grief?' Shakespeare puts these words in the mouth of Viola, who addresses the well-known lines to Orsino, the man she loves. She is speaking of herself, but pretends to be talking of an imaginary sister, comparing her to the stone allegorical figure of Patience which often adorned Renaissance tombstones.

> She never told her love,
> But let concealment, like a worm i' the bud,
> Feed on her damask cheek: she pined in thought
> And with a green and yellow melancholy
> She sat like Patience on a monument
> Smiling at grief.[5]

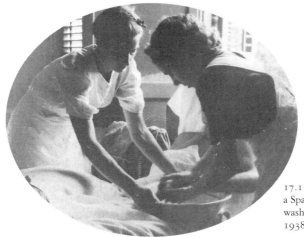

17.1 Patience teaching a Spanish girl how to wash a patient, Valls, 1938.

17.2 Patience unveiling a plaque in memory of the International Brigades, Camden Town Hall, 1995.

17.3 Portrait of Patience at home, 1996, held in the National Portrait Gallery collection.

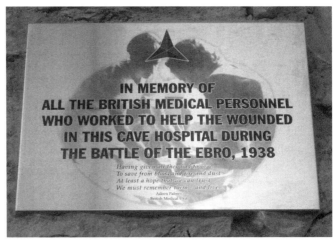

IN MEMORY OF
ALL THE BRITISH MEDICAL PERSONNEL
WHO WORKED TO HELP THE WOUNDED
IN THIS CAVE HOSPITAL DURING
THE BATTLE OF THE EBRO, 1938

*Having given all they had to save
To save from blood and fire and dust
At least a hope that we can trust
We must remember them — and live*
Aileen Palmer
British Medical Unit

17.4 Plaque in the cave hospital with an engraved picture of Patience.

   Viola sees her love for Orsino as serene, silent, and eternally enduring, but such passive notions would certainly not have suited Patience, despite her name. Patience 'concealed' her love for decades, but the extent to which she 'pined in thought' can only be surmised. That she continued to mourn the loss of Robert is evident from her statement to the journalist shortly before her death, and from a story told by her son. One day, Patience, at this time in her sixties, took out a boat on the Regent's canal together with half a dozen old friends from the Brigades. In the narrow darkness of one of the tunnels, the boat somehow capsized, tipping them all into the water. Patience had to keep afloat for about twenty minutes until another boat came along, but by then, she lacked the strength to climb in and her rescuers were unable to haul her aboard. She had to be towed out of the tunnel. An amusing anecdote in retrospect maybe, but an experience that was surely fraught with danger and very frightening at the time. Bob went to collect her from St Mary's hospital where she had been taken for a check-up after the ordeal, and was surprised to find that despite her rather harrowing experience, his mother's overriding emotion was one of anger at having lost her purse in the canal. She was 'livid' remembers Bob, because the purse had contained a photograph of Robert that she had been carrying round with her for years. Only later did he come to understand exactly why this keepsake from Spain had been so precious to her.[6]

   Patience worried she might die and Bob would have no family of his own, so she was delighted when he married and she became a grandmother – 'It's terrible not to have a family'. When asked if she was satisfied with her life, there were certain regrets, but Spain remained inviolable at the heart of her life.

> I'm not satisfied with my life, no. If I look back I think there were lots of things I should have done differently. I was very happy to have a son, but I ought to have married a different man. I don't regret having gone to China, but, on the other hand, there were so many complications there. . . . But it doesn't help to say, 'I shouldn't have done this or that.' That's no help to anyone. Only when I think of Spain, yes! I believe it was a wonderful thing to be able to feel so united. We – the International Brigaders – were so fortunate. We were so lucky that the Spaniards let us go to their country. We were so fortunate to be able to be with people who were committed to such a just cause, people who were really fighting against fascism.[7]

Though beset by melancholy at times, Patience was never disposed to sit and smile mawkishly at grief for long. Action was the answer. I only knew her when she was a very elderly lady, terrorising the pavements of Camden in her electric mobility scooter, but still with the same determination to 'do something' whenever the need arose, just as she had done when volunteering for Spain. And in writing this biography and reading her letters, I feel I have also come to know her as a young woman, caught up in the specific issues of the thirties and struggling with political commitment, though in some ways still very much like a young woman of today – a vibrant mixture of assertiveness and insecurity – writing to her lover and receiving a reassuring reply. Their words seem like dialogue taken from a play – all the world being a stage – a play in which the key acts are set in Spain.

> *Patience:*
> I dreamt last night that you had come
> And I went up to you to kiss you
> And you wouldn't let me: You said 'Not here.'
> I was terribly cross and said,
> 'I shall kiss you when I like.'
> But I was so angry that I woke up,
> So I don't know if I won,
> Or not.[8]

> *Robert:*
> Don't fear that your dream will be realized,
> That I'll be such a fool to say,
> Not here.[9]

I often think of Patience, standing on that stage in Madrid. But now, when I replay the event in my mind, it is suffused with an aura of symbolism to become the final performance in the drama of her life. The curtain descends. The audience rises. Thunderous applause greets the players as they each come forward to take a final bow. The leading lady is presented with an enormous bouquet in recognition of her work on behalf of the clamouring public. She inclines her head towards them graciously, knowing her part is now played, but that there will be new productions with other actors, on different stages. The show will go on.

Notes

I Portraying Patience

1 Patience Edney (PE), née Darton (PD), interview with Angela Jackson (AJ), 18 March 1994.

2 Recent studies cite the figure of 35,000 foreign volunteers, though not all were in Spain at the same time. Richard Baxell, *British Volunteers in the Spanish Civil War: The British Battalion in the International Brigades, 1936–1939* (London and New York: Routledge/Cañada Blanch Studies on Contemporary Spain, 2004), pp. 8–9.

3 The right-wing insurgents, led by Francisco Franco, chose to call themselves 'Nationalists'. Their coalition included the Spanish Fascist Party, the *Falange*. Patience always used the term 'fascists' when referring to Franco's supporters.

4 For more on the role of Spanish women during the war see Martha A. Ackelsberg, *Free Women of Spain: Anarchism and the Struggle for the Emancipation of Women* (Bloomington and Indianapolis: Indiana University Press, 1991), Mary Nash, *Defying Male Civilization: Women in the Spanish Civil War* (Colorado: Arden Press, 1994) and Shirley Mangini, *Memories of Resistance: Women's Voices from the Spanish Civil War* (New Haven and London: Yale University Press, 1995).

5 For a re-examination of Felicia Browne's participation in the war see Tom Buchanan, *History Workshop Journal* 54 (2002), also in *The Impact of the Spanish Civil War on Britain: War, Loss and Memory* (Brighton and Portland: Sussex Academic Press, 2007).

6 Exact numbers of women working for some time in Republican Spain are unknown. References to over seventy women from Britain who were working for some time in the medical and refugee services have been noted by the author. Jim Fyrth estimates that there were more than 170 English-speaking women volunteers involved in this type of work. Jim Fyrth and Sally Alexander (eds), *Women's Voices from the Spanish Civil War* (London: Lawrence & Wishart, 1991), p. 29, fn. 1.

Only one British nurse is known to have worked in the Nationalist hospitals. See Angela Jackson, *British Women and the Spanish Civil War*, (London and New York: Routledge/Cañada Blanch Studies on Contemporary Spain, 2002; paperback edition, Barcelona: Warren & Pell Publishing/Cañada Blanch Studies on Contemporary Spain, 2009) and Priscilla Scott-Ellis, (ed. Raymond Carr), *The Chances of Death: A Diary of the Spanish Civil War* (Norwich: Michael Russell, 1995).

7 For more information on the work of the Society of Friends, the 'Quakers', in

Spain see Farah Mendlesohn, *Quaker Relief Work in the Spanish Civil War* (New York: Edwin Mellen Press, 2002).

8 For more on the work of journalists and MPs such as the Duchess of Atholl, Ellen Wilkinson and Eleanor Rathbone, see Jackson, *British Women and the SCW*, Chapter 5.

9 For information on these campaigns in Britain see Jim Fyrth, *The Signal Was Spain: The Aid Spain Movement in Britain 1936–39* (London and New York: Lawrence and Wishart, 1986), and Jackson, *British Women and the SCW*, Chapter 3.

10 On 27 September 1938, Neville Chamberlain infamously declared in a radio broadcast about events in the Sudetenland and trenches being dug in a London central park, 'How horrible, fantastic it is that we should be digging trenches and trying on gas-masks here because of a quarrel in a far away country between people of whom we know nothing.'

11 My thanks to Bob Edney for allowing me to use his mother's letters and papers to write this biography.

2 Sniffing at Socialism

1 There were very few instances when the involvement of British women resulted from prior knowledge of the country and its problems. Exceptions include Winifred Bates and Helen Grant who had both visited Spain before the war. Felicia Browne was already in Barcelona when war broke out and joined one of the militias. Jackson, *British Women and the SCW*.

2 PE, short untitled memoir, p. 1. She was born on 27 August 1911.

3 Ibid., p. 2.

4 For more on the motivation of other women volunteers, see Jackson, *British Women and the SCW*, Chapter 2.

5 Wells, Gardner, Darton & Co.

6 PE, interview with AJ, 8 March 1996.

7 PE, memoir, p. 7.

8 Ibid., p. 2.

9 Patience was the second child, with one older brother and a younger sister and brother.

10 PE, memoir, p. 4.

11 Jackson, *British Women and the SCW*, Chapter 2.

12 PE, AJ, 8 March 1996.

13 PE, AJ, 18 March 1994.

14 PE, Sound Archive, Imperial War Museum, London (IWM), 8398.

15 PE, IWM 8398. The perspective of a scholarship girl on the segregation of those who were to receive free books can be found in an interview with Bessie Wild by Sue Bruley, 8 September 1977, during the research for a thesis, later published as *Leninism, Stalinism and the Women's Movement in Britain 1920–1939* (New York & London: Garland, 1986).

16 See Jackson, *British Women and the SCW*, Chapter 2.

17 Ibid. See especially Appendix II for references to the term 'composure', attributed to Graham Dawson and discussed by Penny Summerfield in *Reconstructing Women's Wartime Lives* (Manchester and New York: Manchester University Press, 1998) and by Alistair Thomson in *Anzac Memories: Living with the Legend* (Australia and New Zealand: Oxford University Press, 1994).

18 Jackson, *British Women and the SCW*, Chapter 2.

19 PE, AJ, 18 March 1994.

20 Ibid.

21 Ibid.

22 See the chapter on Patience Edney in the collection of interviews with women who went to Spain during the civil war by Petra Lataster-Czisch, *'Eigentlich rede ich nicht gern über mich.' (Lebenserinnegungen von Frauen aus dem Spanischen Bürgerkrieg 1936–1939)*, (Leizpzig und Weimar: Gustav Kiepenheurer Verlag, 1990), pp. 9–105.

23 PE, IWM 8398.

24 Ibid.

25 PE, Lataster-Czisch, *'Eigentlich rede ich nicht gern über mich.'*

26 PE, AJ, 18 March 1994.

27 Ibid.

28 For more on William Roberts and pacifism see Clive Barrett, *Pacifism in the Church of England, 1930–1937* (Leeds: University of Leeds Department of Theology and Religious Studies, 1997).

29 Sarah Miles, *Portrait of a Parson: William Corbett Roberts, Foreword by Storm Jameson* (London: George Allen and Unwin Ltd., 1955).

30 PE, IWM 8398.

31 PE, IWM 8398. She also goes on to make the interesting retrospective observation that although she didn't remember many men doing this, 'they made rather a lot of the men, now I come to think of it, the few who were there.'

32 Other examples are given in Jackson, *British Women and the SCW*, Chapters 2 and 6.

33 PE, IWM 8398.

34 Ibid.

35 Ibid.

36 PE, Lataster-Czisch, *'Eigentlich rede ich nicht gern über mich.'*

37 For further examples see Jackson, *British Women and the SCW*, Chapter 2, and Paul Preston, 'Nan Green: A Great Deal of Loneliness', *Doves of War: Four Women of Spain* (London: HarperCollins, 2002), pp. 121–201.

3 The Road to Spain

1 Margaret Mitchell 'The Effects of Unemployment on the Social Condition of Women and Children in the 1930s', *History Workshop Journal* 1985, 19, Spring, pp. 105–127, quoting Margery Spring Rice, *Working Class Wives* (London: 1981, 2nd edition), p. 19, fn. 1.

2 PE, AJ, 18 March 1994.

3 PE, IWM 8398.

4 PE, Lataster-Czisch, *'Eigentlich rede ich nicht gern über mich.'*

5 Ibid.

6 PE, IWM 8398.

7 Ibid.

8 PE, AJ, 8 March 1996.

9 PE, AJ, 18 March 1994.

10 PE, IWM 8398.

11 The situation changed when she joined the International Brigades serving within the Republican army after which she received 10 pesetas a day.

12 PE, IWM 8398.

13 Ibid.

14 Others who have made similar comments include for example, Rosaleen Smythe, Frida Stewart, Dorothy Rutter.

15 PE, letter to Michael Alpert, March 1982.

16 PE, IWM 8398.

17 PD, letter to Father Roberts, Hotel Pasionaria, Valencia, undated but the contents indicate it was written the day after her arrival.

18 Ibid.

4 Patients and Politics in Valencia

1 For example, Molly Murphy wrote of her train journey to Albacete, during which the nurses were singled out for a special welcome at every stop, and were repeatedly presented with oranges, grapes and dates. Molly Murphy, *Molly Murphy: Suffragette and Socialist* (Salford: Institute of Social Research, University of Salford, 1998), p. 134.

2 See previous chapter.

3 PE, IWM 8398.

4 'Balding, bespectacled and already married, Wintringham, while hardly handsome, had a romantic air,' writes Paul Preston in *We Saw Spain Die: Foreign Correspondents in the Spanish Civil War* (London: Constable, 2008), p. 105. For more on Kitty Bowler and Tom Wintringham, see his chapter 'Love and Politics: The Correspondents in Valencia and Barcelona', pp. 104–113.

5 After recovering in hospital in Valencia, Tom Wintringham served on Brigade Staff. He was wounded again in Quinto and invalided home in November 1937. During the Second World War, he established a school to train the Home Guard in guerrilla tactics.

6 Roser Valls (Coordinator), *Infermeres catalanes a la Guerra Civil espanyola* (Barcelona: University of Barcelona, 2008), p. 23.

7 PE, IWM 8398.

8 Ibid.

9 J.B.S. Haldane, a left-wing scientist and Professor of Biometry at University College London, became well known for his work on protection from gas attacks and prevention of civilian casualties during air raids.

10 PE, IWM 8398.

11 Preston, *We Saw Spain Die*, pp. 105–113.

12 PD, letter to Father Roberts, 22 March 1937, Hospital Pasionaria, Calle Segundo, Valencia.

13 Kate Mangan and Jan Kurzke, 'The Good Comrade', unpublished MS, Jan Kurzke Papers, Archives of the International Institute for Social History, Amsterdam. See also Preston, *We Saw Spain Die.*

14 Kate Mangan (née Foster) was born in Sedgley, Staffordshire in 1904. She married the Irish-American left-wing writer Sherry Mangan in 1931. They divorced in 1935.

15 Kate Mangan had a working knowledge of Spanish, having made several previous visits to Spain. Her sister was married to a Spaniard and Kate had lived in Mexico for some time with her first husband, Sherry Mangan.

16 Mangan 'The Good Comrade', p. 344.

17 Mangan, 'The Good Comrade', pp. 397–98. Kate Mangan changed many of the names when writing her memoirs, probably because at the time of writing, so soon after the war, she was anxious to protect people she had known.

18 Mangan, 'The Good Comrade', pp. 344 and 345–6.

19 PE, IWM 8398.

20 PD, undated notes, probably those she referred to in her letter to Father Roberts, 22 March 1937.

21 Sarah Miles, *Portrait of a Parson*, p. 68.

22 Peter Spencer, Viscount Churchill, was cousin to Winston Churchill. He was in Spain for almost two years, working with Spanish Medical Aid. His memoirs were published as *All My Sins Remembered* (London: William Heinemann, 1964).

23 Letter from PE to Michael Alpert, March 1982. See his article, 'Humanitarianism and Politics in the British Response to the Spanish Civil War 1936–1939', *European History Quarterly*, 14, 4 (1984).

24 Mangan, 'The Good Comrade', p. 407.

25 Ibid., p. 150.

26 Mangan, 'The Good Comrade', p. 352. For more on this episode see Preston, *We Saw Spain Die*, pp. 125–26.

27 Mangan, 'The Good Comrade', p. 352.

28 Mangan, 'The Good Comrade', p. 353.

29 PE, IWM 8398.

30 Mangan, 'The Good Comrade', p. 352.

31 Preston, *We Saw Spain Die*, p. 126.

32 Patience did not say whether the will was actually destroyed or not. However, Basil's mother was well aware of her son's feelings for Patience. See Chapter 12.

33 PE, IWM 8398.

34 See also Hugh Purcell, *The Last English Revolutionary: Tom Wintringham 1898–1949* (Stroud: Sutton Publishing, 2004), pp. 141–142.

35 Winifred Bates, 'Summary and critical survey of my work in Spain since the

outbreak of the war. Barcelona, September 1938', Moscow Archives 545/6/88.

36 PD, letter to Father Roberts, 13 June 1937, and 'Mish teas' in Miles, *Portrait of a Parson*, p. 67.

5 A Modern Woman Making Waves

1 Nurses working primarily with nationalities other than British include for example Penny Phelps, who ran a hospital when there was an outbreak of scarlet fever amongst the Italians of the 'Garibaldi' Battalion. See Penny Fyvel, *English Penny* (Ilfracombe, Devon: Arthur H. Stockwell, 1992), and Jackson, *British Women and the SCW*, Chapter 4.

2 The first hospital set up by the Committee had been in Grañen, but when this was handed over to the Spanish authorities in January 1937, the British nurses were moved together to the unit at Poleñino.

3 Bates, 'Summary and Critical Survey'.

4 Judith Keene, *'The Last Mile to Huesca: An Australian Nurse in the Spanish Civil War* (Kensington, Australia: New South Wales University Press, 1988), p. 12.

5 Ibid., Hodgson diary, 19 March 1937, p. 131.

6 Ibid., Hodgson diary, 18 March 1937, p. 130.

7 Ibid., Hodgson diary, 19 March 1937, p. 131.

8 Ibid., Hodgson diary, 16 June 1937, p. 142 and 21 June 1937, p. 145.

9 Margaret Powell, short untitled memoir, 13 July 1980. My thanks to her daughter, Ruth Muller, for a copy of this document.

10 Ibid.

11 Ibid.

12 PE, AJ, 18 March 1994.

13 PE, letter to Frida Knight (née Stewart), undated, in the personal papers of Frida Knight. The bonds between those who, like Patience and Frida had been in Republican Spain during the civil war, remain clear as the letter closes with the Spanish greeting 'Salud'.

14 PE, IWM 8398.

15 PE, AJ, 18 March 1994.

16 Aurora Fernández (m. Edenhoffer) short untitled memoir written in Prague, January 1983, International Brigade Archive, Marx Memorial Library, London, (MML), Box 29, D/9.

17 PD, letter to Robert Aaquist (RA), 22 July 1938. Nan Green was one of the British women who referred to the attitudes of Spanish women towards the medical staff, see Jackson, *British Women and the SCW*, Chapter 4.

18 Keene, *The Last Mile to Huesca*, Hodgson diary, 9 June 1937, p. 141.

19 PD, letter to Father Roberts, 13 June 1937.

20 Keene, *The Last Mile to Huesca*, Hodgson diary, 11 June 1937 and 12 June 1937, pp. 141–2. The *Canarias* was perhaps the most famous and active of the Nationalist heavy cruisers, entering service in September 1936 to carry out blockading, escorting and bombarding throughout the war.

21 Keene, *The Last Mile to Huesca*, Hodgson diary, 16 June 1937, p. 141.

22 Ibid., Hodgson diary, 24 June197, p. 145.
23 Ibid., Hodgson diary, 9 June 1937, p. 140.
24 PD, letter to Father Roberts, 13 June 1937, though she is uncertain of the exact day.
25 PE, AJ, 18 March 1994.
26 Fyrth, *The Signal was Spain*, p. 100, and PE, IWM 8398.
27 PD, letter to Father Roberts, 1 July 1937.
28 Keene, *The Last Mile to Huesca*, Hodgson diary, 16 July 1937, p. 150.
29 Ibid., Hodgson diary, 25 July 1937, p. 152.
30 Agnes Hodgson recorded seeing her there too during this period. Keene, *The Last Mile to Huesca*, Hodgson diary, 11 August 1937, p. 157
31 PD, letter to Father Roberts, 18 August 1937.
32 See Fyrth, *The Signal was Spain*, p. 88. The Committee agreed to this on 21 July 1937 and the decision was endorsed by a conference in September.
33 Agnes Hodgson records that the unit arrived in Fraga on 8 August 1937. Keene, *The Last Mile to Huesca*, p. 155.
34 PD, letter to Father Roberts, 18 August 1937.
35 Ibid.
36 Ibid.
37 PE, AJ, 18 March 1994.
38 PE, IWM 8398.
39 The bombing of Guernica in April 1937 by German planes is the most widely known early example of the heavy bombing of a civilian town. George Steer's reports were published in the Times and are reproduced in Preston, 'The Sentimental Adventurer: George Steer and the Quest for Lost Causes' in *We Saw Spain Die*, pp. 263–290. For another evaluation of Steer's work see Tom Buchanan, 'Journalism at war: George Lowther Steer, Guernica and the resistance to fascist aggression', in *The Impact of the Spanish Civil War on Britain*, pp. 23–42.
40 PE, IWM 8398.
41 Ibid. See also PE, Lataster-Czisch, *'Eigentlich rede ich nicht gern über mich'*, where Patience mentions that one of the doctors in this incident was Len Crome and that the other nurse who left with her was Lilian Urmston.
42 Margaret Powell, memoir.
43 PE, IWM 8398.
44 PD, letter to Father Roberts, 3 October 1937.
45 PE, AJ, 18 March 1994.
46 Ibid.
47 While working with the Garibaldis, Penny Phelps became their honorary medical officer for about two months and was given the rank of Lieutenant. Fyvel, *English Penny*, p. 38.
48 MASH units were the Mobile Surgical Army Hospitals used extensively by the Americans during the Korean War and subsequent conflicts.
49 For more on the development of triage, particularly by the surgeon Josep Trueta

during the Spanish Civil War, see Nicholas Coni, *Medicine and Warfare: Spain, 1936–1939* (London and New York: Routledge/Cañada Blanch Studies on Contemporary Spain, 2008), pp. 103–104.

50 For more on other medical advances in Spain see Coni, *Medicine and Warfare.*

51 Ibid.

52 PE, IWM 8398.

53 PE, AJ, 18 March 1994.

54 Ibid.

55 Ibid.

56 Spanish Medical Aid Committee (SMAC), Bulletin, May 1938. MML, Box 29/B/3.

57 Rosaleen Ross (née Smythe), interview with AJ, 10 April 1999.

58 SMAC, Bulletin, May 1938. MML, Box 29/B/3. Rosaleen Smythe's extract reproduced as 'Rain', in Fyrth and Alexander, *Women's Voices from the Spanish Civil War*, pp. 83–4.

59 PE, IWM 8398.

60 SMAC Bulletin, May 1938.

61 PE, AJ, 18 March 1994.

62 SMAC Bulletin, May 1938.

6 Blossoming Spring to Bitter Winter

1 Letter from RA read by his sister, Susie, in Eran Torbiner's documentary, *Madrid before Hanita* (2006).

2 Torbiner, *Madrid before Hanita.* The mostly socialist leadership of the Jewish Community in Palestine took great interest in the Spanish Civil War, and even expressed its support in fiery speeches. Yet the slogan of those days was 'First Hanita then Madrid' (Hanita was one of the overnight erected new settlements – the Zionist answer to the Arab Revolt). But the 300 volunteers who chose to fight for the Spanish Republic thought differently, because as internationalists they regarded Fascism to be the biggest threat, not only to the Jews, but to the world. They were often denigrated by the Zionist establishment for abandoning the national struggle in Palestine, and misunderstood by friends and family.

3 The Tschapaiew Battalion was part of the XIII (Dabrowski/Dombrowksi) Brigade. It was made up of volunteers of many nationalities: Ukrainian, Polish, Czechoslovakian, Bulgarian, Yugoslavian, Turkish, Italian, German, Austrian, Finnish, Swedish, Norwegian, Danish, Belgian, French, Greek, Albanian, Dutch, Swiss and Balts. See Anna Ananieva, *Alfred Kantorowicz: "Tschapaiew". Das Bataillon der 21 Nationen* in Bannasch and Holm, *Erinnern und Erzählen: Der spanische Bürgerkrieg in der deutschen und spanishen Lieratur und in den Bildmedien* (Essen: Klartext, 2005), pp. 191–208. The Edgar-André Battalion was part of the XI (Thaelmann) Brigade. Promotion mentioned in RA, letter to his family, 9 August 1937.

4 RA, letter to his family, 2 November 1937.

5 PD to Father Roberts, 13 July 1938.

6 Bates, 'Summary and Critical Survey'.

7 PE, IWM 8398.

8 PD to Father Roberts, 13 July 1938.

9 PE, IWM 8398.

10 SMAC, Bulletin, May 1938. MML, Box 29/B/3.

11 PD to Father Roberts, 13 July 1938.

12 RA, letter to his family, 22 January 1938.

13 Jim Fyrth records that under the overall command of Len Crome, Chief of the 35th Division Medical Services, the doctors at this time included Reggie Saxton, John Kiszely and Gerald Shirlaw, with an American, William Pike, assisting Crome with the administration. Amongst the nurses were Phyllis Hibbert, Dorothy Rutter, Lillian Urmston, Joan Purser and Patience Darton, with the South African Ada Hodson, the Australian Una Wilson, and two Americans, Esther Silverstone and Irene Golding. *The Signal was Spain*, p. 111. For more on Len Crome and Reggie Saxton see Paul Preston, 'Two doctors and one cause: Len Crome and Reginald Saxton in the International Brigades', *International Journal of Iberian Studies*, 19, 1 (2006), pp. 5–24.

14 PE, IWM 8398.

15 Ibid.

16 Margaret Powell (m. Lesser) in the television documentary, *Yesterday's Witness: A Cause Worth Fighting For* 1973. See www.spokenword.ac.uk

17 Lillian Urmston (m. Buckoke), interview with Stewart Rawnsley, 28 February 1978.

18 Aurora Fernández, memoir.

19 PE, AJ, 18 March 1994.

20 PE, IWM 8398.

21 RA to PD, 24.1.38.

22 PE, IWM 8398. The Republican army retreated from Teruel on 21 February 1938.

23 'Rot Front', Red Front salute.

24 PE, Lataster-Czisch, '*Eigentlich rede ich nicht gern über mich.*'

25 PD to Father Roberts, 13 July 1938.

26 PE, IWM 8398.

27 Ibid.

28 Ibid.

29 PE, AJ, 8 March 1996.

30 PE, AJ, 18 March 1994.

7 Retreat and Recovery

1 Hugh Thomas, *The Spanish Civil War* (London: Penguin Books, 1986; first published by Eyre & Spottiswode, 1961), p. 798.

2 RA to PD, 8 March 1938.

3 PD to RA, 9 March 1938.

4 *Chato* was the popular name for the Polikarpov I-15 biplane.

5 PE, AJ, 18 March 1994.

6 PE, IWM 8398.

7 PE, AJ, 18 March 1994. Such painful memories of injured children stand out vividly in the narratives of several nurses. See for example Fyvel, *English Penny*, p. 22, and Jackson, *British Women and the SCW*, Chapter 4.

8 PD to Father Roberts, 14 May 1938.

9 PE, IWM 8398, and AJ, 18 March 1994. For the perspective of a British nurse working on the other side of the lines on the use of morphia to hasten death see Scott-Ellis, *The Chances of Death*, p. 94.

10 Given that the focus of their work was on the patients, and the number of places in which they worked, this is not surprising. Ann Murray, the Scottish nurse who was at Poleñino with Patience, later worked on a hospital train and, when interviewed years later, had similar problems in recalling any place names. IWM 11318.

11 PE, IWM 8398.

12 See also Nan Green in Preston, 'Nan Green: A Great Deal of Loneliness', *Doves of War*, pp. 121–201, and Penny Phelps in Jackson, *British Women and the SCW*, Chapter 6.

13 RA to PD, 8 April 1938.

14 RA to PD, 9 April 1938.

15 Ibid.

16 PD to RA, 30 April 1938.

17 RA to PD, 26 April 1938.

18 RA to PD, 29 April 1938.

19 RA to PD, 9 April 1938.

20 RA to PD, 5 May 1938.

21 See Angela Jackson, *At the Margins of Mayhem: Prologue and Epilogue to the Last Great Battle of the Spanish Civil War* (Pontypool: Warren & Pell Publishing, 2008).

22 The term *Brigada Mixta* was the designated title within the Republican army for those Brigades containing both international volunteers and Spanish troops.

23 PE, IWM 8398.

24 PD to RA, 30 April 1938.

25 Postmarked 8 June 1938. 'Marsá' is the Castilian equivalent of the Catalan, 'Marçà'.

26 PD to RA, c.27 May 1938.

27 PD to RA, 30 April 1938.

28 For more on visitors and fiestas see Jackson, *At the Margins of Mayhem*, Chapter 4.

29 PD to RA, 1 May 1938.

30 PE, IWM 8398.

31 Scott-Ellis, *The Chances of Death*, pp. 68–9. Her father, Lord Howard de

Walden, had sent her the car. This allowed her to visit her childhood friends in the household of the Infante Alfonso d'Orleans Bourbon. For more on Priscilla Scott-Ellis see Jackson, *British Women and the SCW* and Preston, 'Priscilla Scott-Ellis: All for Love', *Doves of War*, pp. 11–118.

32 PD to RA, 30 April 1938.
33 PD to RA, 7 May 1938.
34 PD to RA, 1 May 1938.
35 RA to PD, 2 May 1938.
36 RA to PD, 12 May 1938.
37 RA to PD, 14 May 1938.
38 RA to PD, 12 May 1938. Written in Spanish as *Rojo, cuantas alpargatas tienes? Dos, un par no sera bastante para correr detras ti.*
39 RA to PD, 2 May 1938.
40 PD to RA, 1 May 1938.
41 Ibid.
42 PD to RA, 7 May 1938.
43 See Chapter 9.
44 PD to Father Roberts, 14 May 1938.
45 It is interesting to note that at this point, Patience is using a mixture of Catalan and Castilian Spanish words in her letters. *Equip* is Catalan.
46 PD to RA, 19 May 1938.
47 PE, IWM 8398.
48 PD to RA, 25 May 1938.
49 PE, IWM 8398.
50 Patience is referring to the 308 soldiers of the Republican army, captured on the Asturian front, who were rescued from their imprisonment in the castle known as the *Fuerte de Carchuna*, Granada, on the night of 23 May 1938. Amongst the officers leading the rescue party of 35 was the young North American, Lieutenant Bill Aalto. The audacious and well-planned gaol-break was the subject of a propaganda leaflet published in Madrid in 1938. See http://es.geocities.com/eustaquio5/carchuna.html. My thanks to Helen Graham for this information.
51 PD to RA, 26 May 1938.
52 PE, IWM 8398.
53 Ibid.
54 PD to RA, 27 May 1938/1.
55 PD to RA, 27 May 1938/3.
56 Sometimes nurses returned to England when taken ill, and while recuperating, would speak at meetings to raise funds for Spanish Medical Aid, see for example, Fyvel, *English Penny*. Occasionally, like Molly Murphy, they did not return to Spain afterwards. See Murphy, *Molly Murphy: Suffragette and Socialist*. Others would remain in Spain for treatment and then return to duty, for example, Una Wilson after a breakdown mentioned in Fyrth, *The Signal Was Spain*, pp. 77–78.

57 PE, IWM 8398.
58 PD to RA, 30 May 1938.
59 PD to RA, 3 June 1938.

8 Head and Heart

1 PD to RA, 12 June 1938/1.
2 RA, letter to parents, 12 July 1937, translation by Peter Parmella.
3 PE, Lataster-Czisch, 'Eigentlich rede ich nicht gern über mich.'
4 Letter to RA from his father, 24 June 1938.
5 RA to PD, 14 May 1938.
6 PD to RA, 12 June 38/1. In another letter written later the same day it seems that her anger has subsided a little and she is now 'more disappointed than cross', though still intends to begin 'flirting in earnest'.
7 RA to PD, 14 June 1938/1.
8 Ibid.
9 PD to RA, 18 June 1938/1.
10 PD to RA, 19 June 1938.
11 Ibid.
12 Ibid.
13 Ibid.
14 PD to RA, 18 June 1938/2.
15 Ibid.
16 RA to PD, 20 June 1938.
17 For example, 'Earl Browder's book', the leader of the US Communist Party. PD to RA, 1 July 1938.
18 For more about this period of training see Jackson, *At the Margins of Mayhem.*
19 RA to PD, 24 June 1938.
20 RA to PD, 8 July 1938.
21 PD to RA, 1 July 1938.
22 Ibid.
23 PD to RA, 2 July 1938.
24 PD to RA, 6 July 1938.
25 PD to RA, 5 July 1938.
26 RA to PD, 21 July 1938.
27 The drawings are on the back of a letter from Robert of 10 June 1938. As his letter is in ink and the drawings in pencil, it would seem that they may be later additions, in all likelihood, sketched by Patience.
28 RA to PD, 14 June 1938.
29 PD to RA, 6 July 1938.
30 Ibid. The journal was most probably the Communist Party publication, 'NUMERO ESPECIAL: LA CORRESPONDENCIA INTERNACIONAL', Revista Semanal. Año IX, 10 de Julio 1938. Núm. 26, Barcelona, 1938.
31 PD to RA, 6 July 1938.
32 RA to PD, 2 July 1938 and 11 July 1938.

33 PD to RA, 6 July 1938.

34 RA to PD, 11 July 1938 and 12 July 1938/2.

35 RA to PD, 20 July 1938.

36 RA to PD, 12 July 1938/1.

37 PD to RA, 10 July 1938.

38 T. C. Worsley's 'fictionalised memoir', *Fellow Travellers*, features Stephen Spender and friends and was written in the thirties though not published until 1971 (London Magazine Editions), p. 145. Others who had been in Spain and later drew parallels between religion and communism include Nan Green, who wrote of her growing disquiet in the 1950s with aspects of Soviet and Chinese Communism as 'unlearning blind faith', and Charlotte Haldane, who wrote that 'as spiritual laxatives and opiates, both religion and communism fulfil similar emotional criteria'. See Jackson, *British Women and the SCW*, Chapters 2 and 6.

39 PD to RA, 1 July 1938.

40 See Chapter 6.

41 PD to Father Roberts, 13 July 1938.

42 PD to RA, 12 July 1938. Other letters, for example, 9 July 1938, 13 July 1938, 14 July 1938 and 16 July 1938, contain similar expressions of disappointment.

43 PD to RA, 13 July 1938.

44 RA to PD, 21 July 1938.

45 RA to PD, 22 July 1938.

46 PD to RA, 21 July 1938.

47 Ibid.

48 PD to RA, 23 July 1938.

49 PD to RA, 22 July 1938.

50 Ibid.

51 PD to RA, 21 July 1938.

52 PD to RA, 22 July 1938.

53 PE, IWM 8398.

54 RA to PD, 23 July 1938.

55 PD to RA, 6 July 1938.

56 RA to PD, 23 July 1938.

9 The Ebro

1 PD to RA, 26 July 1938.

2 'Ebro Crossing, 1938', by Jane Durán in *Silences from the Spanish Civil War* (London: Enitharmon Press, 2002). The first two stanzas read, 'How can I restore them, persistently crossing over the spilt milk of that river, on pontoon bridges, in boats or up to their waists in water, a last hope?

3 PE, IWM 8398.

4 For more on the initial setting up of the cave hospital, see the memoirs of Nan Green, *A Chronicle of Small Beer*, (Nottingham: Trent Editions, Nottingham Trent University, 2005), and Jackson, *Beyond the Battlefield: Testimony, Memory*

and Remembrance of a Cave Hospital in the Spanish Civil War (Pontypool: Warren & Pell Publishing, 2005).

5 PE, IWM 8398.

6 PD to RA, 27 July 1938.

7 PE, IWM 8398.

8 Ibid.

9 Techniques for the management of compound fractures (ie. open) had been pioneered by the Catalan surgeon, Josep Trueta Raspall, thereby greatly reducing the number of amputations required. See Coni, *Medicine and Warfare*, pp. 49–57 and the autobiography of J. Trueta, *Surgeon in War and Peace* (London: Gollancz, 1980).

10 See for example the 1938 documentary film by Cartier Bresson, *Return to Life.*

11 Barcelona had more than 14,000 listed donors in 1938, a figure which had doubled by the end of the war according to Nicholas Coni FRCP. For a brief account of medical advances during the war see his article, 'Medicine and the Spanish Civil War', *Journal of the Royal Society of Medicine*, 95, (March 2002), and for more information on blood transfusions during the civil war see Chapter 5 of his book, *Medicine and Warfare*.

12 In addition to travelling round the various hospitals and medical units at the front to check on the welfare of the English speaking nurses, Winifred Bates also took photographs and wrote articles about the work the medical staff were doing. This material was then published in pamphlets to raise funds for Spanish Medical Aid.

13 PE, IWM 8398.

14 Ibid.

15 The Moorish occupation of Spain began in 711. The Reconquest started shortly afterwards but the Moors were not completely expelled until after the fall of Granada in 1492. Moorish troops had been used in the violent suppression of the Asturian miners in 1934. Infamous for their treatment of prisoners and in newly occupied regions, during the civil war they became a focus of terror for civilians in much of Republican Spain.

16 PE, IWM 8398.

17 For more on Spanish attitudes to the war in Morocco see *The Track*, the second part of Arturo Barea's autobiographical trilogy, *The Forging of a Rebel*, (London: Granta Books, 2001; first published by Faber & Faber in the 1940s).

18 PE, IWM 8398.

19 Ibid.

20 Ibid.

21 Ibid.

22 Ibid.

23 Ibid.

24 PE, AJ, 18 March 1994. A similar version is also to be found in PE, IWM 8398, but with two wounded Finns instead of three.

25 PE, IWM 8398.

26 Ibid.
27 See Jackson, *British Women and the SCW*, Chapter 5, 'A Far Cry: Women and the Voice of Empathy'.
28 PE, IWM 8398.
29 Ibid.
30 See previous note [Chapter 6, note 3] with the alternative spelling 'Tschapaiew' Battalion.
31 Translation from the German original by Peter Parmella.
32 Letter from 'Comisario Herbert, Baon Ametralladora no 35, 5ª Cia. Plaza Altozano 355M', to PD, 13 August 1938. Translation by AJ.
33 'Unser Robert', by 'Bert, Feldwebel der MGK', *El Voluntario de la Libertad*, 88 (11 September 1938), p. 4.
34 Letter from PD to the family of RA, 20 August 1938. The word 'as' in the last line was inserted above afterwards. My thanks to Eran Torbiner for a copy of this letter.
35 Bates, 'Summary and Critical Survey'.
36 PE, Lataster-Czisch, *'Eigentlich rede ich nicht gern über mich.'*
37 PE, IWM 8398.

10 Leaving Spain

1 PE, IWM 8398.
2 Ibid.
3 PE, Lataster-Czisch, *'Eigentlich rede ich nicht gern über mich.'* In the same interview, Patience refers to attitudes she encountered when she was in China from the Chinese who viewed the Brigaders' acceptance of the order to leave with a degree of scorn. They thought that the Brigaders should have stayed to fight a guerrilla war, but Patience pointed out that Spain was not as big as China, where this type of warfare could be maintained more easily due to the vast areas in which to hide.
4 For other testimonies from International Brigaders on this subject see Jackson, *At the Margins of Mayhem*, Chapter 6.
5 PE, IWM 8398.
6 Ibid.
7 PE, Lataster-Czisch, *'Eigentlich rede ich nicht gern über mich.'*
8 PE, AJ, 18 March, 1994.
9 PE, IWM 8398.
10 Ibid.

11 A Different Life

1 PE, IWM 8398.
2 PE, AJ, 18 March 1994.
3 PD to RA, 30 April 1938.
4 PE, IWM 8398.

5 PD to RA, 5 July 1938.

6 Reference for PD by Leah Manning (Hon Sec. S.M.A.C.), London, 5 January 1939.

7 Reference for PD by R.S. Saxton M.A., M.B., B. Chir. (Cantab), Brighton, 16 August 1939.

8 The matter was referred to Mr Hastings. Modern Records Centre, University of Warwick, Spanish Medical Aid Committee minutes. Correspondence, 4 January 1939.

9 PD, CV1, 1931–1941.

10 PD, notes for a talk or for memoirs, undated.

11 For more on Nan Green see her memoirs, *A Chronicle of Small Beer*, and Jackson, *British Women and the SCW*. For both Nan and George Green, see Paul Preston, *Doves of War*, pp. 121–201.

12 PE, AJ, 8 March 1996.

13 PE, AJ, 18 March 1994.

14 For more on Isabel Brown see Jackson, *British Women and the SCW* and May Hill, *Red Roses for Isabel* (London: May Hill, 1982).

15 Isabel Brown, IWM 844.

16 PE, IWM 8398.

17 PE, AJ, 18 March 1994.

18 PD to RA, 19 June 1938.

19 Letter from the widow of Charles Goodfellow (2nd in command of the British Battalion), 'Proud of their Husbands', *Daily Worker*, 3 September 1937, p. 4. For more on the subject of women's responses to bereavement see Jackson, *British Women and the SCW*, Chapters 3 and 6.

20 For more on David Guest and his mother, Carmel, including her visit to see her son in Spain, see Jackson, *At the Margins of Mayhem*, Chapter 7.

21 PE, AJ, 8 March 1996 Patience commented that the doctor in question went to China along with others from the Brigades who had come to London after Spain, including the Austrian physician, Dr Fritz Jensen.

22 After the Spanish civil war, Angela Haden Guest qualified as a doctor in America, and worked abroad for the World Health Organisation. She married and had one son.

23 For more on the effects of the policy of non-intervention see Gerald Howson, *Arms for Spain: The Untold Story of the Spanish Civil War* (London: John Murray, 1998).

24 Hopes at this point often centred on the possibility that if the Republic could hold out until the outbreak of a wider conflict, Spain would become an ally to be supported in a war against the Axis powers.

25 PE, AJ, 8 March 1996.

26 The nurses were Patience Darton, Joan Purser, Janet Robertson, Beryl Smithson and Louise Jones. Aileen Palmer also helped to throw the red ink at the Prime Minister's door. Both she and Angela Guest were fined 10 shillings and bound over for six months. See Fyrth, *The Signal Was Spain*, pp. 137–8.

27 PD, notes, undated.

28 PE, AJ, 8 March 1996.

29 PD, notes, undated.

30 PE, IWM 8398.

31 *Manchester Guardian*, Wednesday, 22 February 1939, p. 6.

32 *Manchester Guardian*, Wednesday, 29 March 1939, p. 11.

33 Anthony Aldgate, *Cinema & History: British Newsreels and the Spanish Civil War* (London: Scolar Press, 1979), pp. 190–91.

34 Preston, *The Spanish Civil War 1936–39* (London: Weidenfeld and Nicolson, 1986), p. 166.

35 PE, AJ, 18 March 1994.

36 Ramón Mauri Samada, letter to PD, 12 February 1939.

37 For more on Len Crome, see Preston, 'Two doctors and one cause'.

38 Letter from Reggie Saxton to Len Crome, 15 February 1939. My thanks to Peter Crome for making his father's letters and papers available to me.

39 Conversations and correspondence with Joan Mauri, 2009. Ramón eventually returned to Spain and qualified as a doctor, marrying a girl he had met in the village of El Molar, while working with the transfusion unit. He appears in the photograph with Leah Manning included in Chapter 9.

40 IBA letter headings in the early 1940s give the address as 144 Holborn, E.C.1 (entrance in Brooke Street). The President was Sam Wild, with Malcolm Dunbar as the Vice-President and Jack Brent as Secretary.

41 See the sailing of the SS. *Sinaia* in Jackson, *British Women and the SCW*, Chapter 6.

42 Reggie Saxton, letter to Len Crome, 10 April 1939.

43 See Baxell, *British Volunteers in the SCW*, Chapter 6.

44 According to Eva Barilich, author of the biography *Fritz Jensen: Artz an vielen Fronten* (Vienna: Globus Verlag, 1991), the Dartons also helped Jensen obtain a Spanish passport and Spanish nationality. It is not clear how exactly this was achieved.

45 The Chairman of the China Medical Aid Committee was Lord Horder, and the Secretary, Dr Mary Gilchrist.

46 Arthur Clegg, *Aid China* (Beijing, China: Foreign Languages Press, 2003), p. 103. See also Dr Jensen's pamphlet, cited by Clegg, *Bamboo, Mud and Granite* (1943).

47 André Marty to Harry Pollitt, Paris, 9 May 1939, Moscow Archive, Disc 1/545/6/87, p. 43. My thanks to Jim Carmody for bringing this document to my attention, and to Peter Parmella for the translation from French.

48 PD, notes, undated.

49 Clegg, *Aid China*, pp. 105–106.

50 PD, notes, undated.

51 For example, Celia Baker, see Jackson, *British Women and the SCW*, Chapter 6.

52 PE, IWM 8398.

53 PE, notes from a telephone conversation with the author, 1996. For more on

the question of the Czech funds see CAB/24/288 and CAB/23/100. Also the Czecho-Slovakia (Financial Claims and Refugees) Bill, 17 January 1940, Imperial War Museum, Stopford Papers, Ref RJS 3/13–3/17 (File: RJS 3/16) and Czecho-Slovakia Treaty Series No. 9, 27 January 1939, HMSO, Cmd. 5933. My thanks to Jane Buresova for her assistance regarding these documents.

54 The CRTF was founded on 23 July 1939, replacing the earlier British Committee for Refugees from Czechoslovakia. Miss P. Darton appears on the staff lists at their HQ in Colquhoun House for 23 August 1939 in room 23. PRO – HO 294/203.

55 PE, AJ, 8 March 1996.

56 DADMS 44th (H.C.) Division to Crome, 23 June 1939, cited in Preston, 'Two doctors and one cause', p. 13.

57 PE, Lataster-Czisch, *'Eigentlich rede ich nicht gern über mich.'*

58 Dr Jensen, letter to Len Crome, 16 September 1939, from Hsiang-Hospital, Changshah, Hunan, China.

12 Bombs on Britain

1 See Bill Alexander, *British Volunteers for Liberty: Spain 1936–39* (London: Lawrence & Wishart, 1982), pp. 246–7.

2 PE, IWM 8398.

3 Felix Horowitz was born in 1903 in Vijnit. In 1930 he had qualified as a doctor in Prague and had specialised in neurology. The list of refugees compiled by Yvonne Kapp states that in September 1939 he was living at 21, Orsett Terrace, London, W2.

4 Felix Horowitz, letters to Len Crome 1943, 1944, 1945.

5 Isabel Brown, IWM 844.

6 Bertrand Russell pamphlet, *Which Way to Peace* (London: Michael Joseph, 1936).

7 Stephen Spender, quoted in Peter Ackroyd, *London: The Biography* (London: Vintage, 2001), p. 739.

8 For more on Frida Knight (née Stewart) see Jackson, *British Women and the SCW*.

9 AJ, conversation with PE for an 'Afterword' to the unpublished memoir of Frida Knight (née Stewart).

10 Letter of reference for PD from Sir Henry Bunbury, 19 August 1941.

11 Reference for PD by Lady Mary Murray, August 1941.

12 PD, undated CV letter.

13 Ibid.

14 Diana Gurney also taught art at Toynbee Hall and later at St Martin's School of Art.

15 Pauline Paucker, interview with Diana Gurney, 2008.

16 Letter from Felix Horowitz to Len Crome, 21 July 1943.

17 Letter from Bill Pike to Len Crome, 17 November 1943.

18 PD, undated CV letter. A certificate of employment from UNRRA shows that she was employed by them from 12 June 1944 to 30 September 1946 when her work was 'Terminated for redundancy' with the comment, 'a satisfactory officer in every way.'

19 PE, Lataster-Czisch, *'Eigentlich rede ich nicht gern über mich.'*

20 Allied Military Government for Occupied Territories – form of military rule administered by Allied forces during and after WWII within European territories.

21 PD, undated CV letter.

22 PD, CV letter for work in China, undated.

23 Letter from Nan Green to Len Crome, 7 March 1944.

24 See Chapter 13.

25 Letter from Capt. F. Horowitz, RAMC, C.R.D Toroho, E.A. Command, to Dr Len Crome, undated but relating to the M.C.

26 Letter from F. Horowitz, on active service in Kenya, to Dr Len Crome, 6 April 1945.

27 Ibid. Horo stayed in England after the war and became a British citizen in 1947.

28 PE, Lataster-Czisch, *'Eigentlich rede ich nicht gern über mich.'*

29 Later known as the British Polio Fellowship.

30 PE, CV 2.

31 PD, 'The Eisler Case', *Civil Liberties*, 9, 6 (July/August 1949), pp. 3–4. Eisler eventually settled in East Germany where he became a high-ranking official.

32 PE, IWM 8398.

33 Ibid.

13   Opening the Chinese Puzzle Box

1 Sax Rohmer's book, *The Insidious Dr Fu Manchu,* was amongst the many adventures he wrote that were made into films in the 1930s and a television series in 1956.

2 PE, conversations with AJ, 1996.

3 PE, memoir, p. 7. The visit to Poland was made during her first journey to China.

4 See previous chapter.

5 Buchanan, *The Impact of the Spanish Civil War on Britain*, p. 189. See also Clegg, *Aid China*.

6 David Crook, interview with the author, 16 August 1996. David and his wife, Isabel, lived in China for many years. During the Cultural Revolution, they were accused of spying. David Crook spent five years in prison from 1968 to 1973. See his memoirs, 'Hampstead Heath to Tian An Men', available at: www.davidcrook.net/simple/main.html.

7 David Crook, letter dated 15 November 1996, read out at the funeral of Patience Edney in London.

8 Nan Green, in the MS version of 'A Chronicle of Small Beer', pp. 121–129. No further information is given about the delegate.

9 David Crook, letter 15 November 1996.

10 Nan Green stayed in China till 1960. See *A Chronicle of Small Beer*', and Preston, *Doves of War.*

11 PE, CV2. David Crook referred to Patience's 'incisive criticisms' to rid translations of Chinese-English. David Crook, AJ, 15 November 1996.

12 Anne-Marie Brady, *Making the Foreign Serve China: Managing Foreigners in the People's Republic* (New York and Oxford: Rowman & Littlefield, 2003), p. 99.

13 Ibid., pp. xi–xii.

14 Ibid., p. 99.

15 Ibid., pp. 101–102.

16 Ibid., p. 103.

17 PE, Lataster-Czisch, '*Eigentlich rede ich nicht gern über mich.*'

18 Eric Edney, Obituary, *Morning Star*, 4 July 1989.

19 Moscow Archive 545/6/127, pp. 34–36.

20 PE, Lataster-Czisch, '*Eigentlich rede ich nicht gern über mich.*'

21 Two of his poems were published recently in *Poems from Spain: British and Irish International Brigaders on the Spanish Civil War* (London: Lawrence & Wishart/International Brigade Memorial Trust, 2006), edited by Jim Jump, and with a foreword by Jack Jones. See also the obituary for Eric Edney in the *Morning Star*, 4 July 1989.

22 PE, Lataster-Czisch, '*Eigentlich rede ich nicht gern über mich.*'

23 PE, AJ, 18 March 1994. From 1958–1966, Eric Edney worked in London for ADN, the news agency of the German Democratic Republic.

24 Invitation, 13 July 1954, sent from the Foreign Languages Press by Liu Tsun-chi informing them that Comrade Chu Teh would receive them on behalf of the Central Committee of the CPC in the Tze Kuang Hall, Chung Nan Hai, at 10.00am the following day, and that they would be entertained at a dinner at 12 noon by Comrade Hsi Chung-hsun, Central Committee member and director of the Propaganda Department.

25 My thanks to Michael and Paul Crook for the translation of this document.

26 Hilary's replies were in the form of carbon copies, indicating that originally, it had been Hilary who had saved all Patience's letters, together with her own copies. At some point, they must have all been returned to Patience.

27 PD, letter to Hilary Darton (HD), [1] 31 January 1955.

28 Ibid.

29 Bushey Cemetery, Section A, Row 4, Number 123. See www.theus.org.uk.

30 Fritz Jensen died on 11 April 1955. See Clegg, *Aid China*, p. 184, and Barilich, *Fritz Jensen.* According to Brady, the Bandung Conference was convened for African and Asian nations to discuss the question of neutrality. Chou En-lai gave a speech proposing the 'recognition of racial equality and respect for the rights of peoples to choose their own way of life and political and economic system'. *Making the Foreign Serve China*, p. 105.

31 PD to HD, with additions from Eric Edney, [1] 31 January 1955.
32 PE to HD, [4] undated.
33 PD to HD, [2] undated.
34 PE to HD, [5]26 April 1955.
35 PE to HD, [9]11 July 1955.
36 PE to HD, [4] undated.
37 PE to HD, [6] undated.
38 PE to HD, [4] undated.
39 Ibid.
40 PE to HD, [6] undated.
41 PE to HD, [4] undated.
42 PD to HD, [3] undated.
43 Ibid.
44 Gladys Yang (née Taylor) was a British translator who in 1968 was arrested and detained until 1972, along with her husband, Yang Xianyi, both accused of being British spies. Ruth Weiss was one of several Jewish people who had gone to China to escape Europe. Most of her family died in the Holocaust. See Brady, *Making the Foreign Serve China*, pp. 163 and 103 respectively.
45 Brady, *Making the Foreign Serve China,* p. 102.
46 Ibid. Brady notes that for example that British CP member and journalist Alan Winnington was warned not to have parties where Chinese and foreigners 'mixed, danced, ate and drank and made noise'.
47 Dr Grantly Dick Read (1890–1959) was a pioneer in the field of 'natural childbirth' and his book, *Childbirth without Fear*, first published in 1933, was much read throughout the forties and fifties.
48 PE to HD, [4] undated.
49 Ibid.
50 PE to HD, [6] undated.
51 PE to HD, [14] undated.
52 PE to HD, [5] 26 April 1955.
53 Ibid.
54 Ibid.
55 Ibid.
56 Ibid.
57 Ibid.
58 Chinese puzzle boxes are in reality, Japanese. The 'Himitsu-Bako' (Personal Secret Box), is a traditional Japanese puzzle box that was designed over 100 years ago in the Hakone region of Japan.

14 Falling in Love Again
 1 PE to HD, [5] 26 April 1955.
 2 PE to HD, [7] undated.
 3 Ibid.
 4 PE to HD, [5] 26 April 1955.

5   PE to HD, [7] undated. *Chinese Literature* magazine was founded in 1951 and published in English and French.

6   PE to HD, [8] 11/12 July 1955.

7   Winnie the Pooh was the bear of 'very little brain' in the stories for children by A. A. Milne.

8   PE to HD, [8] 11/12 July 1955.

9   Ibid.

10   PE and Eric Edney to HD, [10] 24 July 1955.

11   PE to HD, [13] undated.

12   PE to HD, [14] undated.

13   Ibid.

14   PE to HD, [15] undated.

15   Ibid.

16   PE to HD, [16] New Year 1956.

17   PE to HD, [17] undated.

18   PE to HD, [18] undated.

19   PE to HD, [19] 21 March 1956, Peking, China, Yang Shih Ta Chieh 41.

20   Ibid. and [18] undated, respectively.

21   PE to HD, [24] undated.

22   Note from Eric Edney to HD, [19] 21 March1956.

23   PE to HD, [20] undated. Address given as FLP, Flat 20, Pai Wan Chuang, Peking, 37.

24   PE to HD, [21] undated. The use of 'suppose' instead of 'don't suppose' suggests that those in the medical profession like Patience can easily identify patients from their posteriors!

25   Brady, *Making the Foreign Serve China*, p. 103.

26   David Crook, letter of 15 November 1996.

27   Anthony Eden (1897–1977) was a Conservative politician who served as foreign secretary in three different decades and became Prime Minister in 1955. His premiership was overshadowed by the Suez Crisis and he resigned after little more than 18 months in office.

28   PE to HD, [24] undated.

29   PE to HD, [9] 11 July 1955.

15   Clouds over the Peking Picnic

1   PE, Lataster-Czisch, *'Eigentlich rede ich nicht gern über mich.'*

2   PE to HD, [26] undated.

3   Undated notes from a conversation between Nan Green and the 'comrades of the Bureau', sent (with official permission) from Nan to Patience.

4   PE to Betty Reid, undated. According to his son, Eric spoke with a noticeable, though not pronounced, West-Country accent.

5   Ibid.

6   Ibid.

7   Transcript of meeting, Thursday 5 December 1957. Present: Patience, Eric,

Wu Wen-tao, Feng Hai-ling (interpreting), Lo Liang, Peng Fei, Yang Chen-fang.

8 Ibid.

9 Nan Green, transcript of meeting with two representatives of the Bureau for Experts' Affairs, 31 December 1957.

10 PE to Betty Reid, undated.

11 PE to HD, [28] undated.

12 Ibid.

13 PE to Betty Reid, undated.

14 Anne Bridge, *Peking Picnic* (London: Penguin, 1932).

15 PE to HD, [30] undated.

16 PE to HD, [32] 2 February 1958.

17 PE, CV 2.

16 Reprise

1 Josephine Herbst to Mary and Neal Daniels, 17 February 1966, Za Herbst Collection, Beinecke Library, Yale University. Quoted in Preston, *We Saw Spain Die*, p. 367.

2 Comments made by Avis Hutt, Pauline Paucker and others in conversations with the author, 2009.

3 Eric Edney, letter of application for a pension from the Novosti Press Agency written to V. Shkalyabin, Managing Editor, Soviet Weekly, 10 May 1979. The letter also cites that after service throughout the war in the R.A.O.C., he returned to join the Industrial Department at the headquarters of the CPGB, where he worked from 1945 until leaving for China in 1954. My thanks to Bob Edney for allowing me to see the papers of his father.

4 Bob Edney to AJ, 17 March 2009.

5 Pauline Paucker, short memoir of PE, January 2000. A letter from Eric's solicitor to Patience of 14 June 1974 states that the final separation dated from 24 March 1973.

6 Ibid. Edmund Evans pioneered printing with coloured woodblocks, enabling him to produce long runs of children's books relatively cheaply.

7 Bob Edney to AJ, 17 March 2009.

8 Bernice Robertson, correspondence with AJ, 2 June 2009.

9 PE, CV 3, c.1976, and PE, letter to DHSS, 1987.

10 PE, letter to DHSS, 1987.

11 For example, the Imperial War Museum began recording a series of interviews in 1976 that includes volunteers from the medical services and civilian activists as well as those who served with the Brigades. See the catalogue, *The Spanish Civil War Collection: Sound Archive Oral History Recordings* (London: Imperial War Museum, 1996). Interviews were also recorded at an IBA reunion in Loughborough in the same year. The tapes are now held in the Tameside Local Studies Library, Stalybridge.

12 For more on the nature of memory and theories concerning the processes of

'composure' in life review, see Jackson, *British Women and the Spanish Civil War*, Appendix II, 'Interviews: Theory and Methodology.

13 PE, IWM, 8398.

14 Green, in the MS of 'A Chronicle of Small Beer', p. 119.

15 PE, AJ, 18 March 1994.

16 Ibid.

17 Green, in the MS of 'A Chronicle of Small Beer', p. 87.

18 PE, IWM 8398.

19 Ibid.

20 The one exception to this seems to be the interview with Petra Lataster-Czisch, presumably because this was for publication in Germany.

21 Short memoir by Pauline Paucker, January 2000.

22 PE in 'Carried Away to War' by Tunku Varadarajan, *The Times*, 2 November 1996, pp. 1–2.

23 Patience had been diagnosed as suffering from the autoimmune disease, Systemic Lupus Erythematosus.

24 'Morir en Madrid', *El Periódico*, 9 November 1996.

25 PD to RA, 23 July 1938.

17 'Patience on a Monument, Smiling at Grief'?

1 Short memoir by Pauline Paucker, January 2000. I confirmed this story with Patience's niece, Mary Wills. She and her husband had taken Hilary to the funeral. Hilary was rather unwell and her memory poor but, at the last moment, she remembered to bring an old coat with her and knew that she had to follow instructions given by Patience to put it in the coffin. It was given to the undertaker on their arrival at the crematorium.

2 Colin Williams, Bill Alexander and John Gorman (eds), *Memorials of the Spanish Civil War:The Official Publication of the International Brigade Association* (Stroud:Alan Sutton Publishing, 1996).

3 Ibid., PE in Spain p. 21; in Camden Town Hall on 25 April 1995, p. 19.

4 PE in Varadarajan, 'Carried Away to War'.

5 William Shakespeare, *Twelfth Night*, Act II, scene iv.

6 Bob Edney to AJ, 17 March 2009.

7 PE in Lataster-Czisch, *'Eigentlich rede ich nicht gern über mich.'*

8 PD to RA, 2 July 1938.

9 RA to PD, 12 July 1938, 2.

Select Bibliography

Ackelsberg, Martha A., *Free Women of Spain: Anarchism and the Struggle for the Emancipation of Women* (Bloomington: Indiana University Press, 1991).

Aldgate, Anthony, *Cinema & History: British Newsreels and the Spanish Civil War* (London: Scolar Press, 1979).

Alexander, Bill, *British Volunteers for Liberty: Spain 1936–39* (London: Lawrence & Wishart, 1982).

Alpert, Michael, 'Humanitarianism and Politics in the British Response to the Spanish Civil War 1936–1939', *European History Quarterly*, 14, 4 (1984).

Barea, Arturo *The Forging of a Rebel* (London: Granta Books, 2001, first published in an omnibus edition of the trilogy, *The Forge, The Track and The Clash* by Davis Poynter in 1972).

Barilich, Eva, *Fritz Jensen: Arzt an vielen Fronten* (Vienna: Globus Verlag, 1991).

Bates, Winifred, 'Summary and critical survey of my work in Spain since the outbreak of the war. Barcelona, September 1938', Moscow Archives 545/6/88.

Baxell, Richard, *British Volunteers in the Spanish Civil War: The British Battalion in the International Brigades, 1936–1939* (London and New York: Routledge/Cañada Blanch Studies on Contemporary Spain, 2004; paperback edition, Pontypool: Warren & Pell Publishing, 2007).

Brady, Anne-Marie, *Making the Foreign Serve China: Managing Foreigners in the People's Republic* (New York and Oxford: Rowman & Littlefield, 2003).

Bridge, Ann, *Peking Picnic* (London: Penguin, 1932).

Bruley, Sue, *Leninism, Stalinism and the Women's Movement in Britain 1920–1939* (New York and London: Garland, 1986).

Buchanan, Tom, *The Impact of the Spanish Civil War on Britain: War, Loss and Memory* (Brighton and Portland: Sussex Academic Press, 2007).

Clegg, Arthur, *Aid China: A Memoir of a Forgotten Campaign* (Beijing: Foreign Language Press, 2007; first published Beijing, New World Press, 1989).

Coni, Nicholas, *Medicine and Warfare: Spain, 1936–1939* (London and New York: Routledge/Cañada Blanch Studies on Contemporary Spain, 2008).

Crook, David, memoirs, 'Hampstead Heath to Tian An Men' available on line at www.davidcrook.net/simple/main.html.

Fernández, Aurora, short untitled memoir, Prague, January 1983, Marx Memorial Library, London, Box 29, File D/9.

Fyrth, Jim, *The Signal Was Spain: The Aid Spain Movement in Britain 1936–39*, (London and New York: Lawrence and Wishart, 1986).

Fyrth, Jim, and Sally Alexander (eds), *Women's Voices from the Spanish Civil War* (London: Lawrence & Wishart, 1991).

Fyvel, Penelope, *English Penny* (Ilfracombe, Devon: Arthur H. Stockwell, 1992).

Green, Nan, *A Chronicle of Small Beer: The Memoirs of Nan Green* (Nottingham: Trent Editions, Nottingham Trent University, 2005).

Haldane, Charlotte, *Truth Will Out* (London: Weidenfeld & Nicholson, 1949).

Hill, May, *Red Roses for Isabel* (London: May Hill, 1982).

Howson, Gerald, *Arms for Spain: The Untold Story of the Spanish Civil War* (London: John Murray, 1998).

Jackson, Angela, *British Women and the Spanish Civil War* (London and New York: Routledge/Cañada Blanch Centre for Studies on Contemporary Spain, 2002; paperback edition, Barcelona: Warren & Pell Publishing/Cañada Blanch Centre for Studies on Contemporary Spain, 2009; Spanish edition, *Las mujeres británicas y la Guerra Civil española*, València: Universitat de València/Cañada Blanch Centre for Studies on Contemporary Spain, 2010).

Jackson, Angela, *Beyond the Battlefield: Testimony, Memory and Remembrance of a Cave Hospital in the Spanish Civil War* (Pontypool: Warren & Pell Publishing, 2005; first published in Catalan as *Més enllà del camp de batalla: Testimoni, memòria i records d'una cova hospital en la Guerra Civil espanyola,* Valls: Cossetània Edicions, 2004).

Jackson, Angela, *At the Margins of Mayhem: Prologue and Epilogue to the Last Great Battle of the Spanish Civil War* (Pontypool: Warren & Pell Publishing, 2008; first published in Catalan as *Els brigadistes entre nosaltres: Pròleg i epíleg a l'última gran batalla de la Guerra Civil espanyola*, Valls: Cossetània Edicions, 2008).

Jump, Jim (ed.), *Poems from Spain: British and Irish International Brigaders on the Spanish Civil War* (London: Lawrence & Wishart/International Brigade Memorial Trust, 2006).

Keene, Judith, *'The Last Mile to Huesca: An Australian Nurse in the Spanish Civil War* (Kensington, Australia: New South Wales University Press, 1988).

Lataster-Czisch, Petra, interview with Patience Edney in *'Eigentlich rede ich nicht gern über mich.'* (*Lebenserinnegungen von Frauen aus dem Spanischen Bürgerkrieg 1936–1939)*, (Leizpzig und Weimar: Gustav Kiepenheurer Verlag, 1990), pp. 9–105.

Mangan, Kate and Jan Kurzke, 'The Good Comrade', unpublished MS, Jan Kurzke Papers, Archives of the International Institute for Social History, Amsterdam.

Mangini, Shirley, *Memories of Resistance: Women's Voices from the Spanish Civil War* (New Haven and London: Yale University Press, 1995).

Mendlesohn, Farah, *Quaker Relief Work in the Spanish Civil War* (New York: Edwin Mellen Press, 2002).

Miles, Sarah, *Portrait of a Parson: William Corbett Roberts, Foreword by Storm Jameson* (London: George Allen and Unwin, 1955).

Murphy, Molly, *Molly Murphy: Suffragette and Socialist* (Salford: Institute of Social Research, University of Salford, 1998).

Nash, Mary, *Defying Male Civilization: Women in the Spanish Civil War* (Colorado: Arden Press, 1994).

Preston, Paul, *The Spanish Civil War* (London: Weidenfeld and Nicolson, 1986).

Preston, Paul, *Doves of War: Four Women of Spain* (London: HarperCollins, 2002).

Preston, Paul, 'Two doctors and one cause: Len Crome and Reginald Saxton in the International Brigades', *International Journal of Iberian Studies*, 19, 1 (2006), pp. 5–24.

Preston, Paul, *We Saw Spain Die: Foreign Correspondents in the Spanish Civil War* (London: Constable & Robinson, 2008).

Purcell, Hugh, *The Last English Revolutionary: Tom Wintringham 1898–1949* (Stroud: Sutton Publishing, 2004).

Scott-Ellis, Priscilla, (ed. Raymond Carr), *The Chances of Death: A Diary of the Spanish Civil War* (Norwich: Michael Russell, 1995).

Thomas, Hugh, *The Spanish Civil War* (London: Penguin Books, 1986. First published by Eyre & Spottiswode, 1961).

Trueta, Dr J., *Surgeon in War and Peace* (London: Gollancz, 1980).

Williams, Colin, Bill Alexander and John Gorman (eds), *Memorials of the Spanish Civil War: The Official Publication of the International Brigade Association* (Stroud: Alan Sutton Publishing, 1996).

Valls, Roser (Coordinator), *Infermeres catalanes a la Guerra Civil espanyola* (Barcelona: University of Barcelona, 2008).

Varadarajan, Tunku, interview with Patience Edney in 'Carried Away to War', *The Times*, 2 November 1996, pp. 1–2.

Index

23694991R00034